Indonesia and ASEAN Plus Three
Financial Cooperation

Eko Saputro

Indonesia and ASEAN Plus Three Financial Cooperation

Domestic Politics, Power Relations, and Regulatory Regionalism

Eko Saputro
Fiscal Policy Agency
Indonesian Ministry of Finance
Jakarta, Indonesia

ISBN 978-981-10-9768-3   ISBN 978-981-10-3029-1   (eBook)
DOI 10.1007/978-981-10-3029-1

Cover illustration: David Collingwood / Alamy Stock Photo

Printed on acid-free paper

This Palgrave imprint is published by Springer Nature
The registered company is Springer Nature Singapore Pte Ltd.
The registered company address is: 152 Beach Road, #21-01/04 Gateway East, Singapore 189721, Singapore

To my parents

Acknowledgements

I am grateful to a number of people—professors, friends, and colleagues—who have encouraged me to transform my dissertation into a book. In particular, I would like to express my appreciation to any institutions who gave permission to use some materials in this book.

I also would like to acknowledge the support of my working institution, the Fiscal Policy Agency, Indonesia, that had already provided me with permission to pursue my doctoral program and complete my dissertation. Furthermore, I should mention that all opinions or views expressed in this book do not necessarily reflect the views and policies of the agency.

Lastly, but equally important, I would like to acknowledge, with gratitude, the support of my family. This book would not be possible without their encouragement and love.

CONTENTS

List of Figures

LIST OF TABLES

CHAPTER 1

Introduction: Indonesia and the Dynamics of Regional Financial Cooperation

Financial regionalism in East Asia has stimulated not only a new architecture for regional governance, but also a transformation in Indonesia's national regulatory framework. As a relatively new phenomenon compared to trade regionalism, financial regionalism has successfully shaped cooperative networks among financial authorities in East Asia. The Executives Meeting of East Asia-Pacific Central Banks (EMEAP) and the Association of Southeast Asian Nations (ASEAN) Plus Three (APT) finance ministers meeting are examples of how financial regionalism stimulates policy networks among state financial agencies in East Asia. Especially in regard to the APT cooperation, Indonesian financial authorities have been collaborating with their counterparts in other member countries (the ten ASEAN states plus Japan, China and South Korea).

The progress of APT financial cooperation has influenced international financial arrangements. APT financial cooperation has not only critiqued the conventional global financial architecture that placed the International Monetary Fund (IMF) at the centre of the world financial system. It has also signalled that East Asian countries are, in their own way, developing their abilities in managing future economic challenges, with less dependency on existing global financial arrangements (De Brouwer 2002). The reluctance of the West, particularly the United States (USA), to provide adequate assistance during the Asian financial crisis became a lesson learnt and a trigger for the APT member countries to consolidate their own strengths to develop better regional mechanisms.

© The Author(s) 2017
E. Saputro, *Indonesia and ASEAN Plus Three Financial Cooperation*,
DOI 10.1007/978-981-10-3029-1_1

From the early establishment to the current process of APT financial cooperation, Indonesian financial authorities have demonstrated their roles in developing this cooperation. Indonesia has indicated its enthusiasm for joining the APT financial initiatives, not only to support its own economic recovery after the Asian financial crisis, but also to develop the future Indonesian financial sector. Indonesia has also paid considerable attention to the APT financial initiatives related to both liquidity support arrangements and bond market development, as well as making effort towards financial market integration (Indrawati 2008). With other APT member countries, Indonesia has agreed to build regional liquidity support mechanisms to deal with future economic shocks, ones that would build stronger economic measures effectively.

Indonesia's success in tackling the 2009 global financial crisis provides an indication of how the regional support mechanism worked and was important to support Indonesia's economy. For Indonesia, the regional liquidity mechanism enables an alternative financial support, and reduces Indonesian dependency on international financial institutions during crises. With capital market development, the former Indonesian finance minister, Sri Mulyani Indrawati (2007), views that East Asian nations should develop local capital markets continuously and integrate them with other regional markets, as well as global markets, to sustain economic growth. The minister's view reflects Indonesian concerns on developing market infrastructure and the harmonisation of regulation, two issues that are currently undertaken within APT financial cooperation.

Like other APT member countries, Indonesian participation in financial cooperation has been led predominantly by state financial agencies. The state remains the primary actor, as Indonesia still regards finance as a sensitive issue related to sovereignty. During this study, the Indonesian Ministry of Finance (IMOF) and Bank Indonesia (BI) were the authorities with mandates to deal with regional arrangements. These institutions held power and mandates for the financial sector, and represented Indonesia in any interaction and collaboration with other financial authorities of APT member countries.

While the state actors remain dominant in the process of APT financial regionalism, the recent development of APT financial cooperation has also provided an opportunity for non-state actors to participate. At the regional level, non-state actors have engaged directly or indirectly in the development of cooperation. Regional organisations such as the Asian Development Bank (ADB) and several research institutes within APT member countries have been involved in APT financial initiatives, initially through research studies. These roles have recently been elevated to a higher level of trust by enabling non-state actors to shape and engage in the regional governance of APT financial cooperation. For example, the ADB has been given a mandate as trustee of the APT initiative on guarantee mechanism, while market players have been collaborating with national capital market authorities to formulate governance for a regional bond market. Thus, the dynamics in shaping regional governance in APT financial cooperation is becoming more complex. It is also leading to a new pattern of regional interaction.

At national level, Indonesian non-state actors have also participated in the development of APT financial cooperation. Under a democratic regime, Indonesian non-state actors have been increasingly participating to develop Indonesia's stance on regional arrangements. Indonesian research centres, think tanks and business organisations have contributed to the progress of APT regional financial projects by providing research studies or knowledge sharing. They have often been critical to Indonesian economic foreign policies. For instance, Indonesian scholars, non-governmental organisations (NGOs) and business associations have argued that regional cooperation—particularly ASEAN—potentially hampers Indonesian interests, especially in economic sectors. This is because Indonesian firms are less competitive than their rivals in neighbouring countries in some industries (Chandra and Hanim 2004). However, on other issues, the non-state actors' views were often parallel with the Indonesian authorities. For example, despite the difference in looking at economic prospects within regionalism, both government and non-state actors shared the same perspective regarding the benefits and roles of regional cooperation in terms of security and bargaining power in international forums (Chandra and Hanim 2004; Natalegawa 2011). These various views as presented by Indonesian non-state actors suggest their sound engagement in regional affairs.

Beside the growing participation of non-state actors, policy coordination also emerges as another feature of APT financial cooperation. It has become an important tool, in the absence of a formal regional institution in APT financial cooperation. Buckley et al. (2011) argue that macroeconomic policy coordination is necessary to address regional governance and transnational issues. Jayasuriya (2010) also notes that regional coordination maintains its strategic function over national boundaries. In Indonesia, policy coordination in the financial sector is conducted predominantly by the two pivotal institutions: the IMOF and BI. These institutions play major roles not only for internal policy coordination, but also for transnational policy coordination.

In addition, the recent progress of APT financial cooperation has also introduced common standards through its initiatives. The project of standardisation has emerged in response to different levels of financial development among APT member countries. Different standards hinder regional market integration. In this respect, standardisation becomes an important instrument for regional and international economic integration (Mattli 2001). While standardisation implicitly entails voluntary action, it sometimes becomes an obligation, to avoid inefficiency in regionalism processes. On this point, standardisation often gains different responses from different countries considering their domestic interests. Reflecting on the previous study on bank supervision, Indonesia's commitment to international regulatory standards remains limited (Walter 2008). It mainly relates to the domestic costs of compliance that are too high and potentially hinder business interests. However, Indonesia's commitment to international standards on capital market best practices is relatively strong. For instance, Indonesian authorities have complied with the standards of the International Organisation of Securities Commissions (IOSCO). Put simply, the different stages of development related to domestic financial issues have shaped different levels of Indonesian commitment towards international financial initiatives. To further progress its commitments, Indonesia has been displaying determination in dealing with structural reforms to facilitate international commitments (Siregar 2011, p. 252).

The development of new regional governance for East Asian financial regionalism has attracted considerable attention (for instance, Grimes 2008, 2009, 2011; Kawai 2005, 2010; Yoshimatsu 2005, 2008a, 2014). However, there has been little analysis of the transformation of national regulatory frameworks in response to financial regionalism in East Asia. Analysis of the financial policy-making process at the domestic level, and the attitudes of state regulatory agencies—particularly in relation to the existing regional arrangements—also remains scant. Even less is known about the participation of non-state actors in the process of East Asian financial regionalism. Investigation of these issues is important, as national dynamics are often excluded from current debates on East Asian financial regionalism that focus more on power-based interaction and institutional building. In this respect, analysing transformations in Indonesia's domestic regulatory framework will be essential to the study of regional cooperation in East Asia.

WHY INDONESIA MATTERS

As the proponent of regional cooperation, Indonesia has been actively participating in APT financial cooperation. Indonesia's success in tackling the 2009 global financial crisis has restored Indonesia's confidence to articulate its stance towards regional and international cooperation (Anwar 2010, p. 127). For Indonesia, the success in dealing with the 2009 global financial crisis is evidence that embracing regional and global economic initiatives are necessary to protect the national economy. In contrast, the lack of engagement with regional and international arrangements means losing potential support. Indrawati (2008) argues that one legacy of the 1997 Asian financial crisis is that failure to create a properly integrated regional and global financial mechanism can result in economic misfortune.

Indonesia operates as a laboratory to explore the political-economic dynamics of financial regulatory bodies in dealing with financial regionalism in the East Asian region. In terms of domestic politics, Indonesia has experienced political transformation from authoritarian rule into a more democratic regime, one that arose in the midst of the economic devastation of the Asian financial crisis. The democratisation of Indonesia has demonstrated better political will and commitment towards the implementation of the rule of law that is essential for sound economic policies and good governance. This new political landscape makes Indonesia different from other victims of the Asian financial crisis—such as Thailand, Malaysia or South Korea—in which the economic depressions were not simultaneously accompanied by political shifts. The political situation in these countries was relatively stable—as stable as two other APT member countries, China and Japan, that were not greatly affected by the Asian financial crisis. Indonesia's experience in the changes of political regimes helps to examine the influence of domestic politics on the structure and power of financial regulatory agencies and their responses to financial regionalism.

In the financial sector especially, the change in Indonesian domestic politics has modified mandates, policy-making processes and policy coordination between financial authorities. The wave of democracy, in particular, has brought power sharing to the financial sector, as marked by the separation of the Indonesian central bank from the government's executive power. It has also contributed to the establishment of a financial supervisory agency. These changes have significantly reduced the exercise of power within the Indonesian financial sector by the elected government. The ability of the president to govern the financial sector in Indonesia has been eroded by *de-politicisation* processes that distanced the president from discretionary power over financial issues. These factors have ensured that the development of policy-making process and policy coordination on financial issues is now more complex.

Moreover, the changes in the types and forms of Indonesian domestic politics have provided impetus as well as constraints for financial agencies to regulatory change. In several parts of this book, especially in Chap. 5, the changes in domestic politics have formed the degree of Indonesian commitments to regional arrangements on financial sector. The distribution of power and more active participation of non-state actors, in particular, have contributed to shape the variety of Indonesian commitments in regional forums.

Naturally, Indonesian domestic politics have been very concerned about protecting domestic market and players. The concerns emerged due to lack of national competitiveness. Besides, Indonesian constitution requests Indonesian government to put national resources for maximum benefits of Indonesian people. In addition, the greater involvement of Indonesian non-state actors as a part of democratic pillars has become another element that influences the decision of Indonesia to support or resist such regional initiatives. Considering these variables, Indonesian regimes have taken regional and international arrangements cautiously to avoid any potential economic and political instability. However, due to several unexpected events and conditions, Indonesian regimes have also been forced to facilitate regulatory change to accommodate regional arrangement in the expense of the domestic market.

In the geopolitical context, Indonesia's position remains important at both the regional and the international level. Indonesia has been widely known as a traditional leader of the Southeast Asian region. Indonesian leadership in ASEAN was pivotal, especially under Soeharto's regime. Garnaut (2012, p. 17) notes that ASEAN influence in international forums was temporarily less significant during the Asian financial crisis, when Indonesia put aside international affairs to deal with domestic political and economic turmoil. This phenomenon shows the importance of Indonesia's position and influence in the region.

Indonesian leadership in the region has fluctuated due to domestic political and economic dynamics. While holding a strong regional leadership during the Soekarno and Soeharto administrations, Indonesia lost its geopolitical position at the end of Soeharto's tenure. Indonesia once again started to search for leadership roles when Soesilo Bambang Yudhoyono (SBY) took power. SBY's interest in foreign relations, supported by stable domestic politics and unique characteristics, has helped Indonesia to regain geopolitical influence in the last decade. Indonesia is the fourth-largest populated nation, with the largest Muslim population in the world, the third-largest democracy and has the largest economy in Southeast Asia. These make Indonesia important on a global scale and have led it into influential international bodies, such as the G20 (Garnaut 2012). From a slightly different perspective, Acharya (2014) argues that Indonesia is an emerging power with an unusual pathway, and does not rely too much on economic and military capacities. Instead, Indonesia's strength is more reliant on an interconnection between democracy, development and stability, while developing an active and independent foreign policy.

Regarding the approach to foreign policy, Indonesia has always tried to restrain from power groupings, while at the same time being active in international development processes. One of Indonesia's objectives in taking a leading role in ASEAN is to reduce its reliance on external powers for regional security (Smith 1999). Indonesian efforts to minimise its dependency on foreign countries reflect its foreign policy approach that avoids alignment with particular power blocs. Indonesia has promoted the value of a non-aligned movement (NAM) that could help it to avoid the segregation of global power and create a balance of power in the region. Indonesia first promoted the NAM at the 1955 Bandung conference (Suryadinata 1996). Since then, Indonesia has continued to promote the movement. In recent attempts, Indonesia welcomed the participation of Russia and the USA in the East Asia Summit (EAS) forum, to accommodate both poles of power in Asian regional cooperation (Wihardja 2011). The participation of Russia and the USA in the EAS is expected to reduce political tensions in the region.

In terms of the economy, Indonesia is a representative of other developing countries in Asia that have successfully combined internal capacity with regional support to recover and build economic fundamentals. During the period of democratic consolidation, Indonesia successfully restored its economy quite well by maintaining its positive economic growth, even as

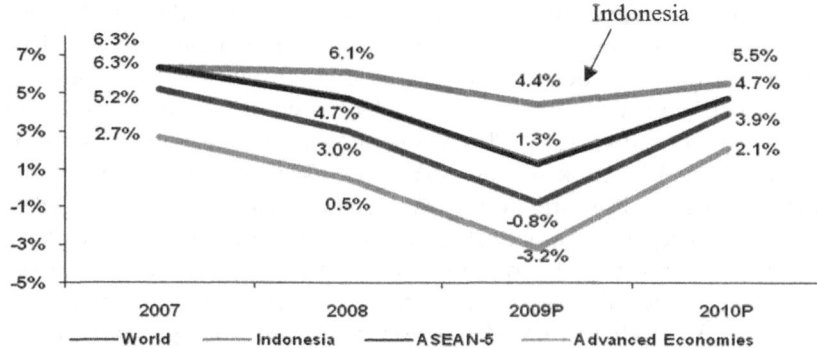

Fig. 1.1 Indonesian GDP rate compared to other groups of countries. Source: IMOF (2010)

other countries experienced recession due to the 2008–2009 global financial crisis. During the same period, Indonesia's economic growth was also higher than other economies in the region. Indonesia's gross domestic product (GDP) was above the aggregate GDP of big 5-ASEAN states; this led Indonesia to be part of G20 member countries representing Southeast Asian region. The data presented in Fig. 1.1 demonstrates that Indonesia successfully maintained a resilient trend of economic growth, even when the world and many other countries were experiencing a sharp decline in economic growth—a condition that makes Indonesia increasingly important for regional economic stability. Due to its economic performance, some have categorised Indonesia as an emerging power, along with countries like Brazil, Russia, India, China and South Africa (BRICS), although it is, in fact, still excluded from this designation.

Indonesia's rising economy may represent small states in the region. Nonetheless, Indonesia has demonstrated its distinct and important economic position compared to other countries. With an abundance of natural resources, a cheap labour force, strong consumption and a wide-scale territory, Indonesia has demonstrated its prominent role in the regional economy, not only as a production base but also as a potential market. This capacity is unique in the sense that not many countries in East Asia possess this potential, although China has all these capacities, except for natural resources.

The combination of political stability and economic fortune has led Indonesia to build its diplomatic roles. To some extent, Indonesia has demonstrated considerable success in dealing with political change, without too much expense to the economy. Particularly regarding relations between the rise of democracy and strong economic growth, Indonesia's experience presents a different story from the usual arguments that often support a positive relation between non-democratic regimes and strong economic growth (such as in China or Singapore). Indonesia has successfully maintained strong economic growth during the emergence of democracy. This unique condition adds to Indonesian confidence in searching for a leadership role—including in financial cooperation—under its new political regime. Overall, these factors also ensure that this study on Indonesia will contribute to filling the gap in the existing literature on East Asian financial regionalism, which predominantly focuses on big economic states such as Japan or China.

Approach and Data

This book provides an analytical discussion to understand financial regionalism within a political-economic context at the national and regional levels. In this regard, I deployed and applied the case study method to explain processes and to discover context. This is relevant to this study, which focuses on only one specific object. Sanders in Green (2011) argues that case studies help to understand processes of events, projects or programs, as well as to discover context characteristics that will shed light on an issue. Further, Gagnon (2010, p. 14) argues that case study research is best suited to practical issues in which the experience of the subject is central and the context of the experience is decisive. The case study approach reflects a researcher's observations and puts them into context. With these strengths, therefore, a case study is able to explain the complex story behind a phenomenon deeply and answer 'why and how', as it applies an intensive approach to monitoring such phenomenon. Green (2011, p. 2) argues that a case study assists in comprehending processes such as describing the context and discovering explanations for a problem being studied.

A case study often suffers from the problem of representativeness. That is, a single case study is often judged as not being representative of general phenomena. However, a case study is still a useful approach for understanding a larger class of similar units although the unit under focus may not perfectly represent the population (Gerring 2007, p. 20). This is particularly due to the ability of a case study to identify detailed processes that potentially can be generalised if new or more data for the case are added. In this respect, the case study approach provides foundation for a broader understanding of such phenomena.

As a research tool that is concerned with detailed processes, the case study has strong relations with *process tracing* methods. Mahoney (2015, p. 200) defines process tracing as a set of procedures to formulate and test explanations with case studies. Process tracing is often used to seek relations or causal inferences about a single case of a small number of cases. Mahoney (2015) argues that high-quality process tracing requires three basic elements: (i) good knowledge of the history of the case, (ii) good knowledge of relevant pre-existing theories and (iii) a strong capacity to carry out plausible reasoning by combining facts about the case with more general knowledge. Further, process tracing can be useful to identify the pattern of such events or phenomena. Waldner (2015) argues that process tracing may allow researchers to construct *causal graphs* that can provide complete statement of causal relations, as well as *event-history maps* that represent unit-level causal effects.

In this book, Indonesia is taken as a case study, focusing on its responses to APT financial cooperation. Thus, Indonesian financial authorities' related reactions in, and experiences of, financial initiatives under APT financial cooperation are at the core of this study. Specifically, this study investigates why and how Indonesian financial agencies exercise their authorities and mandates, coordinate with international counterparts and configure domestic regulatory framework to accommodate regional policy. Considering the complexity of the relevant issues as well as the different levels of analysis of this study, the case study with process tracing method is the best option to be applied as it can explain the processes involved in this study.

Further, this study's findings can be used to understand the responses of other countries to APT financial cooperation, although an intellectual limitation exists. The analytical findings from this Indonesian case study are expected to engender new thoughts about, and better understandings of, the development of financial regionalism in East Asia, simultaneously generating new hypotheses on the study of regulatory regionalism. However, the differences in domestic political economies and institutional configurations may result in this study being inapplicable to other countries.

I proceed this book by asking the main question: *How has Indonesia responded to APT financial cooperation?* Following this key question there are two further questions. First, what factors have affected Indonesia's responses to APT financial cooperation? Second, how, and to what extent, has Indonesia transformed its regulatory framework in response to APT regional financial governance?

To answer these questions, I mainly applied a regulatory regionalism approach, while retaining a neorealist approach to power politics as an important element of the analytical framework. Power relations and domestic politics are included in analytical framework of this study as the APT intergovernmental projects on financial issues largely involve both major powers' and national interests. The interrelations among state regulatory agencies comprise political and economic calculations on a bilateral basis that often influence the formation of national responses towards regional arrangements. Meanwhile, domestic politics are also essential, as they comprise interests, institutional arrangements, power sharing and other relevant factors, as considerations for financial authorities responding to APT financial cooperation.

While the essence of power relations and domestic politics has been used to examine financial regionalism in East Asia, a regulatory regionalism approach is relatively new for a study on financial regionalism. By regulatory regionalism, we mean regional governance as a process of internal transformation that creates the appearance of regional frontiers within the state (Jayasuriya 2009). In this respect, regulatory regionalism provides a basis to view East Asian financial regionalism beyond being a product of regional power politics, or a function of shared common purpose and identity, but as a reflection of the national dynamics of all member countries.

In general, regulatory regionalism is an approach typically influenced by the dynamics of state regulatory agencies, rather than formal regional institutions (Jayasuriya 2009). The concept has been developed intensively to understand the governance of regionalism in the context of the political projects of market-making and state transformation within individual countries (Jayasuriya 2009, p. 335). It represents a breakthrough for the current research on East Asian regionalism that has focused more on power politics and the outcomes of regional cooperation, rather than national dynamics. Regulatory regionalism places more focus on the regulatory project that operates within a state's space (Hameiri 2009; Jayasuriya 2009). In this regard, the process of internal regulatory transformation has an essential role in regulatory regionalism (Jayasuriya 2008). Accordingly, regulatory regionalism overcomes the overexposure of formal regional institutions' roles in regional governance. It also challenges majority views on regionalism that mostly admit regionalism as a result of external, rather than internal, drivers.

A regulatory regionalism approach perceives the new mode of regional governance as a result of international and national interactions, with greater contributions from domestic factors. In the past, such interactions have basically been recognised by Putnam (1988), resulting in the 'two-level games' theory on diplomacy. In this context, regulatory regionalism operates more on Putnam's second stage (Level II) of the game, where national authorities should deal with domestic pressures. While Putnam has successfully identified the need to satisfy domestic pressures and maximise national interests, he failed to clarify how domestic actors collaborate to transform national regulatory frameworks to accommodate international arrangements. On this point, regulatory regionalism offers an analytical framework in response to that gap. Drawing from Jayasuriya (2004, 2009, 2010a), the regulatory regionalism approach comprises four main analytical values:

- *The rise of non-state actors.* The new regional arrangement indicates the growing participation of private or non-state actors that play public or regulatory functions in the region. However, the roles of state regulatory agencies remain essential in the process of regionalism.
- *Policy coordination.* Policy coordination is one of the driving forces in the new mode of regional arrangements. Policy coordination shapes the development of policy networks among actors in the region.
- *Standardisation.* The new mode of regionalism encourages voluntary participation of national authorities to incorporate standards across levels of governance. Standardisation operates to deal with different levels of development, to facilitate regional integration.
- *De-politicisation of particular important areas.* De-politicisation relates to the attempt to insulate particular areas from political influence. De-politicisation minimises the discretionary approach and moves into a rule-based system.

The four features of regulatory regionalism provide a pathway to examine financial regionalism from a national perspective. They contribute to new insights on how national actors respond to regional financial arrangements, how policy coordination is shaped by state agencies and relevant non-state actors, how the standardisation project is perceived by related actors and how the de-politicisation of financial institutions affects the regulatory transformation of national space.

By addressing the above questions, this book makes two contributions to the literature. First, this book provides an analysis of Indonesia's national engagement in APT financial regionalism. It contributes to extending an in-depth study on East Asian regionalism by expanding the empirical research scope to the national level. The existing research in East Asian financial regionalism mainly focuses on the outcomes of regional forums; a very limited analysis of the domestic level exists, except for few studies on Japan and China. Second, in addition to its focus on regulatory regionalism, the book sheds new light on the financial sector, unlike previous studies on regulatory regionalism that mostly focused on education. While regulatory regionalism has helped explain national responses to regional arrangements of education issues, this book also provides an opportunity to broaden the use of regulatory regionalism as an alternative approach to politics and international relations, in the midst of existing dominant approaches, including neo-realism, constructivism and neo-functionalism. Thus, this book is expected to contribute to further develop the concept of regulatory regionalism for future research.

Data collection sites for this book were located in Indonesia, Japan, Singapore and Australia. For primary data, semi-standardised interviews were constructed to facilitate analyses of Indonesian state and non-state actor responses to the APT financial initiatives. The semi-standardised interviews were conducted in Jakarta, Tokyo and Singapore, from April to August 2012, with additional interviews conducted in October 2013. Therefore, the discussion and analysis in this book mainly refer to the situation before 2013. There are some new progresses and changes in Indonesia as well as in East Asian financial regionalism that may not be covered in this book.

In general, the interview participants were selected on the basis of their position, as well as their involvement in the development of APT financial cooperation. For state actors, the interviews were conducted with key officials in the Indonesian financial authorities: the IMOF and the BI. The interview participants from these institutions included low-, middle-, high-ranking and senior officials with various key roles in the development of APT financial cooperation. Beyond Indonesia, this study also includes interviews with key persons in regional organisations to deepen the understanding of several technical issues of APT financial projects, and to update the development of particular initiatives under the auspices of APT financial cooperation.

For secondary data, this study collected several official documents, including official reports, regulations, speeches and statistical data from Indonesian financial authorities. Official documents and reports produced by regional institutions were also collected and analysed to develop a more detailed and comprehensive analysis of the strategic and technical issues related to the APT financial initiatives. In addition, several relevant journals and publications were extensively reviewed to analyse recent debates on East Asian regionalism, regulatory regionalism, APT financial cooperation and the Indonesian political economy.

The structure of this book is as follows. Chapter 2 analyses existing understandings of the development of financial regionalism in East Asia. It reviews the existing research on East Asian financial regionalism, while paying attention to the roles of power relations and domestic factors. These two factors are essential to explain Indonesian considerations to respond to APT financial cooperation. Most importantly, this chapter also explains the regulatory regionalism approach as an analytical framework for this study.

Chapter 3 describes the development of financial regionalism in East Asia. In this chapter, the dynamics of financial initiatives within three regional institutions in East Asia (ASEAN, APEC and APT Cooperation) are discussed to detail the evolution of East Asian financial regionalism. This chapter aims to provide information for readers with limited knowledge of financial regionalism's progress in East Asia.

Chapter 4 examines the changes in Indonesian domestic politics and their influence on the way Indonesia has responded to East Asian financial regionalism. It analyses the different approaches developed by each Indonesian administration to respond to the development of financial regionalism in East Asia. It also examines the influence of democratisation on the decision-making processes of Indonesian financial affairs.

Chapter 5 analyses the influence of regional power relations and bilateral ties on Indonesia's response to APT financial regionalism. The intersections between power relations and bilateral ties between Indonesia and the East Asian power houses—Japan and China—are examined in this chapter, to understand the impacts of power politics at regional and national levels on financial arrangements. Assisted by a neorealist approach to power relations, this chapter delves deeper into the specific roles played by Japan and China in the progress of APT financial cooperation. Meanwhile, Indonesia's bilateral relations with Japan and China are also analysed, as they are understood to contribute to shaping Indonesia's stance towards current APT financial regionalism.

Chapter 6 examines the responses of Indonesian financial authorities towards the APT regional initiative on liquidity support assistance. The chapter particularly analyses the involvement of IMOF and BI in Chiang Mai Initiative Multilateralisation (CMIM), using four features of regulatory regionalism. It covers the pattern of policy coordination between these two financial agencies and internal regulatory transformation that includes issues related to standardisation on crisis countermeasures and the impact of de-politicisation on regulatory transformation.

Chapter 7 analyses the responses of Indonesia's financial authorities in dealing with the progress of APT regional bond market initiatives. As many APT bond market initiatives are still bound up in ongoing processes, this chapter investigates the perspectives of relevant authorities to the Indonesian bond market, as well as the views of Indonesian non-state actors to these ongoing initiatives. Similar to the previous chapter, this chapter also employs the four features of regulatory regionalism. By employing the same approach, this chapter not only provides variation on Indonesia's responses towards different initiatives under the auspices of APT financial cooperation, but also offers comparative evidence related to the application of a regulatory regionalism approach in regional financial affairs.

References

Acharya, A. (2014). *Indonesia matters: Asia's emerging democratic power*. Singapore: World Scientific Publishing Co. Pte. Ltd.

Anwar, D. F. (2010). The impact of domestic and Asia regional changes on Indonesian foreign policy. *Southeast Asian Affairs, 2010*, 126–141.

Buckley, R. P., Hu, R. W., & Arner, D. (Eds.). (2011). *East Asian economic integration: Law, trade and finance*. Chentelham: Edward Elgar.

Chandra, A. C., & Hanim, L. (2004). Indonesia's non-state actors in ASEAN: A new regionalism agenda for Southeast Asia? *Contemporary Southeast Asia, 26*(1), 155–174.

De Brouwer, G. (2002). The IMF and East Asia: A changing regional financial architecture. *Pacific Economic Papers*, Vol. 324.

Gagnon, Y.-C. (2010). *The case study as research method: A practical handbook*. Québec: Presses de l'Université du Québec.

Garnaut, R. (2012). Indonesia in the new world balance. In A. Reid (Ed.), *Indonesia rising: The repositioning of Asia's third giant* (pp. 14–27). Singapore: Institute of South Asian Studies.

Gerring, J. (2007). *Case study research: Principles and practices*. Cambridge: Cambridge University Press.

Green, R. A. (2011). *Case study research: A program evaluation guide for librarians*. California: Santa Barbara.

Grimes, W. W. (2008). *Political economy of bond market initiatives in East Asia*. Paper presented to American Political Science Association 2008 Annual Meeting, Boston, MA, August 28.

Grimes, W. W. (2009). *Currency and contest in East Asia: The great power politics of financial regionalism, Cornell Studies in Money*. Ithaca: Cornell University Press.

Grimes, W. W. (2011). The Asian monetary fund reborn? Implications of Chiang Mai Initiative Multilateralization. *Asia Policy, 11*(11), 79–104.

Hameiri, S. (2009). Beyond methodological nationalism, but where to for the study of regional governance? *Australian Journal of International Affairs, 63*(3), 430–441.

Hidetaka, Y. (2005). Political leadership, informality, and regional integration in East Asia: The evolution of ASEAN Plus Three. *European Journal of East Asian Studies, 4*(2), 205–232.

Indrawati, S. M. (2007). *Developing broader regional financial integration*. Paper presented to East Asia Summit's regional financial cooperation and integration workshop, Jakarta.

Indrawati, S. M. (2008). *Perspectives on Asian economic integration and cooperation*. Emerging Asian regionalism book launch, 41st Asia Development Bank Annual Meeting of the Board of Governors, Madrid.

Jayasuriya, K. (2004). The new regulatory state and relational capacity. *Policy & Politics, 32*(4), 487–501.

Jayasuriya, K. (2008). Regionalising the state: Political topography of regulatory regionalism. *Contemporary Politics, 14*(1), 21–35.

Jayasuriya, K. (2009). Regulatory regionalism in the Asia-Pacific: Drivers, instruments and actors. *Australian Journal of International Affairs, 63*(3), 335–347.

Jayasuriya, K. (2010). The emergence of regulatory regionalism. *Global Asia, 4*(4), 102–107.

Kawai, M. (2005). East Asian economic regionalism: Progress and challenges. *Journal of Asian Economics, 16*(1), 29–55.

Kawai, M. (2010). *East Asian financial co-operation and the role of the ASEAN+3 Macroeconomic Research Office*. Bonn: German Development Institute.

Mahoney, J. (2015). Process tracing and historical explanation. *Security Studies, 24*(2), 200–218.

Mattli, W. (2001). The politics and economics of international institutional standards setting: An introduction. *Journal of European Public Policy, 8*(3), 328–344.

Natalegawa, M. (2011). *Pidato Pernyataan Tahunan Menteri Luar Negeri Republik Indonesia 2011 (Annual Media Statement of Minister of Foreign*

Affairs of the Republic of Indonesia, 2011). Jakarta: Departemen Luar Negeri (Ministry of Foreign Affairs).

Putnam, R. D. (1988). Diplomacy and domestic politics: The logic of two-level games. *International Organization, 42*(3), 427–460.

Siregar, M. (2011). Indonesia's structural reform. *The Indonesian Quarterly, 39*(3), 249–255.

Smith, A. L. (1999). Indonesia's role in ASEAN: The end of leadership? *Contemporary Southeast Asia, 21*(2), 238–260.

Suryadinata, L. (1996). *Indonesia's foreign policy under Suharto: Aspiring to international leadership*. Singapore: Times Academic Press.

Waldner, D. (2015). Process tracing and qualitative causal inference. *Security Studies, 24*(2), 239–250.

Walter, A. (2008). *Governing finance: East Asia's adoption of international standards, Cornell Studies in Money*. Ithaca: Cornell University Press.

Wihardja, M. M. (2011). *2011 East Asia Summit: New members, challenges and opportunities*. East Asia Forum. Retrieved June 1, 2011, from http://www.eastasiaforum.org/2011/06/01/2011-east-asia-summit-new-members-challenges-and-opportunities/

Yoshimatsu, H. (2005). Political leadership, informality, and regional integration in East Asia: The evolution of ASEAN Plus Three. *European Journal of East Asian Studies, 4*(2), 205–232.

Yoshimatsu, H. (2014). *Comparing institution-building in East Asia: Power politics, governance, and critical junctures*. Palgrave Macmillan.

CHAPTER 2

Explaining Financial Regionalism in East Asia

East Asia is a diverse region in terms of politics and economy. The region is characterised by diverse values, political systems and levels of economic development that might seem to constrain any regional cooperation and integration processes between constituent countries. The domestic political configuration in East Asian countries ranges from authoritarian to more open democratic government structures. The region is also subject to various possible political conflicts. While East Asia can be regarded as stable, several intergovernmental disputes remain. Territorial disputes and overlapping claims of sovereignty remain unresolved under the peaceful political surface (Alatas 2001).

Financial regionalism in East Asia is always complex, but not impossible to build. It is complex due to the region's diversity, as well as differences in the level of engagement with the international system (Beeson 2003). The existing political tensions, the lack of regional cohesiveness and the legacy of colonialism also heighten the complexities in achieving effective and efficient intergovernmental arrangements in the region (Komori 2009, p. 321). Despite its complexity, the dynamics of East Asian financial regionalism—in the wake of the Asian financial crisis—have indicated significant progress in recent years. An example of this progress is the Association of Southeast Asian Nations (ASEAN) Plus Three (APT) financial cooperation. Several initiatives, including access to financing, financial stabilisation issues and bond market harmonisation, have resulted

© The Author(s) 2017   19
E. Saputro, *Indonesia and ASEAN Plus Three Financial Cooperation*,
DOI 10.1007/978-981-10-3029-1_2

in concrete programmes being implemented by APT member countries, while some initiatives are still undergoing negotiation.

East Asian financial regionalism can be viewed with three approaches: neo-realism, constructivism and neo-functionalism. From the neo-realist perspective, financial regionalism is perceived as an outcome of the major powers' influences. In general, neo-realists argue that power relations among major countries in the region shape and influence the development of such regionalism. Differing from neo-realism, proponents of constructivism perceive financial regionalism as a project developed or constructed despite complex economic and political situations. On this basis, constructivists emphasise the importance of the process of bringing various domestic characteristics into a common platform. Meanwhile, regionalism is viewed by neo-functionalism proponents as a medium to deal with common problems faced by member countries that potentially leads to political integration. In the neo-functionalist perspective, financial regionalism should provide answers to technical problems. Therefore, neo-functionalists place more importance on technical projects, rather than on other aspects of regional arrangements.

The objective of this chapter is to locate East Asian financial regionalism in the conceptual and theoretical landscape, and also introduce regulatory regionalism as an analytical framework to examine Indonesia's responses to the APT financial regionalism. This chapter begins with a review of the existing approaches to East Asian financial regionalism. It then analyses power relations and domestic dynamics that are understood to influence member states' responses to the development of financial regionalism in East Asia. Finally, this chapter presents the regulatory regionalism approach as a relevant analytical framework for this study.

Reviewing the Research on East Asian Financial Regionalism

Despite its political, economic and social diversity, East Asia has moved to shape regional cooperation. While initially security was the top concern, East Asian regionalism has eventually paved the way for more focus on economic issues, rather than on politics or other issues. East Asian countries tend to restrain themselves from raising political disputes, to maintain their economic cooperation (Shin and Cho 2010, p. 32). The growing interdependence in economic relations and lessons from the Asian financial crisis has encouraged East Asian countries to interact more closely with each other in financial affairs. These factors have contributed to shape various theoretical angles for understanding East Asian financial regionalism.

The first set of studies on East Asian financial regionalism emphasises power politics among the region's great powers. Power politics dominates the studies on financial regionalism in East Asia. In this respect, neo-realism provides a fundamental framework to analyse power relations within East Asian financial regionalism processes. For the proponents of neo-realism (Mearsheimer 1990; Walt 1987), regionalism is understood as a politics of alliance formation that pays more attention to power-political pressures and economic competition. In general, neo-realists argue that weak states remain reliant on the policies and attitudes of the major powers in regional economic arrangements (Hurrell 1995). As such, neo-realists assume that the states are key organising agents of international affairs, and fight for power and survival (Yoshimatsu 2014, p. 11). Accordingly, the proponents of neo-realism perceive that power politics determines the processes of financial regionalism in East Asia. The process of East Asian financial regionalism is viewed (for the most part) as being influenced by power relations. Several scholars (Amyx 2004; Choi 2013; Grimes 2012; Katzenstein 2000; Yoshimatsu 2014) argue that East Asian financial regionalism is greatly influenced by the power politics between three major countries: Japan, China and the United States (US). The power competition between Japan and China, in particular, has affected the long-term prospects of regional financial stability and integration (Amyx 2004, p. 111). Similarly, Choi (2013) emphasises that the political rivalry between Japan and China is an intra-regional factor that defines and exercises regional financial governance.

In addition to Japan and China, power relations in the East Asian region include those resulting from the US's involvement in the region, particularly on economic and security fronts. The long history of the US's interest in Asia has witnessed this superpower's continued engagement in the region's development. US hegemony, in the form of direct encouragement and pressure, plays an important role in spurring regional integration (Hurrell 1995). The involvement of the US, which is mostly indirect, influences the shape of, and mechanisms for, East Asian financial regionalism. Katzenstein (2000) argues that the US has influenced the defining of East Asian financial regionalism. In a broader and more comprehensive coverage, Grimes (2012) has defined three power games that have determined East Asian financial regionalism: those between creditors and borrowers; the contests between East Asia as a region and the global system represented by the International Monetary Fund (IMF) and the US; and the power game contested by Japan and China to gain regional leadership.

Neo-realism has helped identify power relations between the major powers in the development of East Asian financial regionalism. In general, neo-realist perspectives on East Asian financial regionalism are predominantly built upon a balance of power concept that generally resists the emergence of regional hegemony. In this respect, the dominance of Japan as the leading power in the East Asia region is maintained by China as a rising power that leads them into contestation. However, neo-realism places too much focus on power and the interests of major states in the region. This approach overlooks the roles of smaller states in the region, which cannot be excluded in the process of developing regional arrangements, particularly when the small states collaborate in a collective power such as ASEAN.

Moreover, the neo-realist perspective alone is inadequate to explain the effects of power relations on smaller states. In particular, it discounts the influence of power relations between major states on smaller states' policies and stances in regional arrangements. The contributions of bilateral ties between smaller states and the regional major powers in shaping the national stance of small states remain unanswered. Smaller states are often positioned by neo-realists as passive players in regionalism processes, with the major powers as the sole players in regional development.

The second set of studies explains East Asian financial regionalism by employing a constructivism approach. From the constructivist perspective, successful regionalism outcomes are still possible, even though the region faces differences in socio-economic, political and cultural systems. Davis (2010) argues that a distinctive characteristic of regionalism is that it is a constructive process, with the capacity to shift heterogeneity into homogeneity. He emphasises that states can either develop or dismantle regional constructs in order to address economic, socio-political or security challenges (Davis 2010, p. 35). Emmerson (2008) argues that regionalism has an underlying intention of bringing diverse states, societies or economies into a common dialogue around interests, purposes and activities. Another scholar (Stubbs 2002, p. 445) argues that history and cultural factors have combined to shape the development of a distinctive set of institutions and a particular approach to economic development within East Asian countries. For Acharya (2004, 2005), shared norms are critical factors that contribute to promote regionalism. In general, commonalities provide a platform for regional identity and consolidation.

Further, the norms of sovereignty, decision-making style and legalistic approaches are always considered in any discussion on Asian regionalism (He and Inoguchi 2011; Shiraishi and Katzenstein 1997). These norms have been adopted by East Asian regional institutions, like ASEAN, by implementing consensus, voluntarism and non-interference into its governance procedures (Beeson 2006, p. 545). The formation of ASEAN is the example of how regionalism was developed in the midst of diversity. Similarly, Stubbs (2002, p. 453) finds that the APT Cooperation processes facilitate a sense of common purpose and identity for East Asia, thus progressing towards regionalism.

The major contribution of constructivism in viewing East Asian financial regionalism is the recognition of different domestic characters. Constructivists are optimistic that domestic characteristics will not undermine the development of regionalism. However, constructivists do not present viable arguments regarding the level of heterogeneity that can be tolerated to achieve common goals. Further, constructivists also cannot provide sufficient explanation for the process of establishing concrete regional arrangements that are built upon diverse factors. Constructivists seem to simplify the processes in achieving common platforms that often involve 'conflicts' within a state or between states in the region. Constructivists have not effectively explained how the national or regional actors deal with such conflicts, as a result of different norms or regulatory constraints. Particularly in financial issues where economic interests and regulatory systems are critical and sensitive for many governments, creating common purposes and activities can be challenging, as these should encompass various national players, objectives, regulations and expectations. On this point, constructivists fail to discuss the real steps and constraints to bridge the various norms and capacities.

The third set of studies highlights the link between regionalism and regional interdependence based on the purpose of regionalism, by applying a neo-functionalism approach. For neo-functionalists, regional institutions are the most effective means of solving common problems, beginning with technical and non-controversial issues, but potentially leading to political integration (Hurrell 1995). Therefore, in many studies, the proponents of neo-functionalism are focused on creating institutions of cooperation. Some neo-functionalists, including De Brouwer (2002), Kawai (2005) and Soesastro (2006), view East Asian financial regionalism as a means to solve economic problems due to the financial crises faced by member countries. For De Brouwer (2002), developing new forms of regional financial cooperation is pivotal to protect the region from future crises, through technical arrangements for short-term liquidity assistance, followed by other areas, such as capital and bond markets. Kawai (2005, p. 1) argues that the most fundamental rationale behind the emergence of economic regionalism is the deepening of regional economic interdependence in East Asia. He views that deregulating financial systems, opening financial services to foreign institutions and liberalising capital accounts in East Asian countries have led to market-driven economic interdependence. In a clearer view of neo-functionalism, Soesastro (2006) argues that functional initiatives in the areas of finance—such as exchange of information, surveillance processes and development of bond markets—promote financial cooperation and integration. These studies posit that the technical projects of regional cooperation shape East Asian financial regionalism.

The neo-functionalist approach is often used by regionalists to propose a regional initiative or project as a response to financial challenges faced by several countries in the region. While neo-functionalists have successfully ensured the benefits of creating regional projects to solve common financial problems, it is likely that they have overlooked the domestic constraints and capacities faced by each member country. South Korea's option to seek assistance from the US Federal Reserve, instead of activating Chiang Mai Initiative Multilateralisation (CMIM)'s swap facility, demonstrates how regional projects may not be fully functioning for certain conditions. In another case, the existence of a bilateral swap arrangement between Indonesia and Japan after the establishment of CMIM reflects doubts about the effectiveness of regional arrangements. Put simply, there are certain economic problems that might be solved efficiently through non-regional arrangements.

Neo-functionalists have provided insights on the stages of potentially achieving political integration through technical cooperation. However, the concept is seemingly unfinished and gives minimal consideration to other factors that are essential in developing political integration. The neo-functionalist approach may be well applied to explain the development of financial regionalism in Europe that has led to political integration. However, it is worth noting another variable that plays a significant role in Europe's regional development: *democracy*. As a shared norm, democracy has largely contributed to political integration in Europe. In this regard,

East Asia has a different story. While regional technical projects have developed financial regionalism in East Asia, their contribution to establish political integration remains vague due to diverse political ideologies.

This overview of the three approaches presents several factors that influence financial regionalism in East Asia. Among these factors are two prominent elements—power relations and domestic factors—that help examine national responses to East Asian financial regionalism. The political and economic interdependence among East Asian countries accounts for the strong influence of the major powers, namely Japan and China, in the development of East Asian regionalism. Meanwhile, complexity at the national level, including domestic politics, national interests, economic capacities and other relevant factors, suggests contributions to shaping national responses to regional arrangements. Both factors deserve more detailed discussion in this section.

Power Relations

As mentioned earlier, neo-realists emphasise the importance of power relations to East Asian financial regionalism. The development of financial regionalism has been influenced by the power relations between Japan and China, the two major power houses in East Asia. The longstanding political and economic competition between Japan and China has affected the progress and governance of East Asian financial regionalism. Yoshimatsu (2008a) argues that 'great power' politics has built a basic framework for East Asian regional arrangements. In the context of East Asian financial cooperation, regional arrangements have become not only a medium for regional powers to spread their influence, but also a means for small powers to limit the unpredictable actions of great powers. The absence of regional cohesiveness between small and medium powers in East Asia has resulted in an inability to mitigate unexpected reactions of Western countries during the Asian financial crisis.

Beside the contribution of its great economic capacity, Japan's regional power is also built upon two factors: US support as a 'push factor', and the intention of Asian countries to be more inward-looking as a 'pull factor'. Benefiting from its tight political and security engagement with the US, Japan's post-war foreign policy shifted to Asia to build regional stability. Maswood (2001a) has argued that the opportunity to take regional leadership began with US retrenchment from the region. For Japan, regional political and economic stability are essential to support production, and the market for its products. To pursue its objective of regional stability, Japan has been forced to take a more active and assertive political role in the region (Alvstam 2001, p. 188). Hurrell (1995) argues that the containment of Japanese power was achieved by undermining macro-regionalism and a tight extra-regional alliance with the US. In the meantime, many East Asian countries started building their own capacities. Japan provides financial assistance for these countries. Japan has also become an important source of support for many areas of development in many Southeast Asian countries, especially through the provision of investment funds, as well as financial and technical assistance. For example, in 2010 the ASEAN countries received US$8.4 billion of investment inflows from Japan, establishing Japan as the third largest fund provider for ASEAN, after the European Union (EU) and the US (APT 2011). This assistance has promoted the pivotal role of Japan as a major power in the region.

Meanwhile, China has emerged as a new rising power ready to challenge Japanese domination in East Asia. A country is defined as a rising power if it has a strong potential to become a great power (Acharya 2014). In the Chinese context, a strong economy has significantly contributed to build China's power capacity in the region. With its high economic growth, cheap labour and expansive market, China has transformed its capacity to become a major global powerhouse. China's economy was more than half of that of the US and almost double that of Japan (IMF 2013). In recent years, China has been fortunate to enjoy rapid economic growth, which has resulted in it being the world's second largest economy. China has also been on its way to replacing Japan as the major global producer of manufactured products; it will succeed the US as the major player in the global market. The continuity of both its economic growth and overall size of economy has led to China's potential dominance of the region, thus displacing Japan's central occupation of that role in the regional arrangement (Maswood 2001b, p. 17). In this respect, China has become a 'challenger' for Japan as the leading country in the region. The country's strong economy has paved the way for China to define regional development.

In order to maintain its growing economy, China has no choice but to secure its relations with the East Asian countries. For China, regional cooperation will not only secure its economy, but also strengthen its powerful political and competitive position (Breslin 2010). The absence of China in any regional cooperation could potentially create a negative impression of itself as exclusive and self-interested. Particularly with regard to ASEAN, China needs to cooperate with Southeast Asian countries, as its relationship with Japan is not yet completely stabilised (Wanandi 2002, p. 228). At the same time, regional cooperation may also reduce the fear of Southeast Asian countries that has emerged due to China's growing power. He (2004) argues that the traumatic memories of communism as a regional threat during and after World War II are expected to be lessened by tight regional cooperation. Beijing has proactively utilised financial regionalism to increase its influence over regional policy making and polish its credentials as a gentle regional hegemon (Katada and Sohn 2014, p. 154). China's engagement with regional cooperation also shows that its political ideology is compatible with different political ideologies in the region. By maintaining close cooperation with its neighbours, China conveys the message that its political ideology is not a threat to the democracy already flourishing in South East Asia. For instance, China can work closely with Myanmar in bilateral as well as regional cooperation, although Myanmar is in the middle of democratising its political system.

In practice, China has been applying a soft diplomatic approach that enables it to keep a low profile in the eyes of its regional neighbours. Zhu Rongji, a former Chinese premier, understands that an aggressive approach might result in negative outcomes for China. He argues that China should 'give more and take less', and also 'give first and take later', in maintaining regional cooperation (cited in Wang 2011b, p. 203). Increasing Chinese participation in regional institutions is likely to be successful in building trust among other countries and attract positive responses from the region.

Power relations between Japan and China can either facilitate or hinder the development of financial regionalism. On the one hand, Sino–Japanese power relations can expedite the progress of East Asian financial regionalism. Chey (2009, p. 466) argues that the political dynamics between Japan and China have contributed to promote further cooperation within the region. The political rivalry between Tokyo and Beijing provides stimulus for closer regional arrangements, especially in relation to the development of regional economic cooperation. Amyx (2005), in particular, argues that China's proactive stance is a critical force that contributes to accelerate the regionalism process. In contrast, the political stance of East Asia's major powers can constrain the pace of financial regionalism. Japan's proposal on the Asian Monetary Fund (AMF) was opposed not only by the US, but also by China (Grimes 2009). The expansion of the East Asia Summit (EAS) also reportedly involved disagreement between Japan and China, particularly in regard to its membership and basic character (Yoshimatsu 2014). Clearly, Japan's or China's reaction to regional arrangement has influenced the progress of regionalism in East Asia.

Further, Japan–China power relations determine smaller states' positions in East Asian regional arrangements. Most East Asian states are at the development stage regarding their economies. After gaining political sovereignty in the post-colonial era, political-economic interdependence with, and perception of, major powers remain high and influential regarding foreign policy options. As such, political and economic interdependence is often associated with calculating benefits generated from political and economic relations, while perceptions are more related to the ways in which individual countries build their perspectives of their regional counterparts. In the context of international relations, Novotny (2010, p. 31) defines perception as a concept that describes the construction of reality in the eyes of individuals involved in foreign policy decision-making processes. Moreover, a shared perception of belonging to a particular community often defines regional awareness (Hurrell 1995). In East Asia, these perceptions are largely shaped by the interplay between historical trauma, national interests and interpersonal communications.

Overall, while the existing approaches of international studies on power relations have provided valuable insights into East Asian regionalism, they have provided limited tools for a domestic level of analysis. This is particularly the case for financial issues where confidentiality is essential, and understanding the motives of states in joining regional arrangements is critical.

Domestic Factors

In the context of regionalism, there is a mutual correlation between domestic factors and regional arrangements. The dynamics of regionalism often depend on certain domestic prerequisites. Hurrell (1995) argues that domestic policy convergence has been an important factor in the revival of regionalism. The combination of domestic vulnerability and uncontrolled external fragility is understood to act as a catalyst for regionalism (Beeson 2007, p. 217). Similarly, Schirm (2002, p. 6) argues that the centrality of the state is pivotal, particularly as the driving force in international relations and power seeking, which are in line with national interests. The prominent roles of state actors in representing and protecting public interests head the influence of domestic factors on the regionalism process.

On this basis, states naturally use regional arrangements to support their national interests. Simply, states calculate the advantages and disadvantages of intergovernmental arrangements for their national interests. Accordingly, regional integration is not part of a grand project of moving 'beyond the nation-state', but rather is the best means of sheltering or protecting domestic projects (Hurrell 1995, p. 356). Mittelman (2000) similarly argues that regionalism is used to preserve national policy instruments that are difficult to sustain individually. Several developing countries have used regionalism, especially in economic areas, to enhance their bargaining power with transnational corporations or trading partners, and at the same time to constrain the disruptive effects of excessive power (Ravenhill 2011; Yoshimatsu 2008b). With a relatively similar objective, regionalism has also become an alternative medium for nation-states to resist globalisation (Nesadurai 2003, p. 37); although Dieter and Higgott (2003, p. 431) present a different view by arguing that regionalism is an ineluctable part of globalisation.

Domestically, political and economic factors have more influential roles when compared to other domestic factors in affecting national responses to regionalism. On this point, while Beeson (2007) emphasises nationalism and domestic politics, Jiang (2010) presents the domestic economy as an essential element when responding to the development of regionalism. Regarding nationalism, Beeson (2007) argues that it is a powerful force in East Asia that influences the course of regionalism. The early development of political and economic conditions has put pressure on 'young' East Asian countries to pay attention to national interests and sovereignty. To some degree, the keen focus on national interest has stimulated a strong sense of nationalism that potentially jeopardises the regionalism process. Stubbs (2002) argues that attention to regionalism gave way to nationalism during the economic crisis. As an example, in the midst of the global financial crisis, the Indonesian government encouraged its people to consume national products primarily, to sustain the Indonesian market—a policy that can be seen to inhibit the direction of regionalism. Strong nationalism in many Asian countries could decelerate the pace of financial regionalism, as it promotes protectionism and rolls back established market liberalisation measures.

The issue of nationalism is closely related to national sovereignty. Issues surrounding the sovereignty of countries in the East Asian region have also been included in debates on regionalism. With regard to regional arrangements, most East Asian countries perceive that national sovereignty cannot be bypassed by regional or international cooperation. Compared to European countries, East Asian countries are not confident and mature enough to give up some of their sovereign powers (He 2004, p. 118). In this respect, regional financial arrangements are often perceived as a potential threat to sovereignty, despite their overall benefits. Therefore, regional cooperation, such as that developed and implemented by ASEAN or APT, is still far away from pooling sovereignty organisations, as has occurred in the EU (Murray 2010, p. 311). The long history of achieving independence has shaped sovereignty into nationalism as a foremost norm for many Asian countries. Nationalism has become a basic stance to respond to foreign relations.

Economy and security are central to state sovereignty. Therefore, East Asian regionalism only includes regional material, free trade agreements and a security dialogue without intellectual and political commitments (He 2004, p. 118). The threat of colonisation, even if by an Asian neighbour, and consequently the countries' sense of security and prosperity are a major reason why East Asian countries take a prudent approach to policies and actions on security. This is an attempt to safeguard their national sovereignty. The severely oppressive experience during the World War II period of colonialism has meant that Asian countries now highly value, and fight to protect, sovereignty (Cameron 2010, p. 287). The trauma of being colonised by more powerful nations has pushed these countries to respond cautiously to external cooperation. With economic cooperation, the presence of state actors, such as ministries of finance or central banks—as focal points in many East Asian economic cooperation projects—suggests that the sensitivity of economic sovereignty remains high, and any cooperation related to economic matters should be handled by the state.

A high regard for sovereignty has led to the formation of a non-interference norm. East Asian countries hold this principle close, as a way to present their mutual respect for sovereignty. ASEAN, in particular, uses non-interference as a basis for it being a regional institution (Cai 2010, p. 122). The non-interference norm is understood to keep the region free from regional conflict or war. While it is acceptable to respect the sovereignty of a member country, the issue of sovereignty can be a major constraint in handling transnational threats, such as financial shock or terrorism, as other member states are not able to push for any direct action (Acharya 2005, p. 103). On many occasions, ASEAN countries have employed lengthy processes to resolve disputes among themselves, as they understand the imperative to avoid any actions that could be potentially regarded as intervention.

To briefly reiterate, for ASEAN countries in particular, the matter of sovereignty should be at the top of any regional cooperation agenda. The ASEAN member countries prefer to maintain their veto powers in decision-making processes through attempts to develop a consensus mechanism (He 2004). In this respect, such a mechanism may decrease the likelihood that each member state would be forced to follow the majority in the implementation of such an agreement. The ASEAN Charter even allows member countries to abstain from such initiatives, even if the majority agrees on a particular decision (Simon 2008). In the adoption process of ASEAN initiatives, there are no sanctions or penalties for member states that take a different position against the majority. In other words, the internal transformation to facilitate regional arrangements remains reliant on domestic efforts, in the absence of strong regional pressures. The consensus mechanism continues to have a significant place in APT decision-making processes, where ASEAN is claimed as the driver of APT Cooperation. While the voting mechanism has been adopted in the current development of APT financial cooperation, members still rely on a consensus mechanism in their decision-making processes (Suzuki 2004, p. 30).

Domestic politics plays an important role in examining national responses, for two reasons. The first reason is that domestic politics determines the engagement of state agencies at the regional level. Mansfield and Milner (1999) argue that domestic politics should be considered as a major factor in shaping regionalism. In this respect, the dynamics of domestic political situations emerges as a catalyst, as well as a constraint, for regional affairs. Political commitment, in particular, is needed to deal with regional projects, such as the harmonisation of market regulations in the midst of different regulatory models and different stages of economic development (Dalla 2003). He and Inoguchi (2011) similarly note that domestic political systems and culture affect political preferences for future regional cooperation. An example of this is the Thai government's decision to take ASEAN's non-interference approach, instead of the 'flexible engagement' approach it had proposed earlier, when it attempted to avoid foreign interference in its domestic political turmoil. Another example is the Indonesian policy to lessen attention on regional issues, while raising the priority of domestic problems during the internal political distress of 1997 to 1999 (Stubbs 2002, p. 451). These Thai and Indonesian policy options demonstrate how domestic politics affects national commitments to such regional arrangements.

The second reason is that domestic politics determines the implementation of regional arrangements. Domestic politics defines the process of internal transformation in response to such regional arrangements. The legalisation of regional agreements, or the voluntary adoption of regional standards, requires domestic political support. Rosser (2004) argues that political systems matter in the adoption of universal models of governance. Such political systems facilitate the establishment of reforms, in accordance with external models of governance. Kirschner and Stapel (2012, p. 154) have argued for a correlation between regime type and the national commitment to regional arrangements. Using the case of West African economic cooperation, the authors reveal that autocratic states are less committed than democratic ones to regional integration. In a similar area of study, Mansfield et al. (2002, p. 477) argue that the likelihood of a state cooperating on trade policy increases as it engage in more democratic forms of government. Mansfield and Milner (1999, p. 606) argue that democratic reforms become a prerequisite for various Eastern European countries to obtain EU preferential tariff agreement (PTA) membership. These findings accord with Collins' study (2009, p. 276), which reveals that authoritarian regimes tend to oppose or undermine economic regionalism, as this requires a liberalisation that potentially jeopardises the regime's power. However, these findings are challenged by Wang (2011a), who found that the commitment and contribution of the Chinese socialist regime towards a number of regional trade agreements (RTAs) are significant. On this basis, the relation between the type of political regime and the level of commitment to regional arrangements remains debatable. Commitments cannot be symmetric across areas of cooperation. A member country's commitment to financial cooperation is not automatically followed by a commitment to other regional arrangements, such as security or energy cooperation. The influences of domestic politics on the national responses to such regional arrangements are often unique, in the sense that they are different from one another, and cannot be generalised.

Among studies on the intersection between domestic politics and international commitment, Putnam's (1988) summation of the 'two-level games' is considered pivotal when examining national responses to regional arrangements. In general, the theory attempts to explain the domestic constraints faced by negotiators in dealing with international agreements. In a similar study, Milner (2002, p. 20) argues that international cooperation results from political leaders' expectation to be re-elected, and is constrained by the need for domestic ratification of such international agreements. While Putnam has already recognised the importance of domestic politics and its link to international events, his observation merely focuses on how national authorities deal with 'hard law' in a diplomatic context. Putnam places too much emphasis on developing bargaining positions in international negotiations, and overlooks the state actors' coordination process with other actors within the state, or among different states. Putnam's theory of two-level games also leaves the question of interaction patterns between state and non-state actors unanswered. On this point, Putnam (1988, p. 459) basically admits that his work needs further exploration. Therefore, this theory may not be appropriate to analyse current financial regionalism in East Asia, which involves a 'soft law' approach in the dissemination of regional governance, and also includes the critical role of policy coordination among participating actors—not only state, but also non-state actors.

Besides domestic politics, domestic economy also contributes to shape the dynamics of regional engagement. Economic development at the national level determines the degree of state engagement with regional arrangements. There are two elements of domestic economy that contribute to shape national responses to regional arrangements. The first is related to macroeconomic conditions that are reflected in economic indicators, such as the balance of payments, government revenue and expenditure, market infrastructure and economic growth. Domestic economic conditions determine the power potentials that will eventually affect the level of state engagement in regional financial cooperation. For instance, a state that still suffers from balance of payment difficulties will likely participate in regional financial arrangements to seek regional assistance, compared to those states with relatively few, or no, problems with their balance of payments. For instance, economic stagnation has inhibited Indonesia and Japan from preserving their traditional position as leaders of Southeast and East Asia, respectively, with both re-prioritising their regional interests as a second main concern (Stubbs 2002). In contrast, through its national economic success, China has been able to attract regional partners to secure its economy from unwarranted competition, through regional cooperation and collaboration (Breslin 2010, p. 72). Jiang (2010) also states that the domestic economy has made Beijing determined to share power with Tokyo in the decision-making process of regional financial arrangement. These stories attest to the notion that national economic status substantially contributes to shaping regional cooperation between East Asian countries.

The second element regarding the domestic economy relates to the economic openness that is reflected in economic regulation. In today's development, where economic interdependence and integration are increasing, countries have more exposure to one another through free trade arrangements, as well as financial and capital market access. Naturally, states will try to manage the degree of their economic openness to avoid risks and contagion effects as a result of international exposure. In this regard, small states usually tend to manage their economic openness at a minimum level. In comparison, Malaysia, Singapore and Thailand are classified as always open, while Indonesia and the Philippines (as one group) and all new ASEAN member countries are categorised as less open and closed, respectively (Sachs-Warner cited in Hill and Menon 2010, p. 11). Clearly, most ASEAN member countries are likely to maintain and secure their own markets. No wonder the smaller ASEAN economies engage in regional financial arrangements carefully. Similarly, China's participation in regional financial integration faces significant constraints, as it still controls its exchange rate heavily, and its capital account has not yet been liberalised, while integration entails a free flow of capital (Jiang 2010). Put simply, the degree of economic openness to the international economy in each member country affects the various responses to regional initiatives.

Overall, the existing approaches on regionalism have helped identify the importance of power relations and domestic factors when examining national responses to financial regionalism. However, there is a tendency for these existing approaches to experience some level of problematic analysis, in which they isolate the regional from the domestic level, and vice versa. The approaches seem to prioritise one level of analysis over another. The existing approaches also provide insufficient explanation of critical issues related to regional–domestic interaction and internal transformation in response to regional financial arrangements.

On this basis, an analytical framework that can explain the interaction between various levels of analysis is necessary. Accordingly, I adopt a regulatory regionalism approach to fill the gap in examining national responses towards financial regionalism in East Asia.

Regulatory Regionalism

Regulatory regionalism is useful to analyse regionalism processes in which a formal regional institution is absent. Jayasuriya (2010a, p. 103) defines regulatory regionalism as the development of regional regulatory frameworks within political and policy-making institutions of national governments. He notes that regionalism does not emerge above or beyond the state, but appears from inside the political space of the state (Jayasuriya 2008, p. 22). Regulatory regionalism stresses the basics of regional regulatory projects within the space of the state's institutions (Jayasuriya and Robertson 2010, p. 3). Therefore, the new mode of regional governance is typically more influenced by the dynamics of national regulatory bodies in the practices of regulations, rather than by formal regional organisations or international agreements. Jayasuriya and Robertson (2010, p. 24) argue that regulatory regionalism can overcome the overemphasis on formal regional institutions' roles in regional governance, and that most perspectives on regionalism tend to conceive that regionalism is a result of an externally driven process, rather than an internally driven one.

In recent years, regulatory regionalism has been developed intensively to better understand regionalism in the context of political projects, such as market-making and state transformation within individual countries (Jayasuriya 2009, p. 335). Political projects are advanced by social forces with the discursive power and material capability to secure new regional frontiers that, in turn, enable new strategic relational forms, including state organisation and political rule (Robertson 2010). Hameiri (2009, p. 439) echoes Jayasuriya's idea of domestic transformation by emphasising that several new forms of regionalism are embedded within the state, its governing apparatus and its sub-regions, relating to the state's 're-spatialisation'. Again, in regulatory regionalism, the ability of national regulatory agencies to determine the processes and results of regulatory regionalism is critical, as they have the power to transform national space. Hameiri (personal communication, May 2011) clarifies that new modes of governance do not necessarily involve establishing supra-national regional mechanisms as such, but could involve incorporating regional governance into the state itself, so that parts of the state apparatus are 'regionalised', although they retain the appearance of national governance.

There are four features of regulatory regionalism. The first is *a movement from nation and state to region and non-state*. This feature particularly emphasises the growing participation of non-state actors in the regionalism process. Jayasuriya's empirical study reveals the rise of non-state actors in shaping regional governance (2009, p. 335); for example, the involvement of the Asian Development Bank (ADB) in setting up the Chiang Mai Initiative (CMI)—as well as the Asian Bond Market Initiative (ABMI)—indicates a greater engagement of non-state actors in the process of East Asian financial regionalism. Arthurs (in Stone 2008) notes that the emergence of private regimes, global standard setting and transnational policy communities has shaped a so-called soft authority, as distinct from 'hard' or formal authority.

The growing participation of non-state actors in the process of regionalism stimulates the new configuration of public–private actor collaboration; namely, *accountability communities*. Jayasuriya (2010b, p. 8) describes accountability communities as

> An institutional ensemble that brings together a diverse array of public and private actors around specific practices and ideas of accountability that hold to account the conduct of agents within regulatory regime. Accountability communities define the legitimacy of regulatory regimes, and provide the basis on which new forms of state and market-marking are created.

As such, accountability communities operate to achieve public acceptance of regional regulatory regimes. Most importantly, accountability communities operate through institutional forms, such as deliberative forums, markets or network mechanisms (Jayasuriya 2010b). Therefore, legitimation becomes a crucial issue, as the transformation and relocation of public authority are needed to build accountability communities. Jones (2010) argues that interlocking policy domains, mutual interests and commitment to regional and inter-regional activities is central to achieve a certain degree of accountability.

However, the growing trend of non-state actor participation in regionalism does not necessarily mean that the state's role in the process of regional governance is ignored. While there is a growing participation of non-state actors in the development of APT financial cooperation, the roles of state regulatory agencies in the process of cooperation remain significant. Murray (2010) argues that state actors remain pivotal in the East Asian context. In a similar vein, Komori (2009) also emphasises the crucial position of government leaders as primary actors in determining regional architecture in East Asia, despite the growing participation of non-state actors. The state of regulatory regionalism entails connections between international organisations and various national institutions, not just shifts from nation to region (Jayasuriya 2003, p. 207). The state's role remains important in the process of regulatory regionalism, particularly for the transformation of domestic space within a national framework.

The second feature of regulatory regionalism is *policy coordination*. Jayasuriya (2010a) argues that policy coordination is an important driving force in regulatory regionalism. Jayasuriya claims that policy coordination in emerging regional financial governance will enhance the development of transnational policy networks (2009, p. 341). Policy coordination has been recognised as a key element of regional economic cooperation among APT member countries (Choi 2013; Grimes 2012). In line with Jayasuriya, Stone (2008, p. 26) acknowledges that, especially in regional arrangements, some governments and international organisations actively promote cross-border policy harmonisation. Both authors identify that transnational policy networks, or cross-border policy harmonisation, involve public and private actors at various levels: national, regional and global. In this regard, detecting the nature of a policy network will assist observation of regionalism's development (Jayasuriya 2009, p. 344).

Regional policy coordination retains its strategic function over national boundaries. It is a reflection of national collaborative action among authorities. Transnational policy coordination, for instance, can be triggered by domestic economic threats that can potentially destabilise regional economies. This is why managing finance and risks has become the core project of regional governance in East Asia. The Economic Review and Policy Dialogue (ERPD) of the APT financial cooperation initiative is an example of how regional cooperation has responded to vulnerabilities and systemic risks through regional policy coordination (Kawai 2010, p. 51). The policy coordination within the ERPD is expected to facilitate exchange of information and peer review mechanisms on domestic macroeconomic policies of the APT member countries.

The third feature is *standardisation*. As regulatory regionalism operates in the absence of rigid and binding regional agreements, the role of standards as benchmarks has become critical. Jayasuriya (2010b, p. 16) argues that in regulatory regionalism, different national systems may retain elements of their own regulatory architecture, while adopting common standards. In other words, such standards can be adopted as templates for national regulatory governance. Jones (2010, pp. 74–75) provides an example of how the Bologna Process produced well-defined sets of standards and guidelines for the European higher education system. While the Bologna Process was initially set up for European countries, it has been adopted by Kazakhstan and Kyrgyzstan (of Central Asia). Both countries have reformed their higher education systems along the Bologna Process action lines that these countries recognise as international standards. The

Bologna Process action lines have become education standard benchmarks for Kazakhstan and Kyrgyzstan while both countries retain the ability to set their own education systems.

Standardisation is basically a mechanism to bring regional governance into national regulatory frameworks. In financial contexts, the core idea of standardisation is to formulate and disseminate standards or best practices to promote domestic financial reform, particularly in emerging markets (Walter 2008). This is typically a claim that usually follows the standard-setting project, in which standardisation is expected to introduce a new rule or governance. Standardisation is often viewed as reflecting a minimum level of effectiveness (Kerwer 2005). Therefore, if something does not meet the standard, it does not achieve the minimum level of effectiveness.

To comply with agreed standards, standardisation often relies on voluntary participation, or a 'soft law' approach, instead of enforcing a legalistic or 'hard law' approach, to make regional governance effective in national systems. Kirton and Trebilcock (2004) describe hard law as a regime that relies on the authority and power of the state, whereas soft law relates to a regime that is primarily reliant on participation and the resources of non-state actors. In a similar vein, Abbott and Snidal (2000) define hard law as a special mechanism to make legally binding obligations, whereas soft law refers to voluntary action to comply with standards or best practices. Clearly, hard law requests the authoritative power to enforce standards on the national regulatory framework. Such power is needed to ensure that any 'conflict' emerging due to different regulatory systems can be resolved. Therefore, the hard law approach is relatively efficient in terms of time, although it may trigger disputes at the enforcement stage of standardisation. In contrast, the soft law approach is often time-consuming, to compensate for the smooth processes of standardisation.

The fourth element of regulatory regionalism is the *de-politicisation* of several important areas, particularly economic governance. Jayasuriya (2003, p. 206) states that there are three important means of de-politicisation. The *first* is by placing economic institutions beyond the reach of democratically elected office holders. This arrangement is more related to institutional power in economic areas. The separation of the central bank from the executive power of government, such as in Indonesia, is an example of how de-politicisation works. Walter (2008, p. 21) argues that the insulation of economic regulation from politics via an independent agency is the central principle of regulatory neoliberalism. His view reflects the general neoliberal argument that often enforces market-oriented rules that are immune to political opportunism. In a more direct statement, Isaac (2003, p. 247) points out that regulatory regionalism supports the national regulatory autonomy of the various member countries within the region. The *second* is that de-politicisation operates through the economic policy-making process. In this respect, rule-based forms of governance are more applicable than discretionary approaches. Such agencies should be able to enforce transparent governance impartially, within a limited 'zone of discretion' (Walter 2008, p. 21). This process is evident in the way some Asian countries adjust their economic crisis management mechanisms, by introducing an institutional approach to limit the powerful mandate that is usually held by a ministry of finance, and to avoid any potential power abuse and moral hazards during a crisis mitigation processes. The *third* is through the de-contextualisation of 'agency' from relations of economic and social power, and its consequent embedding within frameworks, such as responsibility and community. At the regional level, de-politicised institutions participate in shaping the new mode of regional governance. The involvement of the financial stability agencies of several member countries in the negotiation process of the APT Bond Market Forum (ABMF) suggests that the presence of new and autonomous regulatory institutions is inevitable for the future development of financial sector regional arrangements.

As illustrated in Fig. 2.1, regulatory regionalism operates through 'meta-governance' and policy networks that monitor and enforce a broad set of standards. In this respect, meta-governance brings standards and policy coordination mechanisms across different levels of governance to existing national frameworks, under the shadow of international and national governmental authorities (Jayasuriya 2009, p. 342).

The concept of meta-governance can be complicated and obscure. Jayasuriya clarifies that meta-governance refers to the 'governance of governance', or 'policing governance', in which a particular form of governance supervises another at a different level (personal communication, August 2014). This arrangement indicates the importance of standards and policy coordination to monitor and oversee regional mechanisms at all levels of governance. An example of this concept is the commitment of the Indonesian central bank, Bank Indonesia (BI), to the global issue

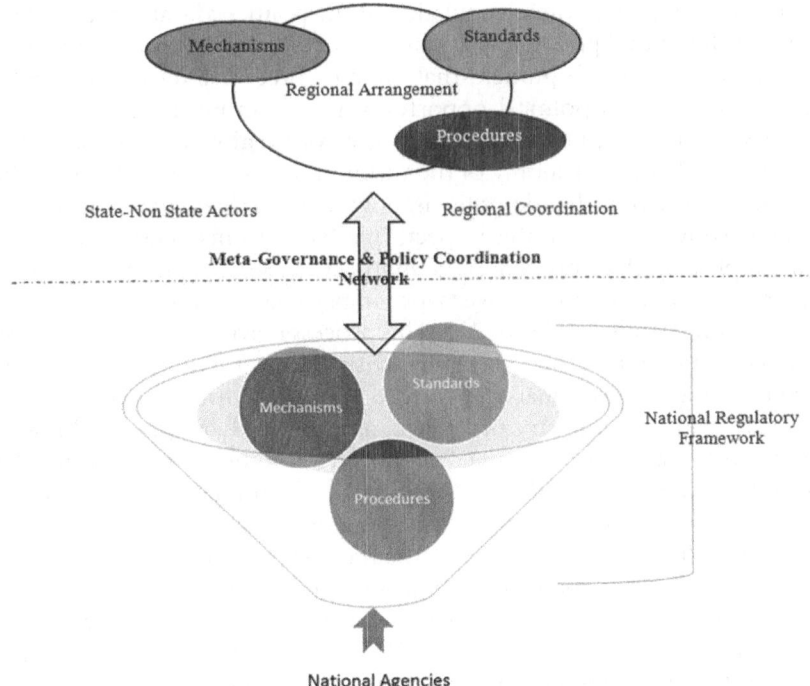

Fig. 2.1   Visualisation of regulatory regionalism. Source: Author's own visualisation

of financial inclusion—an effort to ensure that all households and businesses, regardless of their income level, have access to appropriate financial services. While the World Bank (WB) initially coined the term 'financial inclusion', the issue was then promoted and globally disseminated by G20 member countries as a global agenda. Using its legitimacy derived from the international financial regime, BI released policies related to financial inclusion, such as a 'multi-licensing' policy that pushes Indonesian private banks to provide loans for micro-industries, and also a 'branchless banking' policy, which aims to enhance the coverage of banking services (Shrader 2013). In this respect, financial inclusion indicators produced by the WB become benchmarks for relevant national institutions in promoting financial inclusion in Indonesia.

Further, regulatory regionalism perceives that a policy coordination network is an essential means for transforming the national space, simply because each regulatory agency has a different mandate and range of power. The policy coordination network covers inter- and intra-coordination of governance and policy among actors. Jayasuriya (2010b, pp. 9–10) argues that regulatory regionalism comprises public and private institutions that are able to conduct activities related to decision making about, monitoring of, and compliance with, specific regulatory functions within or beyond national boundaries. He emphasises the rise of policy network mechanisms among the institutions that operate beyond traditional bureaucratic boundaries. This view implies that the establishment of a policy coordination network includes national agencies, as well as regional actors. Stone (2008, p. 7) defines this process as global public policy making, whereby new forms of authority emerge through global and regional policy processes that coexist alongside nation-state processes. Therefore, a policy network is no longer determined solely by the conventional authority of states, but also by international organisations. Jayasuriya (2009) claims that this process is a part of transnational policy networks. Thus, analysing policy networks will assist in identifying not only the participating actors, but also the structure and coordination processes within APT financial cooperation.

Regulatory regionalism is a relatively novel approach to studying regionalism. It has been used to investigate regionalism in several areas, such as education (Jones 2010; Mok 2010) and politics (Jayasuriya 2008). Several scholars (Jones 2010; Mok 2010; Robertson 2010) have applied the regulatory regionalism approach collaboratively to higher education governance in Europe and Asia. Jones (2010) applied regulatory regionalism to analyse the adoption of the Bologna Process in the education reform programmes of Kazakhstan and Kyrgyzstan, while Mok (2010) examined major strategies adopted by the Chinese and Taiwanese governments in shaping their universities' standings in global university leagues.

These studies of education have contributed to further develop the concept of regulatory regionalism. Mok (2010, p. 97) reveals that regulatory regionalism does not necessarily ignore the controls of states in relation to the development of higher education, particularly in China and Taiwan. He argues that regulatory regionalism focuses more on domestic factors, even though external factors also exist in regionalism processes. This finding accords with that of Jones (2010, p. 81), who recognises the importance of a 'host of factors', even though all components related to regionalism have been set up by external actors. Therefore, 'regulatory conflicts' between regional and national governance are somehow inevitable.

Hameiri and Jayasuriya (2011) claim that conflicts between regional political projects and national projects occur within the state.

Regulatory regionalism considers the domestic political economy, as opposed to the dominance of external factors. In this regard, regulatory regionalism provides a tool to investigate points of political-economic contention within financial regionalism projects that may arise between national and regional power holders. Such an investigation contributes to revealing how the roles within, or influences of, the political and economic environment shape the surrounding financial regimes. As most APT financial initiatives comprise state-led projects, the dynamics of the domestic political-economic environment need to take centre stage in the study of regionalism.

Moreover, the features of the regulatory regionalism approach enable scrutiny of the institutional contexts in which such regional financial initiatives are developed. Concerns of regulatory regionalism, in relation to the trend towards the *domestication* processes of regional arrangements, enable better understanding of the implications of domestic institutional changes on regionalism processes. These are often excluded from the consideration of other existing approaches on regionalism. Such attention to the institutional context of regionalism is necessary to comprehend broader perspectives on the transformation of the national regulatory framework, as the major focus of a new mode of regional financial governance.

In this book, the regulatory regionalism approach poses as the main analytical framework to examine Indonesia's domestic political economy, which, in turn, enables its response to APT financial regionalism. The features of regulatory regionalism were applied to examine Indonesia's responses to two APT financial initiatives: CMIM and Asian Bond Market Initiatives (ABMI), which are the most advanced regional arrangements under the auspices of APT financial cooperation. In this respect, the development of APT financial initiatives is viewed as a political project that comprises a dialectical relationship between the multiple scales of political and economic activities of international, regional and national actors.

The next chapter briefly presents the development of East Asian financial regionalism, in the light of financial cooperation in ASEAN, APEC and APT. It provides a 'big picture' of the progress of several regional financial initiatives in East Asia.

REFERENCES

Abbott, K., & Snidal, D. (2000). Hard and soft law in international governance. *International Organisation, 54*(3), 421–456.

Acharya, A. (2004). How ideas spread: Whose norms matter? Norm localisation and institutional change in Asian regionalism. *International Organization, 58*(Spring), 239–275.

Acharya, A. (2005). Do norms and identity matter? Community and power in Southeast Asia's regional order. *The Pacific Review, 18*(1), 95–118.

Acharya, A. (2014). *Indonesia matters: Asia's emerging democratic power.* Singapore: World Scientific Publishing Co. Pte. Ltd.

Alatas, A. (2001). *ASEAN Plus Three: Equals peace plus prosperity.* Paper presented to the 2001 Regional Outlook Forum, Bangkok.

Alvstam, C. G. (2001). Regionalization still waiting to happen? In M. Schulz, F. Soderbaum, & J. Ojendal (Eds.), *Regionalization in a globalizing world* (pp. 173–195). London and New York: Zed Books.

Amyx, J. A. (2004). Political dynamics of regional financial cooperation in East Asia. *Japanese Economy, 32*(2), 98–112.

Amyx, J. A. (2005). What motivates regional financial cooperation in East Asia today? *Asia Pacific Issues,* (76), 1–8.

ASEAN Plus Three. (2011). *The joint ministerial statement of the 14th ASEAN Plus Three Finance Ministers' Meeting.* Ha Noi: ASEAN Plus Three.

Beeson, M. (2003). ASEAN Plus Three and the rise of reactionary regionalism. *Contemporary Southeast Asia, 25*(2), 251–268.

Beeson, M. (2006). American hegemony and regionalism: The rise of East Asia and the end of the Asia-Pacific. *Geopolitics, 11*(4), 541–560.

Beeson, M. (2007). *Regionalism and globalisation in East Asia.* Basingstoke: Hampshire Palgrave Macmillan.

Breslin, S. (2010). Comparative theory, China, and the future of East Asian regionalism(s). *Review of International Studies, 36*(3), 709–729.

Cai, K. G. (2010). *The politics of economic regionalism: Explaining regional economic integration in East Asia, International Political Economy Series.* Basingstoke: Palgrave Macmillan.

Cameron, F. (2010). The geopolitics of Asia—What role for the European Union? *International Politics, 47*, 276–292.

Chey, H. K. (2009). The changing political dynamics of East Asian financial cooperation: The Chiang Mai Initiative. *Asian Survey, 49*(3), 450–467.

Choi, J. Y. (2013). East Asian financial regionalism and the politics of global financial governance: Structural and institutional power in global and regional governance. *Pacific Focus,* No. 3, p. 411.

Collins, K. (2009). Economic and security regionalism among patrimonial authoritarian regimes: The case of central Asia. *Europe-Asia Studies, 61*(2), 249–281.

Dalla, I. (2003). *Harmonization of bond market rules and regulations in selected APEC economies*. Manila: Asian Development Bank.

Davis, J. R. (2010). East Asian regionalism: Origins, development and prospects for the future. *Politikon, 16*(1), 34–49.

De Brouwer, G. (2002). The IMF and East Asia: A changing regional financial architecture. *Pacific Economic Papers*, Vol. 324.

Dieter, H., & Higgott, R. (2003). Exploring alternative theories of economic regionalism: From trade to finance in Asian co-operation? *Review of International Political Economy, 10*(3), 430–454.

Emmerson, D. K. (2008). Critical terms: Security, democracy, and regionalism in Southeast Asia. In D. K. Emmerson (Ed.), *Hard choices: Security, democracy, and regionalism in Southeast Asia*. Stanford, CA: Walter H. Shorenstein Asia-Pacific Research Center.

Grimes, W. W. (2009). *Currency and contest in East Asia: The great power politics of financial regionalism, Cornell Studies in Money*. Ithaca: Cornell University Press.

Grimes, W. W. (2012). Financial regionalism after the global financial crisis: Regionalist impulses and national strategies. In W. Grant & G. K. Wilson (Eds.), *The consequences of the global financial crisis: The rhetoric of reforms and regulation*. Oxford: Oxford University Press.

Hameiri, S. (2009). Beyond methodological nationalism, but where to for the study of regional governance? *Australian Journal of International Affairs, 63*(3), 430–441.

Hameiri, S., & Jayasuriya, K. (2011). Regulatory regionalism and the dynamics of territorial politics: The case of the Asia-Pacific region. *Political Studies, 59*(1), 20–37.

He, B. (2004). East Asian ideas of regionalism: A normative critique. *Australian Journal of International Affairs, 58*(1), 105–125.

He, B., & Inoguchi, T. (2011). Introduction to ideas of Asian regionalism. *Japanese Journal of Political Science, 12*(2), 165–177.

Hill, H., & Menon, J. (2010). *ASEAN economic integration: Features, fulfilments, failures and the future*. ADB Working Paper Series on Regional Economic Integration, No. 69.

Hurrell, A. (1995). Explaining the resurgence of regionalism in world politics. *Review of International Studies, 21*(4), 331–358.

International Monetary Fund. (2013). *Report for selected countries and subjects*. World Economic Outlook Database. Retrieved May 13, 2014, from http://www.imf.org/external/pubs/ft/weo/2013/01/weodata/index.aspx

Isaac, G. E. (2003). Food safety and eco-labelling regulations: A case of transatlantic regulatory regionalism? In G. P. Sampson & S. Woolcock (Eds.), *Regionalism, multilateralism, and economic integration: The recent experience* (pp. 227–252). Tokyo: United Nations University Press.

Jayasuriya, K. (2003). Introduction: Governing the Asia Pacific beyond the new regionalism. *Third World Quarterly, 24*(2), 199–215.

Jayasuriya, K. (2008). Regionalising the state: Political topography of regulatory regionalism. *Contemporary Politics, 14*(1), 21–35.

Jayasuriya, K. (2009). Regulatory regionalism in the Asia-Pacific: Drivers, instruments and actors. *Australian Journal of International Affairs, 63*(3), 335–347.

Jayasuriya, K. (2010a). The emergence of regulatory regionalism. *Global Asia, 4*(4), 102–107.

Jayasuriya, K. (2010b). Learning by the market: Regulatory regionalism, Bologna, and accountability communities. *Globalisation, Societies and Education, 8*(1), 7–22.

Jayasuriya, K., & Robertson, S. (2010). Regulatory regionalism and the governance of higher education. *Globalisation, Societies and Education, 8*(1), 1–6.

Jiang, Y. (2010). Response and responsibility: China in East Asian financial cooperation. *Pacific Review, 23*(5), 603–623.

Jones, P. (2010). Regulatory regionalism and education: The European Union in central Asia. *Globalisation, Societies and Education, 8*(1), 59–85.

Katada, S., & Sohn, I. (2014). Regionalism as financial statecraft: China and Japan's pursuit of counterweight strategies. In L. E. Armijo & S. Katada (Eds.), *The financial statecraft of emerging powers: Shield and sword in Asia and Latin America*. Hampshire: Palgrave Macmillan.

Katzenstein, P. J. (2000). Regionalism and Asia. *New Political Economy, 5*(3), 353–368.

Kawai, M. (2005). East Asian economic regionalism: Progress and challenges. *Journal of Asian Economics, 16*(1), 29–55.

Kawai, M. (2010). *East Asian financial co-operation and the role of the ASEAN+3 Macroeconomic Research Office*. Bonn: German Development Institute.

Kerwer, D. (2005). Rules that many use: Standards and global regulation. *Governance, 18*(4), 611–632.

Kirschner, V., & Stapel, S. (2012). Does regime type matter? Regional integration from the nation states perspectives in ECOWAS. In T. A. Borzel, L. Goltermann, M. Lohaus, & K. Striebinger (Eds.), *Roads to regionalism: Genesis, design, and effects of regional organization* (pp. 141–157). Farnham: Asghate.

Kirton, J. J., & Trebilcock, M. J. (2004). *Hard choices, soft law: Voluntary standards in global trade, environment, and social governance*. Brookfield: Ashgate.

Komori, Y. (2009). Regional governance in East Asia and the Asia-Pacific. *East Asia: An International Quarterly, 26*(4), 321–341.

Mansfield, E. D., & Milner, H. V. (1999). The new wave of regionalism. *International Organization, 53*(3), 589–627.

Mansfield, E. D., Milner, H. V., & Rosendorff, B. P. (2002). Why democracies cooperate more: Electoral control and international trade agreements. *International Organization, 56*(3), 477–513.

Maswood, S. J. (2001a). *Japan and East Asian regionalism, The Nissan Institute/ Routledge Japanese Studies Series.* London: Routledge.

Maswood, S. J. (2001b). Japanese foreign policy and regionalism. In S. J. Maswood (Ed.), *Japan and East Asian regionalism.* London: Routledge.

Mearsheimer, J. J. (1990). Back to the future: Instability in Europe after the Cold War. *International Security,* (1), 5–56.

Milner, H. (2002). Regional economic co-operation, global markets and domestic politics: A comparasion of NAFTA and the Maastricht Treaty. In W. D. Coleman & G. R. D. Underhill (Eds.), *Regionalism and global economic integration: Europe, Asia, and the Americas.* London: Routledge.

Mittelman, J. H. (2000). *The globalization syndrome: Transformation and resistance.* Princeton: Princeton University Press.

Mok, K. H. (2010). Emerging regulatory regionalism in university governance: A comparative study of China and Taiwan. *Globalisation, Societies and Education, 8*(1), 87–103.

Murray, P. (2010). Comparative regional integration in the EU and East Asia: Moving beyond integration snobbery. *International Politics, 47*(3/4), 308–323.

Nesadurai, H. S. (2003). *Globalisation, domestic politics, and regionalism: The ASEAN Free Trade Area.* London: Routledge.

Novotny, D. (2010). *Torn between America and China: Elite perceptions and Indonesian foreign policy.* Singapore: Institute of Southeast Asian Studies.

Putnam, R. D. (1988). Diplomacy and domestic politics: The logic of two-level games. *International Organization, 42*(3), 427–460.

Ravenhill, J. (2011). *Global political economy* (3rd ed.). Oxford: Oxford University Press.

Robertson, S. (2010). The EU, 'regulatory state regionalism' and new modes of higher education governance. *Globalisation, Societies and Education, 8*(1), 23–37.

Rosser, A. (2004). Coalitions, convergence and corporate governance reform in Indonesia. In K. Jayasuriya (Ed.), *Governing the Asia Pacific: Beyond the 'new regionalism'.* New York: Palgrave Macmillan.

Schirm, S. A. (2002). *Globalization and the new regionalism: Global markets, domestic politics and regional cooperation.* Cambridge: Polity.

Shin, D. C., & Cho, Y. (2010). How East Asians understand democracy: From a comparative perspective. *ASIEN, 116,* 21–40.

Shiraishi, T., & Katzenstein, P. J. (1997). *Network power: Japan and Asia.* Ithaca: Cornell University Press.

Shrader, L. (2013). *Latest on branchless banking from Indonesia.* Retrieved November 18, 2014, from http://www.cgap.org/blog/latest-branchless-banking-indonesia

Simon, S. (2008). ASEAN and multilateralism: The long, bumpy road to community. *Contemporary Southeast Asia, 30*(2), 264–292.

Soesastro, H. (2006). Regional integration in East Asia: Achievements and future prospects. *Asian Economic Policy Review, 1*(2), 215–234.

Stone, D. (2008). Global public policy, transnational policy communities, and their networks. *Policy Studies Journal, 36*(1), 19–38.

Stubbs, R. (2002). Asean Plus Three: Emerging East Asian regionalism? *Asian Survey, 42*(3), 440–455.

Suzuki, S. (2004). *East Asian cooperation through conference diplomacy: Institutional aspects of the ASEAN Plus Three (APT) framework.* IDE APEC Study Center Working Paper Series, Vol. 3/4, No. 7.

Walt, S. M. (1987). *The origins of alliances, Cornell Studies in Security Affairs.* Ithaca: Cornell University Press.

Walter, A. (2008). *Governing finance: East Asia's adoption of international standards, Cornell Studies in Money.* Ithaca: Cornell University Press.

Wanandi, J. (2002). The rise of China: A challenge for East Asia. *The Indonesian Quarterly, XXX*(3), 224–233.

Wang, J. Y. (2011a). China and East Asian regionalism. *European Law Journal, 17*(5), 611–629.

Wang, Y. Z. (2011b). China, economic regionalismand East Asian integration. *Japanese Journal of Political Science, 12*, 195–212.

Yoshimatsu, H. (2008a). Japan and regional governance in East Asia. In N. Thomas (Ed.), *Governance and regionalism in Asia* (pp. 66–88). London: Routledge.

Yoshimatsu, H. (2008b). *The political economy of regionalism in East Asia: Integrative explanation for dynamics and challenges.* Hamsphire: Palgrave Macmillan.

Yoshimatsu, H. (2014). *Comparing institution-building in East Asia: Power politics, governance, and critical junctures.* Palgrave Macmillan. Basingstoke, Hampshire, UK.

CHAPTER 3

The Progress of East Asian Financial Regionalism

The study of East Asian financial regionalism is relatively new compared to other regionalism issues, such as security or trade. For many years, East Asian countries have limited financial issues to domestic interests only until the Asian financial crisis wave swept several East Asian countries, effectively forcing them to open a regional dialogue on financial affairs.

In general, financial regionalism in East Asia has been developed based on the progress of financial initiatives under the auspices of the Association of Southeast Asian Nations (ASEAN), Asia-Pacific Economic Cooperation (APEC) and ASEAN Plus Three (APT) Cooperation. These three regional bodies are related. In recent years, the term 'East Asian financial regionalism' has more often been applied to APT Cooperation on financial regionalism. The terms 'East Asian' and 'APT' have been used interchangeably in existing studies to describe the development of financial cooperation in East Asia. For Stubbs (2002), APT Cooperation is the latest manifestation of the evolution of East Asian regional cooperation, after ASEAN and APEC. In a similar vein, Ravenhill (2002) argues that APT Cooperation is a response to ASEAN's lack of financial and human resources, as well as APEC's ineffective commitment in the midst of the Asian financial crisis. Definitely, the progress of financial regionalism in East Asia has been determined by the dynamics of the three regional cooperation bodies.

The central objective of this chapter is to investigate the evolution of financial regionalism in East Asia. While the focus of this study is

© The Author(s) 2017

E. Saputro, *Indonesia and ASEAN Plus Three Financial Cooperation*,
DOI 10.1007/978-981-10-3029-1_3

APT financial cooperation, the development of financial projects within ASEAN and APEC are also reviewed, as they help shape financial regionalism architecture in East Asia. The broader coverage of East Asian financial regionalism is useful to understand the focus of each regional cooperation body and to make comparisons between the three regional institutions. In this chapter, there is a particular focus on surveillance processes, regional financing arrangements, capital market development and financial service liberalisation. These foci represent the major financial issues widely discussed across East Asian regional financial forums even though other financial initiatives have been developed and implemented.

ASEAN

ASEAN is understood to constitute the first step towards the idea of regionalism in Asia (Davis 2010; He and Inoguchi 2011; Murray 2010; Ravenhill 2002). Formally established to stabilise the political tensions of the Southeast Asian region, ASEAN eventually sought to build peace and secure its members against military threats, as well as regional conflicts (Murray 2010, p. 599). In later developments, growing regional stability has expanded the cooperation areas of ASEAN. Currently, ASEAN's scope of cooperation covers cultural, agricultural, defence, economic and technical issues (Davis 2010, p. 38). Regarding the economy, ASEAN economic cooperation was developed based on research conducted by Kansu and Robinson—researchers who were tasked to provide analysis on possible economic cooperation to ASEAN (Anwar 1994, p. 65). Their report recommended that ASEAN should begin with trade liberalisation initiatives through tariff negotiations, package deal arrangements and financial cooperation (Hill and Menon 2010, p. 3).

The emergence of financial regionalism in ASEAN began when financial cooperation became a part of ASEAN's dialogues, particularly when the ASEAN Swap Arrangement (ASA) was established in 1977. The ASA was aimed to manage liquidity difficulties. The development of ASEAN financial cooperation was further bolstered by the sudden emergence of the Asian financial crisis. In 1997, ASEAN finance ministers gathered in Phuket, Thailand, to work on pragmatic cooperation in finance. This included the banking sector, capital markets, customs, insurance, taxation and human resource development (ASEAN 1997). Although unanticipated at the time, this significant meeting was conducted in the early stages of the Asian financial crisis. The ASEAN finance ministers realised the need for sound macroeconomic and financial policies, following deterioration of the Thai currency, which led to the rise of Thailand's current account deficit in May 1997 (De Brouwer 1999, p. 8).

More broadly, ASEAN financial cooperation was concerned with three key points as a response to the Asian financial crisis. The first point was related to regional financial arrangements. In this regard, there was an idea to develop a cooperative financial arrangement as a supplement to IMF financial assistance. However, this idea was somewhat unclear regarding whether it would be a new arrangement or a further development of ASA as an existing scheme of financial assistance. There was no further discussion regarding the use of ASA as an instrument to deal with the financial crisis.

Besides collaborating in liquidity support assistance through ASA, ASEAN member countries also worked on other financial initiatives included in the Roadmap for Monetary and Financial Integration (RIA-Fin). RIA-Fin covers three areas of cooperation, including capital markets, financial service liberalisation and capital account liberalisation. For capital market, the cooperation initiated the establishment of the ASEAN Capital Market Forum (ACMF), which aimed to harmonise the rules and regulations of capital markets in Southeast Asia (Saputro 2012). Operationally, the forum has identified regulatory and infrastructure gaps evident in the capital markets, with the intent to create common standards for the integration of capital markets in the ASEAN region (Singh 2009). The ACMF released the ASEAN 'Standards' and 'Plus Standards' schemes to facilitate cross-border security offerings. On this point, ACMF has emerged as a regional standard-setting project for capital markets in ASEAN member states. Jayasuriya (2003, p. 209) argues that regional regulatory governance provides a mechanism for regulatory standards and policy harmonisation. In this context, standardisation in capital markets was implicit in ASEAN's attempt to deal with various levels of capital market development in the Southeast Asian region.

However, progress in ASEAN capital market development has been gradual, mainly due to the slow adoption of ASEAN 'Standards' and 'Plus Standards'. Until 2011, Malaysia, Singapore and Thailand were the only countries to have implemented these schemes. This means that the majority of ASEAN member states still hold to their domestic schemes. The different levels of capital market infrastructure and national interest were understood as the main contributors to this situation. ASEAN is a regional organisation that maintains a consensus mechanism and a non-interference approach that demonstrates respect for national sovereignty. Although ASEAN is categorised as an organisation that promotes regional cooperation, it was initially established to serve and strengthen national interests (Acharya 2011, pp. 8–9). Therefore, domestic interests are almost always prioritised above ASEAN's interests, something that makes it difficult to achieve regional goals. In this respect, each member state tends to avoid the adverse impacts of ASEAN standards to their domestic markets, as standardisation means subjecting domestic market governance to regional, or even international, exposure. This situation highlights the need to pay more attention to domestic capital market conditions when dealing with ASEAN capital market initiatives.

Alongside capital market development, financial services liberalisation began to attract government concern when it was included within the negotiation processes of the ASEAN Framework Agreement on Services (AFAS), in 1998. Negotiations were conducted in the form of a 'request and offer' mechanism towards particular sub-sectors. In general, the negotiations over financial service liberalisation have also made slow progress. For instance, the fourth round of the negotiation, which was initially expected to be concluded in 2007, was extended to 2008. In this regard, there was a tendency for ASEAN member countries to be vigilant in providing commitments, considering their domestic readiness to liberalise financial services. Rajan and Sen (2002) observe that no single ASEAN member was willing to offer commitment to all financial services sub-sectors. This situation is contrary to the spirit of liberalisation that entails attempts to remove domestic barriers and also the willingness to open domestic markets to foreign competitors (Park and Bae 2002, p. 5).

Meanwhile, regarding capital account liberalisation, the progress here is somehow less progressive, compared to the previous two RIA-Fin areas of cooperation following the Asian financial crisis. Although ASEAN finance ministers have acknowledged the need to work closely on this issue, they have paid less attention to capital account liberalisation. Based on statistical research, Lewer and Terry (2003) argue that ASEAN member countries were basically more responsive to capital account liberalisation compared to the rest of the world before the Asian financial crisis. However, up until 2006, there was no concrete result of the initiative on capital account liberalisation. For this initiative, ASEAN had only succeeded in providing up-to-date information on capital account regimes in each member country (ASEAN 2006).

The gradual liberalisation of capital accounts within ASEAN has been due largely to the commitments of its members to this aim, rather than to the creation of regional arrangements. For several ASEAN members, the liberalisation of capital accounts was not an easy task. On the one hand, they needed capital inflow through investments from foreign investors. Conversely, they did not want to lose their control over domestic financial industries. The severely adverse impacts of the Asian financial crisis have pushed ASEAN member states to develop more robust investment policies, to avoid losing control over the movement of capital. Therefore, in practice, the commitment of ASEAN member states to capital account liberalisation has also worked to preserve national agendas.

In order to accelerate the achievement of capital account liberalisation targets, a Working Committee on Capital Account Liberalisation (WC-CAL) was set up and given a mandate to monitor each member's commitment, based on an agreed work plan (Kanithasen and Watjannapukka 2011). However, it was found that the proposed work plan was impractical and unrealistic with respect to the various levels of economic status, as well as to the complexity of financial sector development among ASEAN member countries (Park and Takagi 2011). Eventually, the ASEAN capital account liberalisation initiative did not reveal an energetic progress.

The second point of ASEAN financial cooperation relates to the notion of regional surveillance. At this point, the ASEAN finance ministers considered that economic interdependence in the region would potentially trigger a contagion effect regarding the crisis. Therefore, the timely and comprehensive exchange of information, as part of a regional surveillance process, was necessary to avoid spreading the economic risk to other countries (ASEAN 1997). ASEAN's project on surveillance was finally formed through the ASEAN Surveillance Process (ASP).

Initially established to deal with the Asian financial crisis, the ASP has come to be perceived as a critical entity in monitoring economic development in the ASEAN region. The surveillance activities include monitoring and analysing macroeconomic situations and developments within the region (ASEAN 1998). The establishment of ASP sparked the further development of standardisation and transnational policy coordination. Manupipatpong (2002, p. 114) argues that ASP has the potential to stimulate ASEAN member countries to adopt international standards and codes, in order to enhance effective market forces and financial system resilience. In its new development, the ASP largely adopted the International Monetary Fund (IMF) and Organisation for Economic Cooperation and Development (OECD) standards and codes. This phenomenon emphasises the argument that reproducing global standards is often conducted through regional governance structures (Jayasuriya 2003).

Moreover, ASP has also stimulated policy coordination among ASEAN member states, as they have had to share macroeconomic data and policy options to support regional cooperation mechanisms, particularly in dealing with crisis countermeasures. Greater policy coordination emerged when Japan, China and South Korea agreed to strengthen the ASP, with continuing support from the Asian Development Bank (ADB). This new arrangement marked the policy coordination of ASEAN member states and their Northeast Asian colleagues in creating a new economic monitoring system. While the initial ASP activity was aimed at monitoring regional economic development, the new mechanism also included non-economic—but still related—issues in its analysis. As a consequence, the ASP policy coordination covered a broader range of issues.

Notwithstanding its intention and structure to deal with such crises, the ASP has been critiqued over several aspects. Anas and Atje (2005) identify several weaknesses of the ASP related to the unbinding commitment of the peer review process, inadequate macroeconomic data, lack of comprehensive reporting processes and human resource issues. In relation to the provision of data on economic indicators, several member countries are less enthusiastic about providing timely and comprehensive data, due to their concerns about possible security and confidentiality weaknesses. Nesadurai (2009a, p. 371) also criticises the ASP by arguing that the subjectivity of experts in interpreting national economic data is frequently questioned by the member countries. While the role of regional economic experts in matters of surveillance is pivotal to support national policy-making process, or to drive financial market action, a limited number of specialists are working on regional financial surveillance, as it is a relatively new field (Takagi 2010, p. 9). That there are few experts in this field raises questions about the quality of these reports.

The third point of ASEAN financial cooperation is related to IMF involvement. Regarding this arrangement, ASEAN finance ministers provided the IMF with a special mandate to lead the Asian financial crisis mitigation process, by emphasising the need to implement the Manila Framework to address the financial crisis impact on several ASEAN member states. The Manila Framework was a framework constructed by APEC finance ministers to promote financial stability in the region (APEC 1997). This mandated agenda represents a significant moment for the IMF to engage in the regional governance of financial cooperation in Southeast Asia. The urgent implementation of the Manila Framework was reiterated in the joint statement of ASEAN finance ministers and their colleagues from Australia, China, Hong Kong, Japan, South Korea and the USA, barely a day after the ASEAN finance ministers' special meeting in 1997. This framework represents the first formal response of ASEAN finance ministers to the Asian financial crisis.

Considering the lack of progress on the economic status of crisis-affected countries during the Asian financial crisis, ASEAN finance ministers expressed their concern that there should be more strenuous efforts to tackle the crisis. Therefore, at their April 1999 meeting, the ASEAN finance ministers emphasised two important points (ASEAN 1999). The first was the intention of ASEAN member countries to take proactive action in response to the Asian financial crisis and to ensure the protection of their interests and priorities. This particular point indicates ASEAN's determination to become a more active player in the region, as opposed to maintaining a strict adherence to IMF policy directions. The second point emphasised was the need to bring about international financial architecture reforms, including a review of International Financial Institutions (IFIs). In this respect, the ASEAN finance ministers sent a strong message to the global community that there were serious shortcomings with how they were being treated by the IFIs, in particular by the IMF. ASEAN members realised that they needed to build alternative arrangements for dealing with the financial crisis, ones that would position them at the centre of any arrangements and thus gave ASEAN greater control. Taken together, these points have led to transformative changes in the way ASEAN financial cooperation has managed the Asian financial crisis in particular and international financial architecture in general. This momentum has also provided impetus for national state agencies to be more active in dealing with regional financial arrangements and to create stronger policy coordination among policy makers in the East Asian region. Ravenhill (2006) argues that this momentum brings East Asia into a new type of regionalism that enhances a state's capacity to deepen regional integration.

APEC

Establishing APEC was a stepping stone towards economic regionalism in the Asia-Pacific. As an economic cooperation body, APEC focuses on three key areas, including trade and investment liberalisation and business facilitation (APEC 2010). APEC's concern with financial issues began in just 1994, when APEC finance ministers met in Honolulu. At that time, APEC was primarily concerned with three main issues: sustaining growth with low inflation, financing investment and infrastructure development and promoting capital market development (APEC 1994).

Despite its capability to facilitate open dialogue related to trade issues, APEC's progress on the development of economic cooperation has attracted criticism on three key fronts. First, according to Ravenhill (2002), APEC failed to maintain its momentum in making progress towards a trade liberalisation agenda during the 1995 summit in Japan. Second, it failed to facilitate trans-regional economic integration to any significant extent after the World Trade Organization (WTO) processes stagnated (Aggarwal and Koo 2007, p. 366). Third, APEC's flawed priority agenda during the 1997 Asian financial crisis weakened APEC Asian members' commitments. At that time, rather than establishing ways of managing the financial crisis in Asia, APEC's Western members were more concerned with trade liberalisation issues—reflection of Western agenda—(Ravenhill 2002, p. 178). This particular concern was irrelevant in the midst of financial shocks that demanded more liquidity support assistance. The Asian members' agenda was singled out from the 1997 APEC finance ministers' meeting. As a result, APEC was unable to provide sufficient political legitimacy to continue the wider liberal economic project in the region (Dieter and Higgott 2003).

In financial-capital markets, the increase in public access to economic and financial information became a significant force in APEC's drive for financial cooperation. For instance, in regional standard-setting projects, APEC endorsed the Special Data Dissemination Standard (SDDS) as a new standard for disseminating macroeconomic and financial data. SDDS was created by the IMF to cover four dimensions: data, public access, integrity and quality (IMF 2007). Therefore, APEC's endorsement of the SDDS reflects another reproduction process of global standards at the regional level, which has also been conducted by ASEAN through the ASP.

Regarding another financial issue, economic-financial surveillance emerged for the first time during the APEC leaders' summit in Vancouver, 25 November 1997, in response to the Asian financial crisis. However, rather than creating an APEC-owned surveillance unit, APEC leaders simply endorsed the Manila Framework as constructed by several countries, plus the IMF, the World Bank (WB), the Bank for International Settlement (BIS) and the ADB. In particular, the Manila Framework endorsed the IMF as the main player in the international monetary system and underlined its role in financial surveillance processes (Ito et al. 2005, p. 10). On that occasion, while the APEC finance ministers realised that the surveillance process was critical, there was little operational discussion on the surveillance mechanism, even during the financial crisis. Most importantly, the mechanism of policy coordination among APEC member states to conduct economic surveillance was not given adequate attention. The decision to place the IMF at the centre of the surveillance mechanism abolished the policy coordination mechanism, as the IMF operated exclusively with its own structure. The issue of surveillance finally disappeared from the finance ministers' statement after their eighth annual meeting in 2001.

APT COOPERATION

The emergence of APT Cooperation as a response to the Asian financial crisis has done much to foster East Asian regionalism. Regional financial stability has driven APT member countries to establish financial cooperation exclusively. Such cooperation is intended to protect the region from further financial crises, while maximising regional financial assets during stable periods. Hence, the notion and practice of financial cooperation seems to take centre stage over other issues (Pempel 2010, p. 219). The APT member countries recognise that they need to find their own way to deal with any financial crisis, as the United States (USA) may not be reliable (Soesastro 2003).

Besides being triggered by the Asian financial crisis, the APT Cooperation was also resulted from the power politics among Japan, China and the USA. Power politics had played an important role since former Malaysian Prime Minister, Dr Mahathir, proposed the East Asian Economic Grouping (EAEG). This proposed grouping was considered controversial, as it excluded the USA and its allies (Tongzon 2004, p. 143). China responded positively to the proposal, while Japan was reluctant, due to its close relationship with the USA (Abbott and Snidal 2000). Following mixed responses from the two Asian major powers towards the EAEG, APT Cooperation was proposed. In a nutshell, the proposal to establish APT Cooperation gained positive responses from both China and Japan. For Acharya (2002, p. 283), APT Cooperation had potential to combine the two Asian hegemons in dealing with regional economic and security issues while not engaging with the West's political demands for human rights, democracy and good governance. Throughout the development of APT Cooperation, power politics—particularly between Japan and China—has flourished.

Several financial initiatives arising from APT financial cooperation have been tabled and implemented. The Chiang Mai Initiative Multilateralisation (CMIM), the ABMI and the Credit Guarantee and Investment Facility (CGIF) represent a number of initiatives endorsed by the APT finance ministers (APT 2010). In this book, these two financial initiatives were selected to examine Indonesian responses to APT financial regionalism, as they have made significant progress.

The CMIM

The most advanced initiative of the APT financial cooperation is CMIM. This initiative was designed as a multilateral liquidity support arrangement, to address balance of payments and short-term liquidity difficulties, using 'regional self-help mechanisms'. It is an APT financial initiative aimed at providing liquidity support arrangements during times of financial crisis, supplementing the existing international support fund provided by the IMF (APT 2009). This initiative represents a first in the establishment of regional pooled funds in response to economic crises. As a regional self-help mechanism, CMIM reflects an attempt of APT member countries to manage future financial crises through a risk-sharing project based on the Asian region's own financial capacity. In other words, instead of dealing with economic risks individually, the regional pooling fund initiative collects potential regional funds, while sharing or shifting potential risks to the member countries. The idea of using regional powers to deal with economic shocks is based on a lesson learnt that some East Asian countries being unable to mitigate the 1998 Asian financial crisis independently. Due to differing stages of economic development, and the absence of robust regional financial cooperation during the financial crisis, the region has become increasingly vulnerable to economic shocks.

The CMIM was expected to strengthen the financial safety net for the APT region. The CMIM was understood to create greater readiness among APT member countries to face future economic shocks; as such, it contributes to better regional market stability over the longer term (Park and Oh 2010). The establishment of CMIM was regarded by regional markets as relatively successful in mitigating the potentially more adverse effects of the 2009 global financial crisis on the East Asian region financial sector, even though several member countries (such as Singapore and Malaysia) had experienced negative growth during that period.

The initial form of CMIM was as the Chiang Mai Initiative (CMI) that operated on a bilateral basis. Operationally, the CMI combined the expanded ASA with a network of Bilateral Swap Arrangements (BSAs) (Sussangkarn 2010, p. 5). The ASA was made by, and only for, ASEAN member states. BSAs included the three Northeast Asian countries (Japan, South Korea and China). Both the ASA and BSAs shared similar aims of providing liquidity support for APT member countries that faced short-term liquidity problems. Their difference lies in the drawing mechanism, in which ASA allows ASEAN members to draw up to a maximum of twice the amount of their contribution, while the basic drawing principle of BSAs allows requesting countries to draw only up to ten per cent of member countries' maximum drawing amount, without any further conditionality (Rana 2002, p. 9).

Initially, the total amount of ASA was US$100 million, to which each of the ASEAN member states contributed US$20 million. In 1978, the total amount of ASA was increased to US$200 million (ASEAN 1978). This change affected the maximum amount of swap provision that participants could request, from US$40 million to US$80 million. Henning (2002, p. 14) claims that Indonesia, Malaysia, Thailand and the Philippines activated this arrangement during 1979 to 1982. The total amount of ASA was expanded in 2000, through the combined increased contributions by ASEAN member countries (including the new ASEAN members), to US$1 billion. The increase reflects a stronger ASEAN member commitment to regional financial cooperation.

Meanwhile, the BSAs were operationally signed in 2001 with all Plus Three countries and three ASEAN countries (Thailand, Philippines and Malaysia) as initial participants. In the following years, the number of BSA agreements, as well as the size of the networks, gradually increased. In 2002, the total amount of BSAs was around approximately US$20 billion. This amount was then increased to US$35.5 billion, covering 16 BSA agreements in 2003 (Wang 2004); it was continually increased up to US$36.5 billion in 2004 (Sohn 2005). Up until April 2009, the total amount of BSAs reached US$90 billion.

A significant change in the regional liquidity arrangement was produced when in Kyoto, all APT finance ministers agreed to govern a 'self-managed' reserve pooling, based on a single contractual agreement (APT 2007). The term 'self-managed' means that the funds allocated for regional liquidity support are not physically collected, as they remain under the management of each member country's central bank (Henning 2009, p. 4). The operational arrangements of CMI were reviewed to further improve regional liquidity support arrangements. The review included consideration of several key elements of CMI, such as size, pooling structure, surveillance, decision-making processes, IMF linkages and types of contract agreements (Sussangkarn 2010). Regarding contract agreements, the ASA and BSAs were perceived as inefficient, as they operated on the basis of numerous bilateral contract agreements.

In a later development, the global financial crisis contributed to expedite the negotiation process on developing better regional liquidity support mechanisms. Although these negotiations were relatively sluggish before the crisis, they have started to show productive results. This slow rate of progress resulted from the particular attention given to technical issues during detailed discussions on the format of the pooling fund and quota of contribution (Yoshimatsu 2014). Eventually, in their twelfth meeting in Bali, the APT finance ministers agreed to launch a *multilateralised* CMI, later known as CMIM. Announcing the CMIM in the midst of the global financial crisis was expected to boost investor confidence and give assurance to the stability and security of the businesses and investment ventures in East Asia during 2009's economic difficulties. The announcement emphasised the 13 APT member countries' commitments to bring the CMIM into force (Siregar 2011). Since then, the provision of regional liquidity support has operated on the basis of a single contractual agreement.

The complete CMIM agreement has not been made publically available. Instead of full disclosure, the APT finance ministers have instead provided selected key points of the CMIM agreement to the public (APT 2010). Such limited public access to the agreement details suggests a lack of transparency. In comparison, ASEAN continuously publicised the ASA articles of agreement, as well as any amendments to these.

In relation to the CMIM size, the total amount has been increased from US$80 to US$120 billion, in the midst of the 2009 APT finance ministers' special meeting in Phuket, in response to the global financial crisis that hampered the US economy (Sussangkarn 2010). In 2012, the CMIM's size was expanded to US$240 billion. This expansion allows a requesting country to receive greater financial assistance during crises. The recent CMIM total fund of US$240 billion represents approximately 19.3 per cent of Japan's international reserves in the first quarter of 2013, or almost double that of Indonesia's reserves in the same period.[1]

Two important elements of CMIM are voting mechanism and surveillance process. From the perspective of maintaining nation sovereignty, the CMIM remarked the first time use of a voting mechanism in dealing with regional cooperation. This arrangement has the potential to put national sovereignty at risk, simply because majority votes may surpass national interests (Hix 2010, p. 29). Meanwhile, surveillance processes assist member countries to deal with macroeconomic conditions and reduce possible economic risks. In this regard, the CMIM surveillance mechanism contributes to developing stronger economic policy coordination among APT member countries, as all members share their awareness of economic vulnerabilities. Without stronger policy coordination, CMIM operations are likely to be undermined by bilateral arrangements (Siregar and Chabchitrchaidol 2013).

The ABMI

While focusing on regional financial stability, the APT financial cooperation also pays attention to the development of regional bond markets. The Asian bond markets increasingly attract APT member countries, as the markets contribute to the development of the regional economy. For example, the local currencies bond market marked US$1.7 trillion or contributed approximately 56.5 per cent of the total gross domestic product (GDP) of emerging East Asian countries at the end of 2013.[2] This figure represents the potential of the Asian bond markets as financing, as well as investment sources.

Prior to the Asian financial crisis, many Asian countries, including the private sector, relied mainly on bank financing schemes to support their projects and operations (Johansson 2008). At that time, bond markets in most Asian countries were not yet well-developed enough to constitute an alternative financing source. High dependency on bank financing becomes an economic problem when short-term foreign currency loans are used to finance long-term investment (Bhattacharyay 2013). Economic problems worsen when bank loan borrowers face currency depreciation that lead to significant increases in debt levels. The fragility of Asian capital markets, due to maturity and currency mismatches, has warned APT member countries regarding the stability of their economy.

Indeed, external factors such as changes to US monetary policies, have also contributed to the creation of currency and maturity mismatches in the Asian domestic financial system. Based on statistical observations, Inoguchi (2007, p. 403) argues that the levels and changes in the rates of Asian bond yields are correlated with those of US Treasury bond yields. From a positive perspective, the dynamics of US financial policies have fostered the development of a well-functioning Asian bond market (Johansson 2008, p. 103). However, as the actual interdependence of most Asian financial markets on the US market is not greater than that on other Asian countries, the level of US financial market dynamics contribution to the development of the Asian bond market is less significant compared to regional factors.

The APT regional efforts on bond market development are mainly conducted under the auspices of the ABMI. The initiative covers several fundamental components of the bond market, including market infrastructure and regulation. In general, ABMI aims to assist APT member countries to develop robust domestic bond markets to avoid a double mismatch of maturity and currency of financing, to maximise regional saving and to promote regional financial sector harmonisation, as well as market integration (Lee 2012). ABMI has been set as an initiative to develop liquid and efficient bond markets in the region, using the region's own savings (Kurihara 2012). In practice, ABMI has mobilised several task forces to facilitate sharing of information and to provide technical assistance in establishing benchmarks for financial market infrastructure (Eichengreen 2006, p. 3). Table 3.1 demonstrates the development of ABMI from 2002 to 2010 that comprises several related projects on bond markets under APT financial cooperation.

The ABMI was reorganised in 2008 by implementing the New ABMI roadmap, proposed by Japan. The new roadmap encouraged member

Table 3.1 Highlights of ABMI processes

Year	Progress
2002	The launch of ABMI as the groundwork organisation for bond development in the region.
2003	The establishment of working groups to undertake further study on several elements of bond market development.
2008	The launch of the New ABMI roadmap, setting up task forces in response to specific issues. The new roadmap facilitates greater access, for issuers and investors, to regional bond markets.
2010	The launch of CGIF, the first regional guarantee and investment mechanism in APT. Initially focused on credit guarantee services, rather than investment facilities. Managed by a non-state actor (ADB) as the trustee.
2010	The launch of ABMF as a common platform to foster development of cross-border bond transactions.

Source: Author's own summary

countries to enhance their own local currency-denominated bonds and also to develop more accessible regional bond markets for issuers and investors (APT 2012). Operationally, the New ABMI roadmap consisted of a coordinating team and four taskforces (TFs). These were TF 1, promoting the issuance of local-denominated bonds; TF 2, facilitating the demand for local currency denominated bonds; TF 3, improving the regulatory framework; and TF 4, improving infrastructure related to bond markets (Lee 2012, p. 3). In addition to the four TFs, a Technical Assistance Coordination Team (TACT) was also formed.

Based on the functions of the TFs, ABMI can be perceived as an initiative that promotes regional bond markets and also provides assistance for domestic bond development. Grimes (2009, p. 177) argues that ABMI operates within two distinct but related projects: the development of domestic bond markets and the creation of regional bond markets. Thus, ABMI introduced a new element of governance that shaped a regional bond market arrangement and, at the same time, operated over domestic markets, particularly through standardisation and harmonisation projects.

Reflecting on the discussion about financial initiatives under the auspices of ASEAN, APEC and APT Cooperation, in general, standardisation and policy coordination have emerged as prominent activities in these three regional forums. As illustrated in Table 3.2, while ASEAN and APT Cooperation cover both activities, only APEC includes standardisation without establishing policy coordination as part of its regional projects on financial cooperation.

In particular, the table reveals how ASEAN member countries perceive policy coordination in the financial sector as an important element to

Table 3.2 Key components of financial cooperation

	Standardisation	*Policy coordination*
ASEAN	Capital market standards (ACMF)	Monitoring macroeconomic policy and financial market surveillance (ASP)
APEC	A new standard for the dissemination of macroeconomic and financial data (SDDS)	None
APT	Standardisation of best practice and harmonisation of regulation in bond market (ABMF)	Fiscal and monetary monitoring; regional macroeconomic surveillance (CMIM)

Source: Author's compilation

stabilise regional, as well as individual, economies. As previously argued by Dieter and Higgott (2003), the ASEAN member countries extend their willingness to enhance economic policy coordination to their dialogue partners in APT Cooperation.

The next chapter examines the influence of domestic politics regarding Indonesia's perspectives on, and stances about, regional financial cooperation. It particularly investigates the approaches of each Indonesian administration towards regional financial cooperation in East Asia. In addition, the chapter also pays attention to the contribution of democratisation to Indonesia's recent position in East Asian financial regionalism.

NOTES

1. The data of Japan's, China's and Indonesia's international reserves are generated from IMF data, accessed on 10 July 2013, http://www.imf.org/external/np/sta/ir/IRProcessWeb/colist.aspx
2. According to Asian Development Bank (2014), 'Emerging East Asia' includes the People's Republic of China, Hong Kong (China), Indonesia, the Republic of Korea, Malaysia, the Philippines, Singapore, Thailand and Vietnam.

REFERENCES

Abbott, K., & Snidal, D. (2000). Hard and soft law in international governance. *International Organisation, 54*(3), 421–456.

Acharya, A. (2002). *Regionalism and multilaterism: Essays on cooperative security in the Asia Pacific*. Singapore: Times Academic Press.

Acharya, A. (2011). *Asia is not one: Regionalism and the ideas of Asia*. Singapore: Institute of Southeast Asian Studies.

Aggarwal, V. K., & Koo, M. G. (2007). The evolution of regionalism in East Asia. *Journal of East Asian Studies, 7*(3), 360–369.

Anas, T., & Atje, R. (2005). *Economic surveillance and policy dialogue in East Asia: Making the ASEAN surveillance process a new*. Jakarta: Centre for Strategic and International Studies.

Anwar, D. F. (1994). *Indonesia in ASEAN: Foreign policy and regionalism*. New York: St. Martin's Press.

APEC. (1997). *Vancouver declaration*. Retrieved September 30, 2014, from http://www.apec.org/Meeting-Papers/Leaders-Declarations/1997/1997_aelm.aspx

APEC. (1994). *First APEC Finance Ministers Meeting: Joint ministerial statement.* Retrieved November 24, 2011, from http://www.apec.org/Meeting-Papers/ Ministerial-Statements/Finance/~/media/Files/MinisterialStatements/ Finance/94_fmm_jms.ashx

APEC. (2010). *APEC at a glance, 2011.* Singapore: APEC Secretariat.

ASEAN. (1978). *The supplementary agreements to memorandum of understanding on the ASEAN swap arrangements.* Retrieved November 1, 2011, from http:// www.asean.org/1394.htm

ASEAN. (1997). *Joint ministerial statement of the special ASEAN Finance Ministers Meeting.* Retrieved November 7, 2011, from http://www.asean.org/6333.htm

ASEAN. (1998). *Terms of understanding on the establishment of the ASEAN surveillance process.* Retrieved November 9, 2011, from http://www.asean. org/739.htm

ASEAN. (1999). *Joint ministerial statement of the 3rd ASEAN Finance Ministers Meeting.* Retrieved November 10, 2011, from http://www.aseansec. org/6311.htm

ASEAN. (2006). *Joint ministerial statement of the 10th ASEAN Finance Ministers'Meeting.* Retrieved November 22, 2011, from http://59.77.27.55/ Article/ShowArticle.asp?ArticleID=639

ASEAN Plus Three. (2007). *The joint ministerial statement of the 10th ASEAN Plus Three Finance Ministers' Meeting.* ASEAN Plus Three. Retrieved December 9, 2011, from http://www.mof.go.jp/english/international_policy/convention/asean_plus_3/as3_070505.htm

ASEAN Plus Three. (2009). *The joint media statement of the 12th ASEAN Plus Three Finance Ministers' Meeting.* Bali: ASEAN Plus Three.

ASEAN Plus Three. (2010). *The joint ministerial statement of the 13th ASEAN Plus Three Finance Ministers' Meeting.* Tashkent: ASEAN Plus Three.

ASEAN Plus Three. (2012). *ASEAN Plus Three New ABMI Roadmap.* Retrieved February 27, 2013, from http://asianbondsonline.adb.org/publications/ adb/2008/abmi_roadmap.pdf

Asian Development Bank. (2014, March). *Asia Bond Monitor.* Mandaluyong City, Philippines: Asian Development Bank.

Bhattacharyay, B. N. (2013). Determinants of bond market development in Asia. *Journal of Asian Economics, 24,* 124–137.

Davis, J. R. (2010). East Asian regionalism: Origins, development and prospects for the future. *Politikon, 16*(1), 34–49.

De Brouwer, G. (1999). *Financial integration in East Asia.* Cambridge: Cambridge University Press.

Dieter, H., & Higgott, R. (2003). Exploring alternative theories of economic regionalism: From trade to finance in Asian co-operation? *Review of International Political Economy, 10*(3), 430–454.

Eichengreen, B. (2006). *The development of Asian Bond markets.* Paper presented to BIS/Korea University Conference on Asian Bond Markets: Issues and Prospects, Seoul, March 21–23, 2004.

Grimes, W. W. (2009). *Currency and contest in East Asia: The great power politics of financial regionalism, Cornell Studies in Money.* Ithaca: Cornell University Press.

He, B., & Inoguchi, T. (2011). Introduction to ideas of Asian regionalism. *Japanese Journal of Political Science, 12*(2), 165–177.

Henning, C. R. (2002). *East Asian financial cooperation* (Vol. 68). Washington, DC: Peterson Institute.

Henning, R. (2009). *The future of the Chiang Mai Initiative: An Asian Monetary Fund?* Washington, DC: Peterson Institute for International Economics.

Hill, H., & Menon, J. (2010). *ASEAN economic integration: Features, fulfilments, failures and the future.* ADB Working Paper Series on Regional Economic Integration, No. 69.

Hix, S. (2010). *Institutional design of regional integration: Balancing delegation and representation.* Manila: Asian Development Bank.

Inoguchi, M. (2007). Influence of ADB bond issues and US bonds on Asian government bonds. *Asian Economic Journal, 21*(4), 387–404.

International Monetary Fund. (2007). *The special data dissemination standard: Guide for subscribers and users.* Washington, DC: International Monetary Fund.

Ito, T., Ogawa, E., Kawai, M., Kawasaki, K., & Murase, T. (2005). *Research papers and policy recommendations on economic surveillance and policy dialogue in East Asia.* Tokyo: Institute for International Monetary Affairs.

Jayasuriya, K. (2003). Introduction: Governing the Asia Pacific beyond the new regionalism. *Third World Quarterly, 24*(2), 199–215.

Johansson, A. C. (2008). Interdependencies among Asian bond markets. *Journal of Asian Economics, 19*(2), 101–116.

Kanithasen, P., & Watjannapukka, K. (2011). The ASEAN economic community in 2015: Some steps move forward but no giant leap. *Focused and Quick,* No. 35.

Kurihara, T. (2012). *Achievements of Asian Bond Markets Initiative (ABMI) in the last decade and future challenges.* Paper presented to OECD-ADBI 12th Roundtable on Capital Market Reform in Asia, Tokyo, February 7.

Lee, I. (2012). *Ten Years of the Asian Bond Markets Initiative (ABMI).* Korean Capital Market Institute. Retrieved February 25, 2013, from http://www.kcmi.re.kr

Lewer, J. J., & Terry, N. (2003). Capital account and foreign direct investment policies in the late nineties: What effect on trade? *Asean Economic Bulletin, 20*(3), 256–271.

Manupipatpong, W. (2002). The ASEAN surveillance process and the East Asian Monetary Fund. *Asean Economic Bulletin, 19*(1), 111–122.

Murray, P. (2010). East Asian regionalism and EU Studies. *Journal of European Integration, 32*(6), 597–616.

Park, Y. C., & Bae, K.-H. (2002). *Financial liberalisation and economic integration in East Asia.* Paper presented to PECC Finance Forum Conference on Issues and Prospects for Regional Cooperation for Financial Stability and Development, Hilton Hawaiian Village, Honolulu, August 11–13.

Park, Y. C., & Takagi, S. (2011). *Creating an integrated market by 2015: Capital account liberalisation in ASEAN.* Paper presented to The 9th NIPFP-DEA Research Meeting on Capital Flows, New Delhi, March 15–16.

Park, Y.-J., & Oh, Y. (2010). *East Asian financial and monetary cooperation and Its prospect: Beyond the CMI.* KIEP Working Paper, Vol. 10, No. 4.

Pempel, T. J. (2010). Soft balancing, hedging, and institutional Darwinism: The economic-security nexus and East Asian regionalism. *Journal of East Asian Studies, 10,* 209–238.

Rajan, R., & Sen, R. (2002). *Liberalisation of financial services in Southeast Asia under the ASEAN Framework Agreement on Services (AFAS).* Centre for International Economic Studies (CIES) Discussion Paper, Vol. 226.

Rana, P. B. (2002). *Monetary and financial cooperation in East Asia: The Chiang Mai and beyond.* Asian Development Bank.

Ravenhill, J. (2002). A three Bloc World? The new East Asian regionalism. *International Relations of the Asia-Pacific, 2,* 167–195.

Ravenhill, J. (2006). Regionalism and state capacity in East Asia. In I. Marsh (Ed.), *Democratisation, governance and regionalism in East and Southeast Asia* (pp. 177–203). New York: Routledge.

Saputro, E. (2012). *ASEAN+3 financial cooperation enters a new phase.* East Asia Forum, May 26. Retrieved November 26, 2013, from http://www.eastasiaforum.org/2012/05/26/asean3-financial-cooperation-enters-a-new-phase/

Singh, D. R. A. (2009). ASEAN capital market integration: Issues and challenges. Retrieved October 10, 2014, from http://www.lse.ac.uk/IDEAS/publications/reports/pdf/SR002/SR002_singh.pdf

Siregar, M. (2011). Indonesia's structural reform. *The Indonesian Quarterly, 39*(3), 249–255.

Siregar, R., & Chabchitrchaidol, A. (2013). *Enhancing the effectiveness of CMIM and AMRO: Selected immediate challenges and tasks.* ADBI Working Paper 403. Tokyo: Asian Development Bank Institute.

Soesastro, H. (2003). An Asean economic community and ASEAN+3: How do they fit together? *Pacific Economic Papers,* Vol. 338.

Sohn, I. (2005). Asian financial cooperation: The problem of legitimacy in global financial governance. *Global Governance, 11,* 487–504.

Stubbs, R. (2002). Asean Plus Three: Emerging East Asian regionalism? *Asian Survey, 42*(3), 440–455.

Sussangkarn, C. (2010). *The Chiang Mai Initiative Multilateralisation: Origin, development, and outlook.* ADBI Working Paper Series, No. 230.

Takagi, S. (2010). *Regional surveillance for East Asia: How can it be designed to complement global surveillance?* Tokyo: Asian Development Bank Institute.

Tongzon, J. L. (2004). ASEAN + 3 and ASEAN economic integration. In K. P. Schönfisch & B. Seliger (Eds.), *ASEAN Plus Three (China, Japan, Korea)— Toward an economic union in East Asia?* Seoul: Hanns Seidel Stiftung.

Wang, Y. (2004). Financial cooperation and integration in East Asia. *Journal of Asian Economics, 15*(5), 939–955.

Yoshimatsu, H. (2014). *Comparing institution-building in East Asia: Power politics, governance, and critical junctures.* Palgrave Macmillan.

CHAPTER 4

Domestic Politics in Indonesia and Financial Regionalism in East Asia

As mentioned in Chap. 2, domestic politics matters in the regionalism process. In this regard, changes in domestic politics potentially shift the direction of a state's involvement in the regionalism process. The national commitments to East Asian regional arrangements are more or less determined by the dynamics of domestic politics.

Chapter 2 also showed that democratisation provided greater opportunity to participate in regional arrangements. Democratisation was understood as a process that promotes a higher degree of accountability, leading to the 'check and balance' mechanism. This mechanism often drove restructuring and the separation of power among relevant actors in the regionalism process. In particular areas, democratic reforms even became a prerequisite for specific regional arrangements.

The central objective of this chapter is to examine the influence of domestic politics on Indonesia's responses to ASEAN Plus Three (APT) financial cooperation. Such an examination is necessary to provide insights into, and a deeper understanding of, the changes in Indonesian domestic politics and their influence on Indonesia's commitments to regional financial cooperation. It examines political changes within different administrations since Indonesian independence to the recent administration under Soesilo Bambang Yudhoyono (SBY). This chapter argues that Indonesian domestic politics have influenced Indonesia's stance towards APT financial cooperation.

© The Author(s) 2017
E. Saputro, *Indonesia and ASEAN Plus Three Financial Cooperation*,
DOI 10.1007/978-981-10-3029-1_4

The chapter is divided into two parts. The first part analyses the approaches of different administrations in Indonesia to the development of financial regionalism in East Asia. The administrations are classified into three eras: *non-democratic, transition* and *democratic*. The second part of this chapter analyses the influence of democratisation on the process of financial regionalism at Indonesia's national level. Specifically, this part analyses a new configuration of policy-making processes and policy coordination among relevant authorities in the Indonesian financial sector under democratic administrations and the contribution of democratisation to a stronger commitment to these regional arrangements. This chapter argues that democratisation has contributed to facilitate regionalism processes within the Indonesian financial regulatory framework, through promoting power sharing, transparency and wider participation.

POLITICAL CHANGE AND VARYING APPROACHES TO REGIONAL COOPERATION

Since its independence in 1945 till 2013, Indonesia has had six presidents. In this section, the presidential eras are classified into two major categories: the non-democratic era and the democratic era, with one transitional era that comprises both classifications. This classification is based on the political approaches that were applied by each administration during its respective era.

The Non-democratic Era

In its newly acquired independence, Indonesia was led by President Soekarno from 1945 to 1967. Under Soekarno, Indonesia had little concern for interests in regional cooperation due to the presence of intense domestic political tensions particularly with Malaysia and Japan. The trauma of colonialism and the threat of capitalism prompted Soekarno to turn to Indonesia's own national strengths and bilateral relations instead of looking to regional cooperation. As a new nation, Indonesia brought political and economic prospects together in its history. Table 4.1 summarises Dick et al.'s (2002) account of the Indonesian political and economic situation from 1930 to 1966.

As illustrated in Table 4.1, the Indonesian economy suffered from Dutch colonialism from 1930 to 1942. Dutch military and political repression pushed the Indonesian economy into severe depression. The

Table 4.1 Indonesia's political and economic situation

Period	Politics	Economy
1930–1942	Repression	Depression and recovery
1942–1949	Occupation, revolution	Catastrophic decline
1950–1959	Party politics	Rehabilitation
1959–1966	Guided democracy	Decline, macroeconomic chaos

Source: Dick et al. (2002, p. 154)

signs of an economic recovery began in the early 1950s, with Indonesia emerging to enjoy higher commodity prices for rubber and oil (Johansson 2012, p. 174). However, the Soekarno administration was preoccupied with its national-political building agenda aimed at consolidating domestic political factions. As a result, the early signs of economic progress could not be utilised effectively to improve overall economic conditions.

The hyperinflation period in 1966, due to a high budget deficit, constituted an important event during the Soekarno period, one that shaped Indonesia's financial-monetary policy significantly. The deficit emerged as a consequence of Soekarno's costly agendas related to the liberation of Papua, the confrontation with Malaysia, rice import issues, subsidies for oil products and monumental building programmes (Adiningsih and Devi 2010, pp. 18–19). To deal with the deficit, Soekarno ordered *Bank Indonesia* (BI)—the Indonesian central bank—to generate government revenue. BI could not reject this order, as it was under the president's executive control. According to Law No. 11/1953 on the Principles of BI, BI was governed by three entities: *Dewan Moneter* (monetary council), directors and an advisory council.[1] The chief of the monetary council was the finance minister, who was appointed by, and was accountable to, the president. Due to his position as leader of the monetary council, the Indonesian finance minister had the authority to stipulate monetary policy and financial policy as its main function. Under the Soekarno administration, the governor of BI was a member of the council. Therefore, in practice, all financial-monetary policies, including those related to regional cooperation, remained under the control of the Indonesian president. The existence of the *Dewan Moneter* remained secured up until Soeharto's administration.[2]

Regional economic-financial cooperation did not receive adequate attention under the Soekarno administration. Soekarno was more concerned with building up the nation's strengths through his programme known as

'Berdikari' (*berdiri di atas kaki sendiri*: 'standing on our own two feet'),
rather than setting up cooperative arrangements with neighbouring countries. In general, the Berdikari movement encouraged Indonesian people
to build the Indonesian economy based on self-reliance (Parinduri et al.
2009). In international relations context, the Berdikari can be understood
as a movement to build economic nationalism and, at the same time, protect the Indonesian economy from foreign intervention. Therefore, one
of President Soekarno's strategie-s to assist Indonesia's nascent economy
was a 'nationalisation' that aimed to take over foreign companies operating in Indonesia. During the nationalisation programme, Soekarno took
over not only Dutch-owned companies (Johansson 2012, p. 183), but
also a number of Malaysian enterprises (Parinduri et al. 2009, p. 247).
The latter action eventually created foreign political tension and worsened
Indonesia's regional relations.

After the collapse of the Soekarno administration, Soeharto took power
in 1967 and ruled until 1998. The main issues during the Soeharto administration were political instability due to military and political factions, as
well as poor economic growth due to hyperinflation. To deal with these
complex political-economic problems, Soeharto attempted to consolidate
political-military fractions by banning *Partai Komunis Indonesia* (PKI)—
the Indonesian Communist Party—and by attempting to fuse a multiparty
system into only three parties representing three political mainstreams:
nationalism, Islam and a bureaucracy military (Eklöf 2004; Mariyono and
Saputro 2009). For the sake of political stability, and with strong military
back up, all political actions were presided over by Soeharto. However,
due to his military approach to government, Soeharto adopted an autocratic leadership style, characterised by the silencing of dissenting voices
and a lack of public accountability.

To recover the Indonesian economy, Soeharto sought foreign assistance. Soon after his appointment as the president of Indonesia, Soeharto
decided to resume Indonesia's membership in the International Monetary
Fund (IMF) and the World Bank (WB). Soeharto also welcomed the establishment of the Inter-Governmental Group on Indonesia (IGGI), a con-
sortium of both donor countries and International Financial Institutions
(IFIs) aimed at supporting the Indonesian economy (Emmerson 2012,
p. 15). The president had few options but to accept international assistance to stabilise the domestic economy as regional assistance for economic
cooperation remained fragile due to political tensions. As a result, programmes of debt relief and new loans were started.

Under Soeharto's autocratic regime, Indonesia demonstrated its support for regionalism processes, particularly through ASEAN. Soeharto included Southeast Asia and ASEAN as his third sphere of influence, after the West and non-aligned movement (NAM) countries (Smith 1999, p. 240). However, Soeharto's backing of ASEAN was aimed not only at creating a way to lessen regional political tension, but it was also for the sake of economic development. Therefore, regarding ASEAN, Indonesia paid more attention to security cooperation, rather than to the economy. Security regionalism is more attractive to autocratic political leaders than economic or political regionalism, as it potentially assists an autocratic regime to survive (Collins 2009, p. 274).

While regional financial cooperation did not emerge as an important issue during the Soeharto administration, Indonesia still maintained regional economic cooperation to demonstrate its leadership in ASEAN. The first attempt to follow a regional financial initiative was in 1977, when Indonesia joined the ASEAN Swap Arrangement (ASA), along with four other ASEAN member countries: Malaysia, Singapore, Thailand and the Philippines (Henning 2002, p. 14). Following ASA, Indonesia started to participate in the negotiation of financial issues under the ASEAN Framework Agreement on Services (AFAS). In this respect, Soeharto demonstrated his commitment to AFAS by promptly ratifying it within an Indonesian regulation framework. At that time, the Soeharto administration needed only 15 days to bring the AFAS into force, such that the regulation established the legal basis for related authorities in Indonesia to work with their counterparts in ASEAN.

The rapid legalisation process of AFAS during the Soeharto administration demonstrates that this autocratic regime effectively proceeded with its commitment to a regional arrangement. The accumulation of power in the hands of the president helped to facilitate this development. During the Soeharto autocratic regime, the Indonesian executive body had greater political power over the legislative body (*Dewan Perwakilan Rakyat*/DPR) (Eklöf 2004). According to Article 7 of the Indonesian Constitution—the *Undang-Undang Dasar 1945* (Constitution 1945)—any international agreements require approval from the DPR, before being legalised by the president. However, in the context of AFAS, President Soeharto directly approved the legalisation process without approval from the DPR. In this case, President Soeharto referred to President Soekarno's letter No. 2826/HK/1960 that had been sent to the head of DPR (containing Soekarno's opinion on Article 11 of the

Constitution 1945). In his letter, Soekarno asked the DPR if international agreements, other than treaties on political or social issues that could potentially shift the direction of Indonesian foreign policy, could be passed without DPR approval. Soekarno thought that if the government had to seek DPR approval for every single international agreement, the process would delay prompt responses from Indonesia and hinder the dynamic of international cooperation. Having this approval arrangement in place, without any complex legal processes, meant that the legalisation process of regional cooperation during the Soeharto administration ran smoothly and efficiently, without any disputes among political parties. In a nutshell, while Soeharto's executive-heavy policy-making processes undermined the democratic principle of maintaining the check and balance principle, these processes eased the way for the *domestication* of a regional arrangement.

Habibie's Transitional Administration

The fall of the Soeharto administration in the midst of the Asian financial crisis not only changed many aspects of Indonesian politics, but also affected the implementation of financial policies. Habibie—Soeharto's vice president, who was appointed as 'an interim president', as he took power due to Soeharto's resignation—made a major change to Indonesian financial sector management. During his short tenure (1998–1999), Habibie made a major shift by separating BI from the Indonesian government's executive power into an independent body. The BI's independence was basically an IMF conditionality imposed on Indonesia to secure the central bank's accountability (IMF 1998). The IMF viewed that a lack of accountability within Indonesia's financial authority had led to mismanagement in the financial sector.

Habibie did not pay enough attention to the development of regional financial cooperation processes. The political and economic crisis had restricted Habibie's administration to playing active roles in foreign relations (Smith 1999, p. 244). Therefore, Habibie did not make any substantial decisions related to regional cooperation in the financial sector. The president even provoked tensions with Singapore, after raising sensitive ethical issues that triggered Singapore's furious reaction and worsened bilateral relations between the two ASEAN member states (Chandra 2008, p. 104).

The Democratic Era

Three administrations within the post-Habibie transitional administration are understood to have promoted democratic values. This era began with the short-term Abdurrahman Wahid administration, who after two years in power was succeeded by his deputy, Megawati Soekarnoputri. Following this, the Indonesian democratic consolidation reached its momentum under SBY, who stepped into office in 2004.

In October 1999, Abdurrahman Wahid, widely known as *Gus Dur*, was elected as the next Indonesian president. Although Gus Dur was not elected through a direct election, the Indonesian people started to experience a free and fair election process for the first time, after years of Soeharto's autocratic regime that had gained legitimation through non-democratic election processes. This momentum sparked the shift in Indonesian domestic politics from non-democratic to a more democratic regime.

After the reform movement, Gus Dur inherited a polarised political system beset with tension. The president also had a difficult task to restore market confidence amidst political uncertainty (Soesastro 2000). In dealing with both issues, Gus Dur implemented massive foreign policy changes to gain support for economic restoration, to maintain national territory and to enhance Indonesia's international reputation (Lahat 2011). In this respect, Gus Dur sought alternative sources of economic assistance from Asian countries, instead of restoring relations with the West. Soon after taking power, Gus Dur announced his Asian-oriented foreign policy by proposing a 'looking towards Asia' approach that focused on China, India, Japan and Singapore (He 2008, p. 48). For Indonesia, the establishment of cooperative arrangements with China and India provided alternative partners, while dealing with Japan and Singapore would help to restore Indonesian relations with financial donors, investors and trading partners. This was expected to support the recovery of Indonesia's economy.

Although Gus Dur's foreign policy emphasised a new era in relation to Indonesia's foreign architecture, he continued to regard ASEAN as the cornerstone of his foreign policy. Particularly in the area of finance, the administration engaged with important initiatives, including APT financial cooperation. It was during Gus Dur's administration when the initial step of APT financial cooperation was established. The first joint ministerial statement of the APT finance ministers was prepared on 6 May 2000, a statement given strong support by Indonesia. This engagement provided some assurance for Indonesia in times of crisis, while constructing a path towards the reinstatement of regional leadership. However, during Gus Dur's administration, there was no single regional financial cooperation legalised into the Indonesian regulatory system.

Due to a controversial corruption allegation, Gus Dur was forced to step down. In July 2001, Megawati Soekarnoputri—the daughter of the first Indonesian president, Soekarno—took power. Having strong political support gained from the 1999 election, Megawati had achieved a relatively high level of legitimation that enabled her to create stable political and economic policies. During her tenure, Megawati placed national sovereignty and territory as her top priorities, with respect to foreign policy, whereas achieving economic recovery remained a second priority (Anwar 2003, p. 77). The influence of her father's political views on nationalism explains Megawati's decision to prioritise a political agenda over the economy. Megawati spent much time and effort on democratic and political consolidation during her administration.

Considering that the Indonesian economy had not yet recovered from the impact of the Asian financial crisis, Megawati sought international support. In a regional context, ASEAN remained indispensable as a foreign policy anchor for the first female Indonesian president (Anwar 2003). To restore Indonesian relations with ASEAN members, Megawati chose to visit ASEAN countries on her first diplomatic mission, a decision reflecting the symbolic significance of ASEAN to Indonesian foreign policy, and to obtain regional support (Soekarnoputri 2001). Megawati also reiterated Gus Dur's foreign policy on Asia by strengthening bilateral cooperation, especially with Japan and China as prominent partners in Indonesia's economic development.

On the issue of financial cooperation, Megawati demonstrated her commitment to the development of ASEAN, as well as to APT initiatives. In 2002, Megawati signed the Presidential Decree No. 81, to ratify the second package of commitments on financial services, which had been a part of the AFAS negotiation process since the second package of services was approved in 1998. Notwithstanding its commitment to AFAS, the Megawati administration cautiously provided specific reservation to maintain the right to withdraw, modify and make technical changes to offers contained within the AFAS commitment package. For comparison, this reservation was not provided by the other ASEAN members at that time. Rajan and Sen (2002) argue that Indonesia did not make any specific commitments in relation to financial services, as Indonesia only mentioned general conditions for the banking sector. The trauma of the Asian financial crisis was a likely key consideration of Indonesian financial authorities under Megawati in their more prudent approach to international commitments.

Another important regional policy taken by Megawati was the release of Presidential Decree No. 48/2004, to ratify the framework agreement on comprehensive economic cooperation between ASEAN and China. This provided an endorsement for Indonesia's engagement with the ASEAN-China comprehensive economic partnership. Although financial matters were not specifically stated as part of the partnership's five priority areas, these matters were covered in the broad area of cooperation. This policy emphasised Megawati's focus on Asia, particularly East Asia, as a buffer region for Indonesian economic development.

Further, the state of the Indonesian political economy entered a new phase when the nation successfully conducted fair and transparent direct elections in 2004, for the members of parliament and for the presidency. The presidential election resulted in SBY becoming the sixth president of Indonesia from 2004 to 2009. SBY was re-elected for a second period of administration from 2009 until 2014.

SBY inherited a relatively stable macroeconomic and political environment when taking over from Megawati, even though national security was still being threatened by domestic separatism and the growing threat of terrorism. With a strong political mandate and an improving economy, SBY introduced what was known as 'Triple Track Strategy' of economic policy (Bremner and Shameen 2005). The strategy was directed towards three major activities: enhancing economic growth through investment and export; creating more jobs through real sectors; and reducing poverty through revitalising the agricultural sector and the rural economy.

Regarding the first strategy, the strengthening of regional and global cooperation was part of SBY's major policy options. At the regional level, SBY conducted essential dialogues with leaders of Malaysia, Singapore, China, Japan and Australia during his first four weeks in office (Yudhoyono 2004). Similar to his two predecessors (Gus Dur and Megawati), SBY positioned Asia—particularly the East Asian countries—as his strategic economic partners. Moreover, ASEAN remained as the main pillar of Indonesia's foreign economic and political relations during SBY's administration. Particularly on finance matters, Indonesia consistently engaged with various initiatives in ASEAN and APT Cooperation. A former

Indonesian finance minister under SBY's administration has argued that financial integration contributes to raising economic growth by reducing the cost of capital, supporting technology transfer, promoting further development of the domestic financial market, enhancing macroeconomic policy making and strengthening institutional capacity (Indrawati 2007a). Therefore, Indonesia was active in its participation in regional integration projects.

Reflecting concrete action, Indonesia offered commitments in the areas of commercial banking businesses, such as acceptance of deposits, lending, mortgage, money transmission services and foreign exchange, for the third package of financial services under AFAS. This commitment was legalised by Presidential Decree No. 51 in 2008 and focused on the banking sector. In this commitment, Indonesia offered foreign ownership of Indonesian private banks of up to 99 per cent of the total shares (Government Regulation No. 29/1999). This offer implies Indonesia's growing confidence in the liberalisation of financial services, compared to the initial commitment in the previous AFAS package negotiation process.

Another commitment to financial services liberalisation under AFAS was marked by the release of the Presidential Decree No. 6/2009, on the implementation of the fourth package of commitments on financial services. As distinct from previous commitments, in this commitment Indonesia made a more limited offer, particularly in relation to factoring services; this is a complete financial package that combines credit protection, credit management and account receivable bookkeeping and collection services (Fiordelisi and Molyneux 2004). In addition, the SBY administration also supported the establishment of regional initiatives in many areas of finance under the auspices of APT Cooperation. Indonesia joined the Chiang Mai Initiative Multilateralisation (CMIM), Asian Bond Market Initiative (ABMI) and other financial projects during the SBY administration.

However, despite the growing trend towards financial services liberalisation, the contribution of this sector to Indonesia's economic growth was basically limited. A study conducted by the Indonesian Capital Market and Financial Institution Supervisory Agency—*Badan Pengawas Pasar Modal-Lembaga Keuangan* (Bapepam-LK)—revealed that financial services have not had a significant impact on Indonesian economic growth (Bapepam-LK 2008). Therefore, Indonesia recently urged ASEAN member states to work more closely on regional development, so that tangible benefits could emerge. In the 2011 ASEAN Finance Minister Meeting (AFMM), SBY appealed to ASEAN member states to unify and become more competitive in taking the driver's seat in East Asian regionalism (Theo 2011). This appeal was plausible, as ASEAN member states could not stand alone to compete with their Plus Three colleagues who were already regarded as enjoying higher economic status.

In 2014, Joko Widodo (whose popular name is Jokowi) was elected as the new Indonesian president, taking power from SBY. He won the first Indonesian 'head to head' election in which there were only two candidates running; that divided the nation into two blocs. Different from his six predecessors who had usually built their leadership based on aristocracy, political parties or military background, Jokowi formed his leadership from a massive popularity that saw him lead the polls before the election (Saputro 2014). His supporters placed high hopes on Jokowi's shoulders, especially to fight against corruption and economic inequality.

In terms of international relations, Jokowi seems to have less interest and focus compared to his predecessor, SBY. Jokowi's vision is more domestic-oriented, rather than international. Jokowi posits himself as a domestic reformer, not an international statesman (Connelly 2014, p. 5). Therefore, for international relations—including regional cooperation of financial affairs—Jokowi relies on his advisers and related ministries. As his inauguration has only just been held on 20 October 2014, there has not been much progress made on Jokowi's commitment to regional arrangements. The only commitment he nominated was Indonesia's support for the establishment of the Asian Infrastructure Investment Bank (AIIB), a new regional bank led by China. While Indonesian commitment to AIIB might not favour its Japanese counterpart—as AIIB potentially jeopardises the existence of the ADB—the commitment has demonstrated Indonesia's more practical approach in dealing with financial initiatives in the region. For Indonesia, the AIIB provides financial support to run its infrastructure programmes.

THE IMPACT OF DEMOCRATISATION

The growing movement towards democracy in Indonesia, in the wake of the Asian financial crisis, was understood to have had a positive impact on national performance in terms of the economy. Indonesian democracy has provided a platform for developing better economic policies and has contributed to a sound economic climate (OECD 2010, p. 25). During the democratic era, Indonesia has enjoyed positive trends in economic growth, larger capital inflows and more transparent budget-making processes.

Besides playing an important role in Indonesia's domestic economic performance, the strong democratic movement has also contributed to the country's further involvement in financial regionalism. Indonesia has embraced more diverse ways of enhancing regional and global economic cooperation since the Asian financial crisis, when at that time calls for more democratic forms of government were growing louder (Indrawati 2008, p. 50). The values of democracy have influenced the stance taken by Indonesian financial authorities when promoting the regional initiatives.

The following section aims to analyse both the influence of democratisation on Indonesian domestic political affairs and its impact on Indonesia's involvement in East Asian financial regionalism. This analysis includes discussion on policy-making processes under Indonesian democratic administrations, policy coordination mechanisms among national actors and the rising participation of non-state actors.

Separation of Power under Democratic Regimes

The most important contribution of democratisation to Indonesian domestic politics is the change in political institution and power configuration. Due to democratisation, the 1945 Constitution has been amended four times between 1999 and 2002. The amendments have focused particularly on fundamental issues, such as enhancing check and balance mechanism among state institutions, defining the separation of powers between the executive, legislative and judicative institutions, and on the new arrangements between the central and local governments (Lubis 2003). The major influential shift occurred with the restructuring of state institution organisation and modification of their functions. Following the amendments to the 1945 Constitution, the sovereignty of the Indonesian people was no longer represented by the People's Consultative Assembly (*Majelis Permusyawaratan Rakyat*/MPR), but was now reflected in the constitution itself. Therefore, as illustrated in Fig. 4.1, the position of MPR is now considered to have equal status with other state institutions in the organisational framework.

Another significant change occurred in relation to the limitations of executive power. Executive power in the non-democratic era, especially during the Soeharto administration, was perceived as too great; as such, it created political trauma, as evidenced in the new configuration between the executive and legislative. This trauma then became the foundation for strengthening the power of the DPR, to meet the check and balance

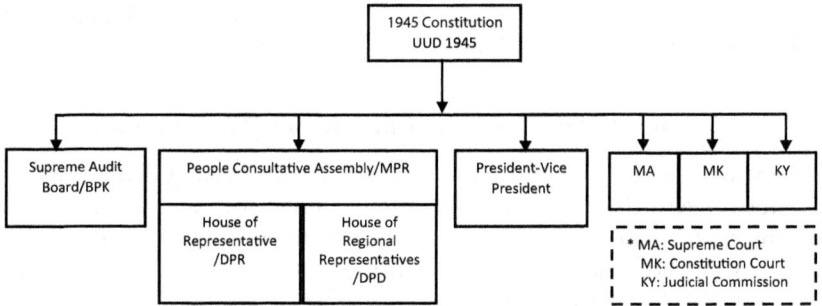

Fig. 4.1   Indonesian state institutions post-amendment of the 1945 Constitution. Source: Author's own visualisation

mechanism (Centre for Strategic and International Studies 2002). As the DPR represents the Indonesian people, this institution should have equal power with the president. The enhancement of DPR's power might ensure that the diversity of Indonesian voices would be accommodated by a democratic administration (Crouch 2010). Therefore, the DPR should be entitled to carry out particular mandates and functions, to make it possible for the Indonesian people to engage in issues that affect their interests, including issues to do with financial and monetary matters. However, the current political power configuration suggests that the policy-making process in Indonesia is 'legislative-heavy', in the sense that the legislative body (DPR) has more power over policy-making processes compared to the executive body (i.e., the DPR has power to determine the operation of any programmes that normally are under executive control in any democratic regimes in the world).

Further, under democratic regimes, the exercise of Indonesian executive power over particular areas, such as education and public health, has also been devolved into sub-national governments at the provincial and district levels. This devolution process was aimed at enhancing greater participation of the Indonesian people in national development. The devolution of power from the Indonesian central government also played out in public finance areas, in which local governments were given a mandate and the authority to manage their own budgets (previously centralised by the then President Soeharto's autocratic administration) (Brodjonegoro 2003). However, under more democratic administrative procedures, the Indonesian central government retains control over the national budget and other sensitive areas, such as security, foreign policy, religion affairs and defence (Law No. 32/2004 on Local Government).

Changes to Financial Institutions and Policy Making

The major changes in Indonesia's financial policy-making process identified above were also marked by the establishment of Law No. 23/1999, relating to BI. This law established a new momentum in the power divisions within the financial-monetary authority framework. Since then, the role of the IMOF in the banking sector, particularly for issuing and revoking bank licences, and the establishment of new branches, has been almost entirely abolished (McLeod 1999, p. 148). Under the current regulation, the position of BI in the national institutional framework is quite unique. It is an independent body located outside the executive sphere; however, it is not parallel with other high-level national institutions, such as the DPR, the Supreme Court (*Mahkamah Agung*/MA) or the State Auditory Board (*Badan Pemeriksa Keuangan*/BPK). As an independent body, BI is no longer directly responsible to the president. Instead, it is responsible to the DPR that represents the Indonesian people. In practice, BI is obliged to report to the DPR every three months, to account for its performance. As part of that process, the bank has to be open to a special auditing mechanism conducted by BPK, should the DPR require further investigation.

The separation of powers in the Indonesian financial sector reflects the check and balance principle that was limited under non-democratic administrations. The new financial institutional arrangements in a democratic Indonesia are more reliant on governance, rather than discretion, as occurred under the previous administrations. However, this separation does not mean that the Indonesian Ministry of Finance (IMOF) and BI are fully disengaged. In several areas, such as those related to the bond or capital markets, both institutions remain connected, as they have particular areas that affect each other. In general, BI has a single function to maintain the stability of the value of the *rupiah* (BI 2014).[3] This function is reflected in BI's organisational framework, as illustrated in Fig. 4.2.

A further landmark in the Indonesian financial sector was the establishment of Law No. 17/2003, related to public finance. According to this law, the Indonesian president has a mandate to manage public finance. In practice, the president delegates this power to the minister of finance. The mandate does not include monetary areas, as BI already has the authority to conduct this function. Under the law, the IMOF is authorised to

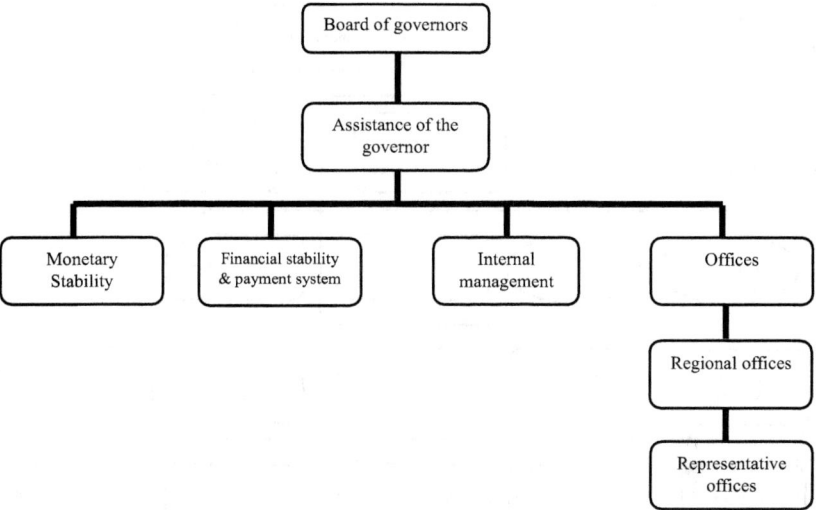

Fig. 4.2 BI organisational structure. Source: BI official website, <www.bi.go.id> (2014)

conduct several activities, such as stipulating fiscal and macroeconomic policies, setting the national budget, generating revenue and making international agreements related to the financial sector (Article 8, Law No. 17/2003).

Based on its latest organisational framework, as illustrated in Fig. 4.3, the IMOF comprised wider organisations, including seven directorate generals, one policy office and two agencies. The IMOF had three units involved in APT financial cooperation: *Badan Kebijakan Fiskal*, Fiscal Policy Office (FPO); *Direktorat Jenderal Pengelolaan Utang*, the Directorate General of Debt Management (known as the Debt Management Office/DMO); and *Badan Pengawas Pasar Modal dan Lembaga Keuangan*, Indonesian Capital Market and Financial Institution Authority (Bapepam-LK).

In the context of financial regionalism, the IMOF and BI were the main government bodies with major roles to play. However, IMOF had more roles in dealing with regional cooperation compared to BI, as most financial issues were under the IMOF's authority. BI only had power over the Indonesian banking sector, while the rest of this financial sector was governed by the IMOF. After its separation from executive power, BI was equipped with a mandate to build cooperation with other central banks,

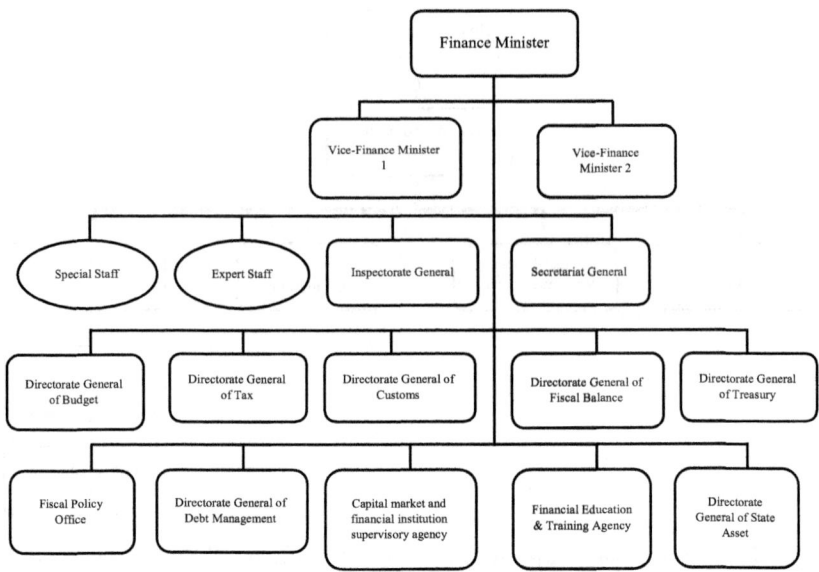

Fig. 4.3 IMOF organisational structure. Source: Finance Minister Regulation No. 184/PMK.01/2010

international organisations or foreign institutions (Article 57, Law No. 23/1999 on BI). The mandate also included the possibility for the BI to act on behalf of Indonesian interests in monetary areas. Operationally, the International Directorate of BI was in charge of regional cooperation. One of the directorate's duties involved dealing with ASEAN studies and cooperation, including APT Cooperation. In 2012, APT Cooperation had gained special attention from the directorate, particularly on the issue of the advancement of a regional safety net (BI 2012, p. 35).

Another relevant institution in the financial sector is the DPR. As a national body that has power over legislative areas, the DPR holds important roles within the financial sector and in the implementation of international cooperation initiatives. As illustrated in Fig. 4.4, DPR has significant power over financial sector management. For example, the Indonesian central government is required to discuss and seek approval from the DPR to release national budgets, including details of programmes and expenditures (Article 15, Law No. 17/2003 on Public Finance). This authority is not ordinary, as the details of such programmes would normally be

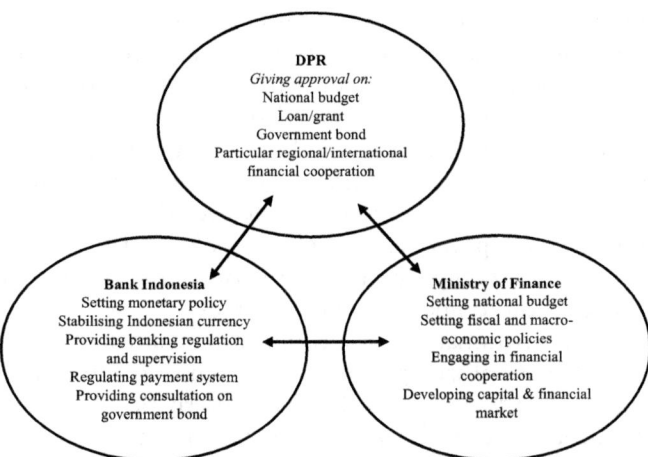

Fig. 4.4 Indonesian major institutions in the financial-monetary regulatory framework. Source: Author compilation, based on Law No. 23/1999, Law No. 17/2003 and Law No. 24/2000

managed by the executive, rather than the legislative body. Without the DPR's approval, the government is only able to work from the previous financial year's budget. This is evidence that the current policy-making process in Indonesia is legislative-heavy, in the sense that the parliament has stronger power than the president.

The DPR also has the power to deal with the government on bond issuance. According to Law No. 22/2002 on Government Bonds, the IMOF is required to seek approval from the DPR, particularly in relation to the maximum net value of government bonds released in one financial year. This arrangement suggests that the DPR, as a legislative body, intends to reduce the economic risks that may result from excessive government bond issuance. Besides working closely with the DPR, the IMOF also has to coordinate with BI regarding the issuance of government bonds to support the national budget, to deal with short-term liquidity and to manage government debt (Article 6, Law No. 24/2002). Regarding government bonds, BI has a mandate to manage the administration of government bonds on issues related to ownership, clearing and settlement processes and payment agencies for the principal and interests. At the operational level, BI also can act as an agent in the primary market (Article 12–14, Law No. 24/2002). While these arrangements are time consuming and to some extent ineffective, the arrangement is necessary to avoid the potential abuse of power in generating public funds that eventually may generate an economic burden. The separation of control over government bond issuance ensures that the amount raised by government bonds will not become a means for the ruling political party to generate excessive funds for the party's interests, thus adding a burden to Indonesian economy. However, giving partial power to the DPR over the issuance of government bonds has also potentially become a political tool for opposition parties in Indonesia to engage in political bargaining, if the ruling party seeks fiscal expansion to finance its programmes.

Within the international financial cooperation context, the role of DPR in international financial arrangements has become more well-defined since the establishment of Law No. 24/2000 on International Agreements. As specified in the law, such international agreements on loans and/or grants need to be stipulated by a government bill to be effective in Indonesian territory. This arrangement enhanced the existence of the DPR in international/regional financial cooperation, one that under the previous Soekarno or Soeharto regimes appeared vague.

Independence and Coordination

As discussed earlier, before the separation of BI from the Indonesian government's executive sphere, both the financial and monetary authorities were controlled by the finance minister, who was also in charge as the head of monetary council. Therefore, policy coordination was not a big issue, as all relevant bodies were under the control of the same person at that time. A problem emerged when politics seemed to intervene to an excessive degree in financial policy-making processes. The lack of independence inhibited financial authorities, particularly BI, to undertake effective policy action. For example, during the Asian financial crisis, BI proposed to close several banks to avoid further economic deterioration. In response to this proposal, President Soeharto rejected the proposed policy, to avoid social and political instability (Djiwandono 2004, p. 62). Due to the president's intervention, BI could not take the proper measures, as it would do normally. Soeharto's decision to intervene eventually led to a worsening of the Indonesian banking sector's performance, which then contributed to further economic deterioration. However, since BI became an independent body, the ruling government and other parties have been prohibited from intervening in monetary policy (Article 4 and 9, Law No. 23/1999).

Further, the separation of financial and monetary authorities has affected the way the IMOF and BI shape their policy coordination. As policy coordination between the Indonesian financial and monetary authorities is such a crucial issue, it is stipulated in Law No. 17/2003 on Public Finance. Boediono, cited in Adiningsih and Devi (2010), argues that, operationally, a fiscal policy has consequences for monetary policy, and a monetary policy has consequences for fiscal policy. As finance and monetary policies are interconnected, policy coordination is important to avoid negative implications for broader economic policies. According to Law No. 23/1999 on BI, there are at least four areas that need policy coordination between IMOF and BI. The first is related to broader economic policies, in which the government needs to seek opinions and inputs from BI, related to its functions. The second area of policy coordination relates to the national budget. In this regard, the IMOF may seek opinions and consideration from the BI in dealing with the national budget plan. The third area is regarding government bond issuance. In this area, the government is also obliged to consult with BI if the government plans to issue bonds. According to this law, BI is tasked operationally with providing services related to government bond issuances, such as clearing and settlement processes. The fourth area of policy coordination relates to foreign loans. In this regard, BI can represent the government to receive, administer and settle foreign loans.

In the context of financial regionalism, policy coordination between national authorities has become more crucial, as regional cooperation may expose the Indonesian economy to external shocks. A higher degree of integration in the financial sector will greatly influence policy coordination (Kurniati and Budiman 2011). In relation to regional arrangements, the biggest challenge faced by the IMOF and BI was when they developed national agendas or position that required a common stance and the immolation of partial interests. To deal with this challenge, the IMOF and BI conducted coordination and consultation meetings, mostly at the technical/staff level. In APT financial cooperation, BI coordinated with the IMOF if the regional initiatives included monetary aspects, such as foreign reserves or capital accounts. However, the Indonesian focal point for processes within APT financial cooperation remained IMOF. A high-ranking official of BI realised that in international financial cooperation, the finance minister should represent Indonesia, as there was a political aspect embedded in the minister's position (Interview, April 2012). As the presidency is a political position, the finance minister (who is appointed by the president) gains political support as well. Such political support is not reflected in the position of the BI governor, as the governor is not elected by the Indonesian people, being an independent position.

Further, while policy coordination within APT financial cooperation was predominantly conducted by the IMOF and BI, financial policy coordination also included the other state actor, the Indonesian Ministry of Foreign Affairs (IMOFA). The participation of the IMOFA in APT financial cooperation has emerged, as the ministry has a mandate to determine Indonesian policy on international cooperation. A senior official of BI argued that IMOFA should define Indonesia's targets for regional cooperation, as the IMOFA was the policy maker for Indonesia's international relations (Interview, April 2012). However, this official felt that the IMOFA could not perform the expectation appropriately. Therefore, in fact, inter-ministerial coordination on regional financial cooperation that included IMOFA was quite limited.

Historically, the involvement of the IMOFA in international economic affairs, including financial cooperation, was significant before 2001. At that time, the IMOFA had a directorate general on economic affairs, the Directorate General for Foreign Economic Relations (*Hubungan Ekonomi Luar Negeri*/HELN), which dealt with economic diplomacy. However, HELN was abolished in 2001, when Hassan Wirajuda became the Indonesian Minister of Foreign Affairs (Wuragil 2001). The minister transformed the organisation of the IMOFA from a sector-based structure (i.e., economic, social and politics) into a region-based structure that includes the Asia-Pacific and Africa, Europe and the USA (Nabbs-Keller 2013). Since 2001, the involvement of the IMOFA in foreign economic affairs had declined, and politics has become the ministry's main concern. The restructuring attracted critique, as it hindered the ability of the IMOFA to deal with Indonesia's foreign economic agenda (Kartasasmita 2005). Therefore, the role of IMOFA in maintaining the current high standard of financial diplomacy was very limited (interview with a high-ranking official of IMOFA, July 2012). This official also observed that policy coordination with the financial authorities—IMOF and BI—was inadequate, even when the IMOFA needed to take on a more critical role, such as in the mitigation process during the 2008–2009 global financial crisis.

Transparency and Economic Openness

Financial matters are generally considered confidential. Many countries are often reluctant to disclose their financial status to public scrutiny, as such disclosure may adversely impact on their national interests. However, financial regionalism operates in a rather different way. Instead of keeping financial issues confidential, financial regionalism requires several aspects of finance to be disclosed. In this respect, transparency becomes critical. Mattli (2001) argues that principles of openness and transparency create a basis for the political acceptability of standardisation, a project that is currently often adopted by supra-national cooperation.

At the national level, efforts to achieve transparency have led Indonesian financial authorities to reform their businesses to facilitate foreign investor expectations of transparency and to provide predictability for long-term investments, including investments in capital markets (OECD 2010, p. 28). Since the establishment of Law No. 25/2007 on Investment, economic information should be disclosed and distributed equally between domestic and foreign investors. This information-sharing arrangement encourages Indonesia to be more open and prompts the Indonesian government to participate in market liberalisation projects within regional cooperation arrangements. Transparency and consistency in regulatory policy design are prerequisites for building successful economic activities (Indrawati 2007b, p. 26). Under the new democratic era, Indonesia has successfully enhanced its attractiveness for investment destination.

Greater financial transparency is also expected to have a strong presence in regionalism initiatives, whereby more open information sharing and procedures are essential. In APT financial cooperation, the demand for greater transparency is inevitable. As cooperation is concerned with maintaining regional economic stability, the transparency of economic data, particularly for surveillance mechanism, is a pivotal requirement that can make the implementation of such APT initiatives proceed more smoothly. Only with candid and frank discussions can regional surveillance mechanisms induce good policy outcomes (Kawai and Houser 2007).

In the midst of critiques directed towards the willingness of some East Asian countries to provide cogent and convincing economic information, Indonesian financial authorities have responded positively to the demand for transparency. In the APT surveillance project, Indonesian financial authorities always disclosed their economic data for scrutiny, either in the Economic Review and Policy Dialogue (ERPD) report or in the ASEAN Plus Three Macroeconomic Research Office (AMRO) report. Valid and timely reporting of economic data is an integral part of the IMOF's commitment to developing a regional surveillance unit (interview with a middle-ranking official of IMOF, April 2012). The commitment to make the reporting of economic data more transparent was also demonstrated by

Indonesian financial authorities for other APT projects, such as the Asian Bond Online (ABO), that became a platform for the dissemination of bond market development information in APT member countries. By publishing the progress of the Indonesian bond market on the ABO website, Indonesia establishes its commitment to promoting greater transparency within the county's financial sector. In addition, the need for greater transparency has also pushed Indonesian financial authorities to openly publicise the outcome of APT financial processes on particular initiatives. Thus, the Indonesian public may understand the nature of ongoing regional negotiations and provide feedback on all issues. Put simply, democracy has brought financial regional cooperation into a wider arena of public scrutiny.

Wider Participation

The trend towards democratisation has allowed greater involvement of the Indonesian private sector to play a more significant role in Indonesia's economic development. The contribution of private companies to Indonesian gross domestic product (GDP), for example, began to grow during the SBY democratic administration. The Indonesian market capitalisation of listed companies demonstrated positive trends across SBY's first period of administration. Figure 4.5 presents the market capitalisation of private companies, which represented approximately 28.5 per cent of the GDP in 2004 and increased to 50.9 per cent in 2010. This figure indicates that

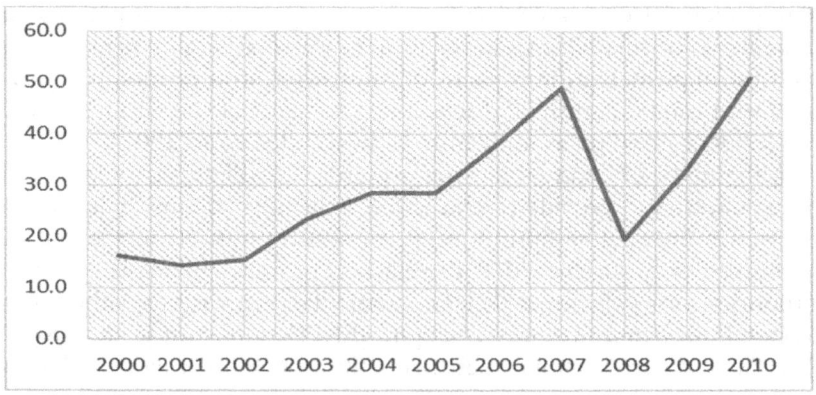

Fig. 4.5   Market capitalisation of listed companies. Source: Generated from *World Development Indicators 2013* (WB 2013)

the SBY democratic administration successfully nurtured an economic environment conducive to conducting businesses, such that the private sector could participate and contribute, to a greater extent in Indonesia's economic development.

The democratisation of Indonesian government policies and increasing regional integration have also stimulated the wider interests of domestic actors (Chandra and Hanim 2004). The roles of the private sector, including market players, academic communities or think-tank organisations in economic development—including those involved in regional financial cooperation—have become increasingly important. Particularly in the context of free market operations, the interests of the private sector in relation to influencing policy-making processes have emerged.

General public in Indonesia has been granted legal right to participate in the regulation-making process since the issuance of Law No. 10/2004 on Formulating Laws and Regulations, including in the financial sector. In this regard, the involvement of the Indonesian private sector in the financial policy-making process has become crucial as it is in the best position to know the implications of such government regulations or policies. Under Law No. 10/2004, the private sector also has the opportunity to advocate or promote policy initiatives that affect their businesses to the government. Simply, democracy has provided social and legal foundation for groups related to financial sector to be more active in shaping Indonesian financial architecture.

At regional policy context, democratisation has provided an opportunity for Indonesian non-state actors to participate in the development of financial cooperation. In this respect, there was an intention of Indonesian financial authorities to set specific mechanisms to accommodate and facilitate the roles and interests of non-state actors in financial regionalism. As a further indication of their greater participation, a few Indonesian market players have engaged directly with APT financial projects. The involvement of Indonesia's *self-regulated organisations* (SROs), such as the Indonesian Central Securities Depository (KSEI) and the Indonesian Stock Exchange (IDX), was an example of the way Indonesian democratic authorities provide opportunities for market players to participate more actively in the process of financial regionalism.

In particular, the IMOF has started to invite market players and research centres to provide recommendations on several regional projects. However, there were only a few non-state actors capable of engaging with the authorities. Along with several economists from Indonesia's prominent universities, such as the University of Indonesia (UI) and Gadjah Mada University (UGM), academic experts from the CSIS, economists from the local rating provider (*Pemeringkat Efek Indonesia/ PEFINDO*) and the Indonesian Bond Price Agency (IBPA) were invited to offer their perspectives and opinions on the ongoing processes inherent in APT financial cooperation. In 2012, UI and the Bogor Institute of Agriculture conducted a joint study on commodity price volatility in East Asia. This collaboration followed the previous participation of the UI in 2011, on a study focused on the possibilities for establishing a regional monetary unit, and UGM's 2009 research on trade, foreign direct investment trends and monetary flows in East Asia (ASEAN 2013).

The following chapter examines the influence of power relations and bilateral ties on the national responses to East Asian financial regionalism. It particularly focuses on the effects of cooperation and competition between Japan and China, and also Indonesian bilateral ties with both East Asian major powers, and on Indonesian responses to APT financial cooperation.

NOTES

1. The monetary council consists of the finance and economic ministers and the Central Bank governor. Meanwhile, the directors consists of the Central Bank governor and at least two other directors. The governor might propose to the government to have a maximum of four directors. Last, the advisory council consists of nine economists appointed by the government. Under this system, Soekarno had exclusive power over the monetary and financial sectors.
2. In 1968, Soeharto released Law No. 13/1968 on the Central Bank that maintained the function of the monetary council to provide assistance to the government, to stipulate financial-monetary policy.
3. *Rupiah* is Indonesian currency. Ideally, the value of the currency should be stable against the value of goods and services and also against the value of other currencies.

REFERENCES

Adiningsih, S., & Devi, L. Y. (2010). Dinamika koordinasi kebijakan fiskal-moneter in Indonesia [The dynamics of fiscal-monetary policy coordination in Indonesia]. In S. Adiningsih (Ed.), *Koordinasi dan interaksi kebijakan fiskal-moneter: tantangan ke depan (Fiscal-monetary policy coordination and interaction: Future challenge)* (pp. 13–42). Jogjakarta: Kanisius.

Anwar, D. F. (2003). Megawati's search for an effective foreign policy. In H. Soesastro, A. L. Smith, & H. M. Ling (Eds.), *Governance in Indonesia: Challenges facing the Megawati presidency* (pp. 70–90). Singapore: Institute of Southeast Asian Studies.

ASEAN. (2013). 2011/2012 ASEAN+3 Research Group final report and summary. Retrieved August 14, 2013, from http://www.asean.org/communities/asean-economic-community/item/20112012-asean3-research-group-final-report-and-summary

Bank Indonesia. (2012). *Menjaga keseimbangan, mendukung pembangunan ekonomi yang berkelanjutan (Keeping the balance, supporting the sustainable economic development)*. Jakarta: Bank Indonesia.

Bank Indonesia. (2014). Bank Indonesia's function. Retrieved October 24, 2014, from http://www.bi.go.id/en/tentang-bi/fungsi-bi/tujuan/Contents/Default.aspx

Bapepam. (2008). *Studi tentang liberalisasi jasa keuangan non-bank di Indonesia (A study on non-banking services liberalisation in Indonesia)*. Jakarta: Bapepam.

Bremner, B., & Shameen, A. (2005). Yudhoyono's "Triple-Track Strategy". *Bloomberg Businessweek Magazine*. Retrieved April 4, 2013, from http://www.businessweek.com/stories/2005-07-03/online-extra-yudhoyonos-triple-track-strategy

Brodjonegoro, B. (2003). Fiscal decentralisation in Indonesia. In H. Soesastro, A. L. Smith, & H. M. Ling (Eds.), *Governance in Indonesia: Challenges facing the Megawati presidency*. Singapore: Institute of Southeast Asian Studies.

Chandra, A. C. (2008). *Indonesia and ASEAN free trade agreement: Nationalist and regional integration strategy*. Lexington: Lexington Books/Rowman & Littlefield Pub.

Chandra, A. C., & Hanim, L. (2004). Indonesia's non-state actors in ASEAN: A new regionalism agenda for Southeast Asia? *Contemporary Southeast Asia, 26*(1), 155–174.

Collins, K. (2009). Economic and security regionalism among patrimonial authoritarian regimes: The case of central Asia. *Europe-Asia Studies, 61*(2), 249–281.

Connelly, A. L. (2014). Indonesian foreign policy under President Jokowi. *Lowy Institute Analyses*. Lowy Institute for International Policy, March 5, 2015. Retrieved from http://www.lowyinstitute.org/files/indonesian-foreign-policy-under-president-jokowi_0.pdf

Crouch, H. A. (2010). *Political reform in Indonesia after Soeharto*. Singapore: Institute of Southeast Asian Studies.

CSIS. (2002). Indonesia's new constitution: A peaceful reform. *The Indonesian Quarterly, XXX*(3), 252–262.

Dick, H., Houben, V. J. H., Lindblad, J. T., & Wee, T. K. (2002). *The emergence of a national economy, ASAA Southeast Asia Publications Series*. Australia: Allen & Unwin.

Djiwandono, J. S. (2004). Liquidity support to banks during Indonesia's financial crisis. *Bulletin of Indonesian Economic Studies, 40*(1), 59–75.

Eklöf, S. (2004). *Power and political culture in Suharto's Indonesia: The Indonesian Democratic Party (PDI) and decline of the New Order (1986–98)*. Copenhagen: NIAS.

Emmerson, D. K. (2012). Is Indonesia rising? It depends. In A. Reid (Ed.), *Indonesia rising: The repositioning of Asia's third giant* (pp. 49–76). Singapore: Institute of South Asian Studies.

Fiordelisi, F., & Molyneux, P. (2004). Efficiency in the factoring industry. *Applied Economics, 36*(9), 947–959.

He, K. (2008). Indonesia's foreign policy after Soeharto: International pressure, democratization, and policy change. *International Relations of the Asia-Pacific, 8*(1), 47–72.

Henning, C. R. (2002). *East Asian financial cooperation* (Vol. 68). Washington, DC: Peterson Institute.

Indrawati, S. M. (2007a). *Developing broader regional financial integration*. Paper presented to East Asia Summit's regional financial cooperation and integration workshop, Jakarta.

Indrawati, S. M. (2007b). *Opportunities and challenges facing new systemic players*. Paper presented to Institute of International Finance, Washington, DC, October 2007b.

Indrawati, S. M. (2008). *Perspectives on Asian economic integration and cooperation*. Emerging Asian regionalism book launch, 41st Asia Development Bank Annual Meeting of the Board of Governors, Madrid.

International Monetary Fund. (1998). *Indonesia—Memorandum of economic and financial policies*. Retrieved April 23, 2013, from http://www.imf.org/external/np/loi/011598.htm

Johansson, A. C. (2012). China's growing influence in Southeast Asia—Monetary policy and equity markets. *World Economy, 35*(7), 816–837.

Kartasasmita, A. G. (2005). Diplomasi dan restrukturisasi Deplu (Diplomacy and restructurisation on the Ministry of Foreign Affairs). *Suara Karya Online*. Retrieved April 24, 2013, from http://www.suarakarya-online.com/news.html?id=118419

Kawai, M., & Houser, C. (2007). *Evolving ASEAN+3 ERPD: Toward peer reviews or due diligence?* Tokyo: Asian Development Bank Institute.

Kurniati, Y., & Budiman, A. S. (2011). Embracing ASEAN economic integration 2015: A quest for an ASEAN business cycle from Indonesia's point of view. In A. Ananta, M. Soekarni, & S. Arifin (Eds.), *The Indonesian economy: Entering new era* (pp. 31–344). Singapore: Institute of Southeast Asian Studies.

Lahat, L. (2011). How can leaders' perceptions guide policy analysis in an era of governance? *Policy Sciences, 44*(2), 135–155.

Lubis, T. M. (2003). Constitutional reforms. In H. Soesastro, A. L. Smith, & H. M. Ling (Eds.), *Governance in Indonesia: Challenges facing the Megawati presidency* (pp. 106–113). Singapore: Institute of Southeast Asian Studies.

Mariyono, J., & Saputro, E. N. (2009). Political determinants of regional economic growth in Indonesia. *The Asia Pacific Journal of Public Administration, 31*(1), 39–56.

Mattli, W. (2001). The politics and economics of international institutional standards setting: An introduction. *Journal of European Public Policy, 8*(3), 328–344.

McLeod, R. H. (1999). Crisis-driven changes to the banking laws and regulations. *Bulletin of Indonesian Economic Studies, 35*(2), 147–154.

Nabbs-Keller, G. (2013). Reforming Indonesia's foreign ministry: Ideas, organization and leadership. *Contemporary Southeast Asia: A Journal of International & Strategic Affairs, 35*(1), 56–82.

OECD. (2010). *OECD investment policy reviews Indonesia 2010*. Organisation for Economic Co-operation and Development. OECD: Paris.

Parinduri, R. A., Thangavelu, S., & Rajan, R. S. (2009). *Exchange rate, monetary and financial issues and policies in Asia*. Singapore: World Scientific.

Rajan, R., & Sen, R. (2002). *Liberalisation of financial services in Southeast Asia under the ASEAN Framework Agreement on Services (AFAS)*. Centre for International Economic Studies (CIES) Discussion Paper, Vol. 226.

Saputro, E. (2014). Transforming popularity into confidence. *The Jakarta Post*, October 27. Retrieved March 3, 2015, from http://www.thejakartapost.com/news/2014/10/27/transforming-popularity-confidence.html

Smith, A. L. (1999). Indonesia's role in ASEAN: The end of leadership? *Contemporary Southeast Asia, 21*(2), 238–260.

Soekarnoputri, M. (2001). *Pidato Presiden Republik Indonesia pada Sidang Tahunan MPR 2001 (Presidential speech at the annual meeting of People Assembly 2001)*. Retrieved November 25, 2014, from http://kepustakaan-presiden.pnri.go.id/uploaded_files/pdf/speech/normal/megawati16.pdf

Soesastro, H. (2000). The Indonesian economy under Abdurrahman Wahid. *Southeast Asian Affairs*, 134–144.

Theo, R. (2011). *SBY: ASEAN motor pertumbuhan ekonomi dunia (SBY: ASEAN the engine of growth for the world)*. Kontan. Retrieved May 27, 2011, from http://nasional.kontan.co.id/v2/read/Nasional/64339/SBY-ASEAN-motor-pertumbuhan-ekonomi-dunia

World Development Indicators. (2013). Washington, DC: World Bank.

Wuragil, Z. (2001). *Tiga Dirjen di Departemen Luar Negeri dihapus (Three director-generals of the Ministry of Foreign Affairs abolished)*. Tempo Interaktif. Retrieved April 23, 2013, from http://www.tempointeractive.com/hg/nasional/2001/10/28/brk,20011028-07,id.html

Yudhoyono, SB 2004, *Pidato Presiden RI: Mengenali masalah, menetapkan agenda dan arah (Speech of Indonesian President: Identifying the problem, setting the agenda and direction)*, Bogor, Indonesia.

CHAPTER 5

Power Relations, Bilateral Ties and Indonesia's Responses

Power relations between Japan and China are significant for the development of East Asian financial regionalism. Indeed, the involvement of the United States (US) and Russia, along with Japan and China, has also been recognised as a part of the regional concert of power (Shirk in Väyrynen 2003, p. 30). However, particularly in relation to East Asian financial regionalism, US and Russian power is relatively invisible. Especially regarding ASEAN Plus Three (APT) financial cooperation, while all members have contributed to the development of the APT financial initiatives in various ways, Japan and China have played distinctively significant roles in the progress of regional financial cooperation. Yoshimatsu (2014) argues that Japan's commitments to East Asian financial regionalism are always prominent, from proposing the Asian Monetary Fund (AMF) to accelerating the progress of APT financial cooperation. Parallel with Japan, China has also been increasingly important to the development of East Asian regional financial architecture. The development of APT financial cooperation might have disappeared at a very early stage if China had not given its support.

In addition to power relations between major countries in East Asia, the development of regionalism in the region has been more or less influenced by bilateral relations. Alvstam (2001, p. 186) argues that, in the absence of a solid regional institution, the regionalisation of East Asia is represented by accumulated bilateral relations. This is particularly due to the type of

© The Author(s) 2017
E. Saputro, *Indonesia and ASEAN Plus Three Financial Cooperation*,
DOI 10.1007/978-981-10-3029-1_5

Asian regionalism that is like a network, rather than a formal institutional type of regionalism (Shiraishi and Katzenstein 1997). As regionalism processes (between member countries of APT Cooperation) are conducted mainly through active collaboration among national actors of the member countries, bilateral ties among APT member countries remain essential in developing national responses to regional arrangements. In this respect, bilateral political-economic interdependence and perceptions can determine the preferred stance of national agencies.

Indonesian financial authorities have maintained bilateral ties with both Japanese and Chinese regulatory agencies, while also still collaborating on a regional basis. These mixed connections are understood to have developed the proximity, and shaped the dynamics, of the political economy interactions and perceptions of Indonesian actors towards their Japanese and Chinese colleagues. In this regard, this chapter seeks to examine two issues. First, it analyses the effects of Sino-Japanese power relations on the regional governance of APT financial cooperation, and also on Indonesia's responses to the cooperation. Second, it examines the influence of Indonesian bilateral ties with Japan and China on Indonesia's responses to APT financial cooperation.

This chapter is divided into three sections. The first section provides an overview of Sino-Japanese power relations in APT financial cooperation. This part offers a broader narrative of Sino-Japanese power relations and, in particular, gives attention to the cooperation and competition between Japan and China in several APT financial initiatives. This section argues that the dynamics of Sino-Japanese power relations affect the development of APT financial cooperation governance. The decision-making process and the operations of APT financial initiatives are influenced by the interests of both powerhouses. The second section discusses Indonesia's bilateral relations with Japan and China. In this regard, special attention is given to issues related to cooperation within the financial sector. This section argues that Indonesia has more robust cooperation in financial areas with Japan, compared to China. The third section examines the influence of Indonesia's bilateral relations with Japan and China on the responses of the Indonesian financial authorities to APT financial initiatives. This section argues that Indonesia's political-economic interactions with, and perceptions to, the two major countries have shaped the dynamics of the Indonesian financial authorities' stance on APT financial cooperation.

JAPAN, CHINA AND THE APT: COOPERATION, COMPETITION AND COMPROMISE

The development of East Asian financial regionalism involves the dynamics of political and economic relations between Japan and China, with the rest of the East Asian countries. In the economic sphere, Japan and China's commitments to provide financial packages to the region during the Asian financial crisis sent a strong message that the Asian major powers were willing to collaborate in building up a new regional architecture on financial safety net. This commitment also implied that both Japan and China recognised that economic dynamics in the region would affect their economic interests significantly, as the region is an important market and part of their economic production chain.

Moreover, the cooperation between Japan and China was also demonstrated by the establishment of APT Cooperation. Initially, Japan was not enthusiastic about the concept of East Asian regionalism, as it was more concerned with an Asia-Pacific model of integration (Inoguchi 2011, p. 236). Considering its close relations with the US, Japan was originally less enthusiastic about the concept of APT Cooperation as proposed by ASEAN. In contrast, China responded positively to the proposed concept. China's positive response triggered Japan's concern about China's intention to tighten its relations with ASEAN, and potentially take on a leadership role for the whole of the East Asian region (Amako 2007, p. 14). Eventually, both Japan and China presented their support for the establishment of APT Cooperation.

In the context of financial cooperation, Japan and China have emerged as prominent actors in shaping the regional governance of financial initiatives (Chung 2013). Japan, in particular, has provided financial support and technical assistance and has developed a conceptual framework for APT financial initiatives. Japan has played important roles in APT financial initiatives, such as the Chiang Mai Initiative Multilateralisation (CMIM), the Asian Bond Market Initiatives (ABMI) and the Research Group. Throughout the implementation of these initiatives, Japan has played multiple roles in developing various schemes and programmes to promote financial cooperation (Yoshimatsu 2008, p. 65). With its high-performing human resources, advanced institutional experience and substantial financial support, Japan has mobilised experts, research institutions and the private sector to support the Japanese government's agendas in APT financial cooperation (Terada 2007). The Japanese Ministry of Finance (JMOF) was the initiator of the APT Research Group, a group of experts that conducts particular studies on financial issues, as ordered by APT finance ministers, aimed at supporting financial cooperation through academic inputs from researchers and research institutes in APT member countries (Yoshimatsu 2014). Data gathered from the ASEAN Secretariat (ASEC) revealed that Japanese research institutions were dominant in conducting research projects managed by the APT Research Group. From 2004 to 2012, 23 studies were conducted under the APT Research Group (ASEAN 2014). Of these, six Japan institutions were involved in 16 projects. In comparison, two Chinese institutions participated in two studies. This research effort, as demonstrated by Japan, implies that Japan was the key actor in supporting APT financial cooperation through research studies. In this respect, although ASEAN claims to be in the driving seat, there is no doubt that Japan plays a dominant role in creating most APT financial cooperation initiatives (Saputro 2012). China has recently started to take on critical functions within APT financial cooperation. Although China was not as active as Japan in formulating APT financial initiatives, it has taken a decisive stance in setting up regional governance of APT financial cooperation. APT financial cooperation has become a medium through which Japan and China can contribute to the promotion of economic and financial interdependence among East Asian countries (Chung 2013). For Japan and China, financial regionalism in East Asia allows them to expand market coverage while simultaneously channelling excessive domestic capital.

Apart from the cooperation context, power relations between Japan and China also often emerged as competition. At least three major events in the development of APT financial initiatives demonstrated the presence of competition. The first was related to the operational arrangement of CMIM. In the process of allocating member countries' contributions, Japan and China differed in their initial views. The process of calculating the CMIM total size reportedly was delayed due to protracted negotiations between China and Japan in relation to their respective contributions. Both countries insisted on making larger contributions, out of consideration of their economies' sizes and international reserves. If the foreign reserve became the weighting factor, then China would be the biggest contributor. However, if the contribution was based on the size of a country's gross domestic product (GDP), then this formula would make Japan the largest contributor (Sussangkarn 2010, p. 9). After a series of negotiations, Japan and China eventually agreed to make equal con-tributions, even though the Chinese contribution would be shared with Hong Kong, as it had its own monetary authority, which was separated from China's monetary authority, and contributed separately from China. However, for the decision-making process, Hong Kong had to cast its vot-ing power together with China, as it did not have a finance minister who was entitled to vote. This arrangement is regarded as a win-win solution in which, on paper, China's contribution is equivalent to Japan's. However, in reality, Japan has become the biggest contributor to CMIM. Regarding China, its contribution to CMIM provides an opportunity to contribute as much as Japan in international forums. As such, it allows China to share equal voting powers with Japan (Chung 2013). These equal contribu-tions imply that neither power is willing to be visibly defeated in regional arrangements. Practically, this arrangement created both Japan and China as key players in the decision-making process of CMIM, as they hold equal voting power.

The second arena of competition between Japan and China still relates to contributions made to APT financial initiatives. However, in this event, competition related to the Credit Guarantee and Investment Facility (CGIF). In CGIF, Japan (represented by the Japan Bank for International Cooperation/JBIC) and China contributed an equal amount of US$200 million. The competition in CGIF contributions between both these Asian major powers was triggered by the voting power given to each contributor of CGIF. This was weighted based on their contribution. The amount of these countries' respective contributions significantly affected the alloca-tion of voting rights for each contributor in decision-making processes, particularly those made in the Meeting of Contributors (MOC). Again, equal contributions provided an incentive to both Japan and China to maintain relatively equal power.

The issue of providing equal contributions within APT financial coop-eration extends to the previously related competitive context, in which the question 'who is paying more?' between Japan and China becomes rel-evant. One year before contributing to the CMIM, Japan and China were competing to support South Korea's liquidity problem, which was a result of the massive devaluation of the Korean *won*. Terada (2009) reports that during the Trilateral Summit of Plus Three countries, both Japan and China competed in their bids to give more funding to South Korea. Eventually, after a series of tough negotiations, they agreed to inject South Korea with US$30 billion each.

The competitive aspect of the contributions to APT financial projects provides examples of how Japan and China each maintain their power in the region. China's persistence in making identical contributions to Japan's can also be perceived in terms of China's growing confidence against the backdrop of Japanese leadership in the region. Through its larger contributions to CMIM and CGIF, China exhibits greater political leadership prospects for, and economic influence on, the region.

The third example of Sino-Japanese competition within the APT financial project is related to the appointment of the ASEAN Plus Three Macroeconomic Research Office (AMRO) leadership. The pivotal role of AMRO in dealing with regional macroeconomic monitoring makes AMRO leadership important to both Japan and China. In this respect, Japanese and Chinese candidates competed and received relatively equal support from APT member countries. The Japanese candidate reportedly gained slightly more votes than the Chinese candidate. Causing some tension, the Chinese delegates strongly objected to the Japanese candidate, and proposed to postpone the leadership selection process until the 2011 APT Finance Ministers' meeting (Rathus 2010). Similar tensions arose incidentally during the territorial dispute between China and Japan over Senkaku/Diaoyutai Island. Eventually, the APT meeting decided to split the tenure of the AMRO director into two terms (AMRO 2011). The first term of one year was presided over by a Chinese candidate, while in the second term, a Japanese candidate took over the administrative period of two years. This arrangement was accepted by both parties, although it broke with the proposed continuous three years tenure, as previously set up and agreed to by all APT member countries.

By putting representatives forward as AMRO leaders, both Japan and China had the opportunity to set a specific agenda for governance of the first regional surveillance unit in the East Asian region. Although the Chinese national had only one year to lead the early development of AMRO, he had power to create a platform for regional governance of macroeconomic surveillance. Meanwhile, the two-year term of administration allowed the Japanese leader to formulate the standards and mechanisms of regional surveillance activities, as well as implement policy actions. In their seventeenth meeting, the APT finance ministers and central bank governors agreed to extend the Japanese national's term of office by two years (APT 2014); this further allowed Japan to mobilise its agenda within the regional surveillance body.

Sino-Japanese competition within APT financial cooperation came to an end with a compromised solution. Sharing equal contributions to CMIM and CGIF, as well as splitting tenure for the AMRO leadership, was accepted by both countries as a satisfactory solution. The compromise option reflects two points. First, Japan and China realised that they needed each other for financial cooperation to be successful. Sino-Japanese bilateral cooperation in financial areas is always robust, as both countries need to behave pragmatically for the sake of broader financial interests (Interview with a high-ranking Japanese diplomat for Indonesia, April 2012). In this regard, Japan and China share similar interests in making the APT region stable in financial sector development, as well as in foreign currency matters (Interview with a leading Japanese thinker, June 2012). Second, shared interests in regional financial cooperation should not be expected to undermine either of the giant countries' leadership positions. Although China and Japan will compete for regional dominance, at the same time, they will maintain a certain level of mutual economic and political contact (Alvstam 2001, p. 189). Sino-Japanese competition has delayed the progress of such initiatives, but it has not impeded the progress of any financial initiatives.

While issues around competition were more likely to be associated with prestige or influence, rather than any intention to exert financial control, Sino-Japanese power relations, to some degree, have affected East Asian financial regionalism, especially at the regional level. As discussed in this section, bilateral political-economic relations between Japan and China have affected their responses to the progress of APT financial cooperation. On this point, the competitive aspects of contribution processes (as occurred with CMIM and CGIF), as well as those inherent in the AMRO leadership battle, have displayed how power relations have affected the progress of such regional initiatives.

Further, bilateral relations coexist with regional cooperation. Putnam (1988) argues that while nurturing regional relations, a country also develops and maintains relations with a particular country. Thus, bilateral ties potentially influence the responses of a particular state towards regional cooperation. In the following section, bilateral relations between Indonesia and the two Asian major powers are discussed; they are understood to contribute to the shaping of Indonesia's stance towards APT financial cooperation.

INDONESIA'S APPROACH: MAINTAINING JAPAN AND WELCOMING CHINA

In the context of bilateral relations with Japan and China, Indonesia has a unique position. Indonesia has expanded and deepened its strategic bilateral relationships with major powers, including Japan and China (Sukma 2012, p. 91). Indonesia has close relationships with both Japan and China, formed either in the past or in recent times. The bilateral relations include economic and political areas that mostly occurred in the wake of World War II. In the economic context, Indonesia has maintained tight economic relations with Japan, and has also developed stronger economic ties with China, as the emerging Asian economic power. In the political context, there was a time when Indonesia was deemed a nation who enjoyed a closer relationship with China, particularly during Soekarno administration. However, there was also a time when Indonesia was recognised as a close friend of Japanese politics, as Soeharto's political vehicle, *Golongan Karya* (Golkar), had maintained a tight political partnership with the long-standing political party, the Japanese Liberal Democratic Party (LDP).

He and Inoguchi (2011, p. 170) argue that there are two dimensions of power relations: the political economy and perceptions. According to these authors, the political economy is a fundamental element within the regionalism process, while power can affect perceptions about regional leadership. Moreover, perceptions often affect the state authorities' foreign policy options. Yoshimatsu (2014, p. 19) argues that state policy makers' perceptions and preferences have a significant influence on the means through which the pressures and opportunities of international environments are translated into a state's external policies. Against this backdrop, this section examines Indonesia's bilateral ties with Japan and China, mainly focusing on political-economic relations and perceptions.

Reciprocity with Japan

Post-World War II, Japan has tried to restore its relations with Indonesia as a part of its reciprocation policy. The Indonesian-Japanese relationship was inaugurated in 1958, by signing the Treaty of Peace between the two countries (Ministry of Foreign Affairs of Japan 2011b). Their relations focus extensively on economic and social cooperation, rather than on politics (Anwar 1990). The trauma of political conflict during World War II has deterred Indonesia and Japan from highlighting any political issues. In the wake of its independence, Indonesia has neither had any political disputes, nor experienced any tensions with Japan, although Indonesia suffered heavily under Japanese occupation from 1942 to 1945. Compared to other Japanese ex-colonies, Indonesia has eased its position towards the Japanese. Japan's commitment to assist and provide supports to Indonesian development programmes underpinned Indonesia's political stance towards Japan. Controversial issues, such as border disputes, human rights abuses, property right disputes or any other disagreements that potentially triggered diplomatic tension, were sidelined from discussions between Japan and Indonesia.

In economic areas, the bilateral relations between Indonesia and Japan were sparked by the establishment of Japanese manufacturing companies in Indonesia. In its early development, Indonesia faced economic difficulties, such as high inflation and high unemployment, despite the country's rich natural resources. To solve these problems, Indonesia invited advanced countries, including Japan, to establish their businesses in Indonesia. At the same time, the private sector in Japan faced domestic problems, such as high labour costs and growing protests over environmental degradation issues. The increase in Japanese income per capita caused a decrease in the supply side of labour, which led to increases in the cost of labour. In the meantime, due to massive industrial development in Japan, environmental degradation emerged as a public concern in Japan—a concern that eventually put pressure on Japanese companies to consider environmental issues (Hall 2002, p. 22). In response to public pressure, the best option for Japanese companies was to relocate their production operations away from the protests. One option was to relocate their businesses to Indonesia.

Over time, Indonesia and Japan have maintained two major economic initiatives: the Official Development Assistance (ODA) and the Economic Partnership Agreement (EPA). The ODA aims to provide development assistance in the form of loans, grants and technical assistance, while the EPA is set up to enhance cross-border movements of goods, services, investments and natural persons between Indonesia and Japan (Ministry of Foreign Affairs of Japan 2008).

Japan began to provide ODA for Indonesia from 1960, in the form of US$14.28 million grants. The ODA has been increased over the years. In 2009, Indonesia received US$115.41 million in the forms of grants and technical assistance, as well as US$1,928.69 million as a loan (Ministry of Foreign Affairs of Japan 2011a). Shiraishi (1997, p. 180) argues that following the 1966 Ministerial Conference for the Economic Development of Southeast Asia, Japan provided Indonesia with US$30 million for economic recovery, representing one-fourth of Japan's foreign aid and one-third of its non-food aid, delivered under the auspices of the IGGI. As a result, Indonesia became the largest recipient of Japan's ODA for many years, until China took over that position in 1982 (Akrasanee and Prasert 2003, p. 67). In 2009, China and Indonesia were ranked first and second respectively, regarding Japan's bilateral ODA.

The area covered by Japan's ODA for Indonesia has shifted from time to time. In its early operations, the ODA business sector focused mainly on industry, communication/transportation, health and agriculture (Ministry of Foreign Affairs of Japan 2012). In 2004, the focus shifted onto three priority pillars: the achievement of sustainable growth by the private sector; the establishment of a democratic and fair society; and a supporting peace and stability. Among these priorities, the development of sound government financial policy gained special attention, along with macroeconomic and fiscal policies. This change indicates an alteration in Japan's perspective towards a development approach in Indonesia. In this respect, issues related to Indonesian politics and the economy have become more important to Japan, particularly in relation to maintaining regional stability.

Japan and Indonesia entered a new phase of economic relations in 2007, when Prime Minister Shinzo Abe and President Soesilo Bambang Yudhoyono (SBY) signed the Indonesia-Japan Economic Partnership Agreement (IJEPA). This agreement covered a wide range of economic activities, including energy, government procurement, competition policy and intellectual property. For Indonesia, the agreement offered greater opportunities to access and attract more investment from Japanese markets. As a result in 2011, Japanese Foreign Direct Investment (FDI) to Indonesia reached US$3,611 million—an increase of more than six times from the previous year (JETRO 2012). Likewise, for Japan, IJEPA provided a better business environment and facilitated greater transparency, as well as wider areas of cooperation. In practice, the agreement pushed the Indonesian government to improve several business-related areas, including customs services, tax administration and legal certainty—improvements that have facilitated Japanese business in Indonesia. However, despite apparent benefits for both countries, the establishment of IJEPA has also meant promoting Japan's economic dominance in Indonesia. For several Indonesian elites, this dominance is more of a threat than any revival in the Japanese military (Anwar 1990, p. 243).

Japan remains Indonesia's largest trading partner. In this respect, Indonesian-Japanese trade transactions are mostly conducted in the form of non-oil/gas products. Table 5.1 illustrates that from 2007 to 2010 Indonesian-Japanese bilateral trade showed a positive trend, with an 11.9 per cent increase annually. Even though in 2009, there was a decline in total trade, due to the global financial crisis that adversely affected both countries, overall Indonesia gained a surplus in its balance of trade with Japan. Until April 2011, Indonesian exports of non-oil/gas to Japan were approaching US$5,828.2 million (11.65 per cent of total export), followed by the USA with 10.47 per cent and China with 10.39 per cent (Statistics Indonesia 2011). These figures show that Japan is economically important for Indonesia compared to other major countries.

The robust relationship between Japan and Indonesia is also demonstrated in liquidity support arrangements. In terms of liquidity support, Japan has almost always supported Indonesia when the country faced difficulties. For example, Japan provided Indonesia with US$5 billion under an International Monetary Fund (IMF) package to deal with the Asian financial crisis. This Japanese financial assistance was initially offered as part of a bilateral arrangement. However, the US forced Japan to inject its support funds into the IMF's package to make Indonesia subject to the IMF's loan conditions (Sujatmiko 1999, p. 112). In recent years, Japan has also provided Indonesia with US$1.5 billion, as part of a precautionary measure in relation to the 2009 global financial crisis (Haswidi and Suharmoko

Table 5.1 Indonesia's balance trade with Japan (in US$ billion)

Description	2007	2008	2009	2010	Trend 2007–2010 (%)
Total trade	30.1	42.9	28.4	42.7	11.97
Oil and gas	10.6	14.2	6.6	9.3	3.47
Non-oil and gas	19.5	28.6	21.8	33.4	15.75
Export	23.6	27.7	18.6	25.8	6.58
Oil and gas	10.5	13.9	6.6	9.3	3,56
Non-oil and gas	13.1	13.8	11.9	16.5	8,89
Import	6.5	15.1	9.8	16.9	25.82
Oil and gas	0.1	0.2	0	0.1	−0.42
Non-oil and gas	6.4	14.8	9.8	16.9	26.06
Balance of trade	17.1	12.6	8.7	8.8	−6.95
Oil and gas	10.5	13.7	6.6	9.2	3.64
Non-oil and gas	6.6	−1.1	2.2	−0.4	0.00

Source: Generated from Ministry of Trade, Republic of Indonesia official website (www.kemendag.go.id) (2012)

2009). At that time, Japan's financial support was disbursed through a guarantee facility in the form of yen-denominated foreign bonds, namely the 'Samurai Bond'. The scheme boosted Indonesia's confidence to face the financial crisis and contributed to protecting the nation from a second round of economic turmoil. Up until 2012, Indonesia had issued Samurai Bonds amounting to US$350 million in 2008, and US$723.3 million in 2012 <www.businessnews.co.id, 2012>. By providing such substantial financial assistance, Japan remained the biggest creditor for Indonesia. Japan's financial assistance to Indonesia exceeded financial support from other countries or international financial organisations. As of April 2012, Japan was ranked as the top lender to Indonesia, with IDR274.68 trillion (approximately US$299 billion), or 44.4 per cent of Indonesia's total foreign debt (Daniel 2012).

Financial-monetary relations between Indonesia and Japan are not only conducted on a bilateral basis, but also under regional arrangements. Under the APT framework, Indonesia and Japan have established the Bilateral Swap Arrangement (BSA). This arrangement is aimed at supporting and stabilising the Indonesian economy through preserving foreign reserves. A 'one-way' BSA agreement was signed in February 2003 between Japan and Indonesia, with a total funding contribution of US$3 billion (Japanese Ministry of Finance 2011).[1] The BSA has been renewed and increased twice. In 2005, it was increased to a maximum of US$6 billion, and in 2009 the amount was doubled again to US$12 billion (Japanese Ministry of Finance 2009). In 2011, Japan agreed to extend the continuity of the BSA until 2013, even though Japan had a right to terminate the arrangement after the CMIM was established. This extension could be perceived as a means of tightening bilateral cooperation in the financial-monetary sector between Indonesia and Japan. In December 2013, Bank Indonesia (BI) and Bank of Japan (BOJ) agreed to increase the BSA to up to US$22.76 billion (Bank of Japan 2013). This agreement also included a new feature allowing Indonesia to use the swap facility for crisis prevention purposes—a feature at this point found only in the Indonesia-Japan BSA.

Under the APT financial cooperation framework, Japan also provided Indonesia with technical assistance. For instance, Indonesia was among the recipient countries under the Bond Financing for Infrastructure Project funded by the Japanese government (ADB 2008). This project aimed at promoting the development of infrastructure bonds denominated in a recipient country's local currency, facilitating bond issuance and supporting investment, as well as trading cross-border infrastructure bonds. In addition, Indonesia also received Japan-ASEAN financial technical assistance under the fund for the promotion of the Asian Medium-Term Note (MTN) programme, which was expected to reduce administration costs through simplifying bond issuance procedures (Nomura Research Institute 2009). Clearly, Indonesia has maintained tight economic and financial cooperation with Japan in several ways, not only on a pure bilateral basis, but also through a regional framework.

Further, the close political-economic relations between Indonesia and Japan have contributed to create positive perceptions of Japan's influence by Indonesia. The 2013 BBC Country-Rating Poll indicates that 82 per cent of Indonesian respondents are in favour of Japan's influence (BBC World Service 2013). However, Indonesian perceptions of Japan's positive influence do not seem to accord with perceptions of Japan's leadership status in the global economy. According to the 2011 Pew Research Centre's Global Attitudes Project, only 18 per cent of Indonesians perceive Japan as a current leading economic power (Pew Research Centre 2011).

Ideology, Pragmatism and Relations with China

Officially, Sino-Indonesian relations first commenced in 1950. The relations between Indonesia and China at that time were influenced largely by both political dynamics and the economic situation. In the early stages of national development, the Indonesian political regime had close affiliations with socialist and communist countries, such as the Soviet Union and China. Soekarno, as the first Indonesian president who was well known for his role in establishing close relationships with Moscow and Beijing, sought to fight against neo-colonialism, colonialism and imperialism (Vaughn 2007, p. 84). During the early period of Indonesian development, Soekarno's concepts of NASAKOM (*Nasionalisme*/Nationalism, *Agama*/Religion, and *Komunisme*/Communism) were associated with his design of a political consolidation that included three major political factions: nationalism, Islam and communism. However, this concept was challenged, predominantly, by Islamists who perceived communism as a threat to religious life (Mietzner 2009). Likewise, the involvement of a communist faction in Soekarno's power circle also worried neighbouring countries, such as Singapore and Malaysia.

Sino-Indonesian relations ceased in 1967, after the Indonesian Communist Party (PKI)'s Movement on 30 September 1965 (G30S/PKI coup), in which several Indonesian army generals were killed. The PKI, assumed to be closely connected to Soekarno and the Chinese Communist

Party (CCP), was allegedly involved in that coup. However, until now, the role of China in the coup has remained unclear. In fact, the coup had destabilised Indonesian politics and initiated political and security tensions. The coup also triggered a response from the US, intervening in Indonesia's political battles because of concerns about communism's spread throughout Southeast Asia. The USA viewed that communism could jeopardise potentially not only its own interests, but also those of its allies, such as Japan and Singapore. Finally, the US decided to stall the spread of communism in Indonesia by supporting Soeharto's efforts to overthrow Soekarno, after leading the fight against communism in Indonesia (Scott 1985). Soeharto then banned the PKI and proclaimed the suspension of Indonesian relations with China (Suryadinata 1996).

In further action, Indonesia followed the US's policy to isolate China from the global arena. For many years, Indonesia had no official contact with China and was suspicious of Chinese political actions. The trauma of the PKI's political movement produced political distrust in Indonesian society regarding China. This trauma also shaped negative perceptions among Indonesian elites towards China as an expansionist power (Novotny 2010, p. 179). Tragically, negative perceptions of China have been followed by negative perceptions of ethnic Chinese-Indonesians, who are perceived by ordinary Indonesians to be individualist, economically exclusive and 'stingy' (Laksmana 2011, p. 25).[2] These negative perceptions were regarded as somewhat exaggerated; they reached their peak in a 1998 riot that gained momentum from the collapse of the Soeharto regime in its attack on ethnic Chinese-Indonesians, who were believed to be Soeharto's cronies (Storey 2000).

Indonesian relations with China were re-developed in 1990, when Jakarta started to restore its diplomatic relations with Beijing. These relations were enhanced by the actions of Abdurrahman Wahid (Gus Dur), who became president of the newly formed Indonesian democracy. Gus Dur endorsed his foreign diplomatic project by choosing Beijing for his first foreign visit, symbolising his strong intention to rebuild relations with China (Smith 2000). Indonesian political ties with China have been continually strengthened by Megawati and SBY (Sukma 2009). To show the new approach towards ethnic Chinese-Indonesians, Megawati and SBY appointed economists of Chinese descent as ministers. The appointment of ethnic Chinese-Indonesians as ministers never occurred during the 32 years of Soeharto's regime. During Megawati's administration, Kwik Kian Gie was appointed as National Development Planning Minister, while

Mari Elka Pangestu became Minister of Trade under the SBY administration. These appointments were understood not only to improve relations between the Indonesian government and ethnic Chinese-Indonesians but also to build political trust in the government of China, which had been sympathetic with the 1998 riot in Indonesia.

In 2005, Hu Jintao and SBY agreed to widen Sino-Indonesian cooperation by establishing a strategic partnership agreement. The partnership covered a broad range of issues, including energy, security and defence (Jize 2005). It also inaugurated development of a new comprehensive process of economic cooperation and signalled a new era of political commitment between the two countries.

The series of attempts to create closer political and economic relations has resulted in increased positive perceptions of the Chinese by Indonesians. The Pew Research Centre project on Global Attitudes 2011 showed trends in positive perceptions of China by Indonesians have increased in favourability from 2002 to 2011. Although this trend dropped in 2008, Indonesian's favourability trend regarding China remained at more than 55 per cent and showed signs of growing again in 2011. Positive Indonesian views of China are parallel with the trend of Indonesian views about China's influence. The 2013 BBC rating poll presents that 55 per cent of Indonesian respondents have positive views of China's influence, while 27 per cent have negative views. These two sets of data regarding perceptions of China indicate that many Indonesians appear less suspicious of, or have less negative thoughts about, China.

While Sino-Indonesian political relations have experienced difficulties, Indonesia and China have maintained economic interactions, even during times of political dispute. During the period when diplomatic ties were terminated, Sino-Indonesian trade activities basically still continued (Suryadinata 1996). Trade between both countries remained active; these activities were facilitated by a third country, such as Singapore or Hong Kong. Sino-Indonesian direct trade transactions resumed again in 1985—five years before the reactivation of diplomatic relations—when the Indonesian government offered the business community opportunities to initiate trade activities (Chongbo 2011, p. 122). Close connections between President Soeharto and ethnic Chinese-Indonesian conglomerates influenced these activities.

In recent years, China has become an important major trading partner of Indonesia. In 2011, China became the second-largest trading partner for Indonesia, after Japan. According to Table 5.2, trends in Indonesia's

Table 5.2 Indonesia's balance of trade with China (in US$ billion)

Description	2007	2008	2009	2010	2011	Trend 2007–2011 (%)
Total trade	18.2	26.8	25.5	36.1	49.1	25.59
Oil and gas	3.6	4.1	3.0	2.3	2.1	−15.23
Non-oil and gas	14.6	22.7	22.4	33.7	47.0	31.43
Export	**9.6**	**11.6**	**11.5**	**15.7**	**22.9**	**22.45**
Oil and gas	3.0	3.8	2.5	1.6	1.3	−21.98
Non-oil and gas	6.6	7.8	8.9	14.1	21.6	34.23
Import	**8.5**	**15.2**	**14.0**	**20.4**	**26.2**	**28.80**
Oil and gas	0.6	0.3	0.5	0.7	0.7	14.56
Non-oil and gas	7.9	14.9	13.5	19.7	25.4	29.71
Balance of trade	**1.1**	**−3.6**	**−2.5**	**−4.7**	**−3.2**	**0.00**
Oil and gas	2.4	3.5	2.0	0.8	0.6	−34.40
Non-oil and gas	−1.2	−7.1	−4.5	−5.6	−3.8	0.00

Source: Generated from Ministry of Trade, Republic of Indonesia official website, <www.kemendag.go.id> (2012)

exports to China have demonstrated average increases of 22.45 per cent per year from 2007 to 2011. However, in the same period, the increase in Indonesia's imports from China was higher than exports (28 per cent on average/per annum), leading to a negative balance of trade on the Indonesian side. In this respect, Indonesia mainly exported natural products, such as palm oil, paper and timber, while it imported electrical machinery and electronic equipment from China.

China's participation in the Indonesian economy is mainly through trade and investment. This is an intriguing phenomenon as China was initially Indonesia's competitor as an investment destination of advanced countries (Surbakti 1999). The initial phase of sizable Chinese investment in Indonesia began in 2002. At that time, President Megawati—who had close relations with China due to her father's connections—visited Beijing to boost bilateral investment and trade. One important event during her visit was the signing of a Memorandum of Understanding (MoU) on the Indonesia-China Energy Forum (ICEF). The MoU was aimed at strengthening bilateral cooperation in the oil and gas industry, as well as providing a foundation for oil exploration cooperation (People Daily, 25 September 2002). This agreement not only heightened investments from China, but also marked a new phase in Sino-Indonesian cooperation regarding the energy sector. This initiative was also understood to be a reason behind the great increase in Chinese investment in Indonesia, in 2003. From that time, Chinese oil and mining companies started to operate in Indonesia.

Table 5.3   Investment realisation in Indonesia 2002–2008 (in US$ million)

Country	2002	2003	2004	2005	2006	2007	2008	Average per year
ASEAN	299	464	916	225	927	4.028	1.855	373.4
China	6	83	81	37	31	28	139	57.9
Japan	432	738	1.041	1.144	908	618	1.365	385.7
USA	60	148	78	88	65	144	151	104.9

Source: Generated from Indonesian Investment Board/BKPM official website (2012)

Chinese investment in Indonesia has been growing steadily, although in aggregate it remains less than other countries. The data illustrated in Table 5.3 demonstrates that Japan, the US and the ASEAN states (as a bloc) have larger investments in Indonesia when compared to China. However, the average amount of Chinese investment per annum is quite significant, amounting to US$57.9 million.

In regional economic cooperation, China and Indonesia are bound by the China-ASEAN Free Trade Agreement (CAFTA). Intriguingly, many Indonesians apparently did not pay much attention to CAFTA's negotiation process, even after the agreement's ratification was released by the Megawati administration. Based on a survey conducted by *Lingkaran Survei Indonesia* in 2011, only 26.7 per cent of respondents knew about CAFTA <www.okezone.com, 3 May 2011>. The majority of respondents argued that CAFTA would hinder Indonesia's economy, instead of generating benefits, due to the massive importation of Chinese products. More than 75 per cent of the respondents said they were concerned about the presence of a massive number of low-cost Chinese manufactured products in Indonesian markets, which could potentially outsell Indonesian products. The respondents were also concerned with potential increases in the unemployment rate as a result of workplace efficiency schemes adopted by Indonesian companies to compete with low Chinese production costs.

However, the Indonesian perception of CAFTA was not parallel with the way Indonesians perceive China's economy. According to the Pew Research Centre's Global Attitudes Project (2011), many Indonesians (62 per cent) perceived that progress in the Chinese economy would be constructive for Indonesia, while 25 per cent disagreed.

Compared to Japan, Indonesian bilateral relations with China in financial sector are relatively limited. Initially, Indonesia maintained a one-way BSA with China, amounting to US$1 billion under the CMI framework signed in December 2003. Two years later, this agreement was renewed and increased to US$2 billion (Jhaveri 2005). In 2006, the amount was further increased to US$4 billion. China discontinued the BSA with Indonesia after the establishment of CMIM in 2009, as the result of the multilateralisation of the financial swap arrangement. China ceased the BSA to reduce use of the US dollar, while at the same time promoting the *renminbi* (RMB) as the foremost international currency. Since then, both countries no longer had specific bilateral arrangements in relation to liquidity support.

Instead, Indonesian and Chinese central banks had established Bilateral Currency Swap Arrangements (BCSA) to promote bilateral trade between, and investment in, the two countries (BI 2009). The total size of the BCSA was RMB100 billion, equivalent to US$16.2 million. To further support the trade facilitation agenda, China has also provided Indonesia with US$2.8 billion in preferential export buyer's credits, and a US$6.5 billion commercial loan for power plant projects (Jiabo 2011). This assistance was expected to ease the costs for trading transactions and construction respectively. Moreover, the use of the *renminbi* instead of the US dollar implies that China strongly intended to boost its *renminbi* internationalisation programme in various ways. Considering that many Chinese products dominate world supply, the Chinese government has an opportunity to force its trading partners into using the *renminbi* strategically, instead of the US dollar, in international transactions. Put simply, once a country depends heavily on Chinese products, it will soon also become heavily dependent on the type of currency requested by China to progress the transaction.

An Independent Stance?

In general, Indonesian state agencies realised that power relations between Japan and China were obvious in the development of APT financial cooperation. While state agencies realised the roles of both countries in supporting many projects that were part of the cooperation, the authorities also admitted that competition between the two Asian powerhouses often emerged in APT financial initiative processes. However, Sino-Japanese competition has fewer consequences for Indonesia's responses to APT financial cooperation. Indonesian financial authorities viewed any competition as being more concerned with showing regional leadership, rather than with the core business of APT financial cooperation. This can be seen in the participating FPO official's interview:

> In my opinion, the rivalry (between China and Japan) is only limited to demonstrate greater influence in the region. It does not have any direct effects to Indonesia. As you can see, we have BSAs with either China or Japan. (Interview with a middle-ranking official, April 2012)

Although Indonesian financial authorities were aware of competition in regional financial cooperation, they made an effort to avoid any adverse impacts of such rivalry. Indonesian authorities attempted to collaborate with either China or Japan to pursue Indonesia's national interests. For instance, BI personnel tried to communicate and cooperate with any dialogue partners, especially those who can offer maximum benefits for the country (Interview with a high-level official of BI, April 2012). A similar position was also expressed by the senior official of the FPO, who argued that the IMOF had to be neutral in maintaining economic relations with any countries, including Japan and China. This official stated that:

> Our point is that we should not be in the position to take sides since, after all, they are all members of APT Cooperation. We have to be neutral, we must be objective, and we take any benefits from their superiorities. (Interview, July 2012)

Indonesian financial authorities calculated the positive and negative effects of the relations with both major powers in APT financial cooperation. Yoshimatsu (2008) argues that a state has the ability to identify policy preferences and political goals in collaborative economic arrangements. Therefore, the Indonesian financial authorities attempted to establish close collaboration with both Japan and China. For Jayasuriya (2003), close collaboration with national and other levels of governance is necessary to build policy coordination mechanisms. At this stage, the financial authorities viewed that close relations with both major powers would not jeopardise Indonesia's interests. In other words, placing Indonesia in a neutral position is perceived as the most strategic position to maximise Indonesia's agenda.

However, the responses of the participating respondents from BI and IMOF imply two basic principles that lead to slippage between reality and rhetoric. The first is that of being neutral towards any rivalry, and the second is being active in making efforts to pursue national interests. These two principles have the potential to be conflicting. They may lead to serious questions about whether Indonesia will treat the two economic giants (Japan and China) equally, while simultaneously giving priority to creating opportunities from any countries that offer more benefits for Indonesia. Putting national interests at the forefront is a far from neutral stance, and is close to 'pragmatism'. For example, it is not plausible for Indonesia to reject any financial assistance from a particular country when, at the same time, no other country is offering support, just to remain neutral. Hatta (cited in Emmerson 2012) argues that Indonesia cannot adopt an attitude of neutrality as, in practice, the country's stance is determined by national interests. A consideration of national interests should become the starting point for foreign relations.

The option of taking a neutral stance on foreign relations is not a new policy direction for Indonesia, as it has been applying the jargon of 'neutrality' for its foreign policy approach, namely *politik bebas aktif* (independent and active foreign politics) since its early development as a nation. The foreign politics mantra was initially created to assign Indonesia's position during the Cold War (Alami 2008). By adopting this approach, Indonesia initiated a non-allied movement in 1955, to create an alternative bloc in the midst of global power segregation. Since then, foreign policy jargon has been in continual use, in various expressions. For example, SBY refers to using this jargon as 'a way of making a million friends and zero enemies'. In another expression, former Indonesian Foreign Minister, Marty Natalegawa, coined the term 'dynamic equilibrium' to express the spirit of *politik bebas aktif* (Acharya 2011). Although the Soviet Union as a bloc no longer exists, Indonesian foreign policy jargon remains relevant, as China may potentially take a Soviet-like stance to challenge the US position in Asia (Emmerson 2012). The presence of China *vis-à-vis* Japan in APT financial cooperation then is deemed as a Cold War-like rivalry that should be addressed by the same foreign policy principle.

There was a tendency that Indonesian financial policy makers intended to reflect the Indonesian foreign policy principle, but they likely defined the term '*bebas*' as neutral, instead of independent. The appropriate term that reflected the position of Indonesian financial authorities towards Sino-Japanese rivalry was independent. Being independent is slightly different from being neutral. The term 'independent' refers to a self-assigned position that provides Indonesia with options to determine its foreign partners, and the autonomy to undertake any policy action to deal with international relations. Put simply, the term independent puts Indonesia in a position to choose.

Being independent in response to Sino-Japanese power relations has provided Indonesian financial authorities with enough space to manoeuvre if necessary. A state of independence contributes to a reduction in economic dependency on one particular country. For example, during Indonesia's development projects, Japan was Indonesia's top partner; this made Indonesia relatively dependent on Japanese assistance for decades. Despite the numerous benefits of Japan's support for Indonesia, strong economic dependency on Japan (and its ally, the West) has limited Indonesia's opportunities to build economic cooperation with other partners, including China. The problem of economic manoeuvres emerged when the West was unwilling to support the Indonesian economy during the Asian financial crisis. Indonesia eventually found limited room to access alternative financial assistance. Therefore, maintaining independence towards Sino-Japanese power relations provides Indonesia with a 'substitute power', as well as a bargaining position, should one of the Asian major powers be reluctant to cooperate.

Further, independence was not only motivated by foreign policy principles, but was also triggered by the absence of a national strategy in relation to regional arrangements. A high-ranking official of BI claimed that Indonesian grand strategy with respect to international financial relations remained unclear. As a result, Indonesia's interests remain blurred in any regional forum. The BI official stated that:

> If we have a well-defined interest, we may sometimes be flexible. Sometimes we lean to 'here' [but sometimes we lean to 'there']. So far, our diplomacy runs in [a] grey position, without guidance or strategy to play. (Interview, April 2012)

A lack of national guidelines on regional economic cooperation has led Indonesia to follow the operational developments of many APT financial projects, without pushing for particular strategic actions. The unclear of a national grand policy had eventually forced financial authorities to build cooperation with many parties, without any sharply defined objectives and priorities. In this respect, the regional stance developed by Indonesian financial authorities was predominantly correlated to the results of APT financial cooperation negotiation processes.

Indonesia has tried to implement a Master Plan for Acceleration and Expansion of Indonesia Economic Development (*Masterplan Percepatan and Perluasan Pembangunan Ekonomi Indonesia*/MP3EI), as a strategic guideline to foster and expand Indonesian economic development from 2011 to 2025 (Article 1 Point 2, Presidential Regulation No. 32/2011 on

MP3EI). However, the plan did not clearly mention anything in relation to regional financial cooperation. Indonesia could provide support for a particular country if the national strategy required to take this position (Interview with a high-ranking official of BI, April 2012). However, as there were no clear guidelines to inform how support might be provided, there was no strong reason to take any partial endorsement of alignment.

Although Indonesian financial-monetary authorities have presented an independent stance as the basic position in developing collaboration with Japan and China in APT financial cooperation, the country has basically paid more attention to Japan, rather than China. In reality, Indonesian financial authorities have made a 'limited alliance' with Japan, meaning that if Indonesia sticks to the position of 'no alliance', it will remain slightly turned towards Japan. Indonesia's preference for Japan was mainly influenced by strong mutual political-economic interests between Indonesia and Japan. For instance, since Soeharto took over the Indonesian leadership, Indonesia and Japan have jointly maintained stable political relations (Anwar 1990). Both countries agreed that political stability was essential to maintain regional security, to keep up the supply and production chains, and to develop new market potentials. In contrast, the idea of having stable political relations between Indonesia and China is relatively new, coming after a long period of absence of such relations.

Obviously, Indonesia remained dependent on Japan to a large extent, in terms of the size of its borrowings from Japan, the FDI and other types of financial assistance. These financial dependencies contribute to develop and sustain the Indonesian economy and strengthen Indonesia's ties with Japan (Wie 1994). An influential Japanese scholar claimed that Japan can be expected to always support Indonesia in every unexpected situation. For example, in connection to the threatening global financial crisis in 2008, Japan provided Indonesia with financial assistance just within two weeks after Indonesia proposed it (Interview with a prominent thinker at a Japanese university, June 2012). This sentiment shows that Japan is confident enough to provide Indonesia with financial assistance without deep, lengthy and detailed assessments, as are usually required by international donors. Again, Japan was able to provide financial support to Indonesia through simple processes.

In comparison to China, Japan is taking the lead in providing assistance to Indonesia's financial sector. Based on the current bilateral position with Indonesia, Japan offered a higher degree of financial assistance in the form of liquidity support assistance, crisis countermeasures and access

Table 5.4   Sino-Japanese economic-financial assistance

Type of economic-financial assistance	Japan	China
BSA for liquidity	Yes	No
Crisis countermeasure	Yes	No
Financial market access	Yes, Samurai Bond	No
Economic partnership	Yes	Yes, indirect (through CAFTA)
BCSA for trade	No	Yes
FDI	Yes, the highest provider	Yes, limited

Source: Author's own summary

to financial markets than China. As illustrated in Table 5.4, Indonesia had more economic-financial arrangements with Japan compared to China. These types of financial ties suggest that Indonesia has a higher level of economic interdependence on Japan.

Up to this stage, there were two identified features of Indonesia's interaction with Japan and China in financial cooperation. Firstly, the interaction was based on an impartial approach, following Indonesia's foreign political approach. The Indonesian foreign political policy, which generally put Indonesia in a 'non-alliance' position, has been adopted by Indonesian financial authorities to maximise their interests. The independent position was believed by authorities to provide them with 'alternative counterparts'.

Secondly, Indonesian financial authorities built their interactions with East Asian major powers mainly based on 'costs-benefits', or economic calculations. The domestic economic situation, particularly ones that challenge the national economy, stimulated the configuration of transnational collaborations. The nature of these interactions also explained the way that Indonesian financial authorities perceived the rivalry between Japan and China as being 'only' about demonstrating political leadership in the region—a view that seemingly underestimated the effect of political influence on regional financial cooperation.

Why Perceptions Matter

Another factor that makes Japan financially attractive to Indonesia is the positive perceptions that Indonesian officials have of Japanese attitudes in dealing with such intergovernmental arrangements. Perceptions of power and how it will be used are important issues in regionalism contexts (He and Inoguchi 2011, p. 170). For Indonesia, Japan's bureaucracy is perceived as having a higher degree of certainty than China's. Japan had more clarity in terms of its financial and political agenda and expectations, if Indonesia proposed such a bilateral initiative (Interview with a high-ranking official of BI, May 2012). Although the official observed that Japan's bureaucratic system may produce delays in dealing with particular aspects of cooperation, the Japanese authorities would at least take a clear and firm position towards any ongoing negotiated issues. Japan always attempted to work on the basis of mutually agreed rules reached by Indonesia and Japan.

Further, Indonesian financial authorities also gave credit to Japanese capabilities in terms of communication and collaborative efforts. As mentioned in Chap. 2, regionalism in East Asia was more reliant on communication among officials of member countries, as cooperation arrangements had no institutionalised regional organisation. In this regard, Japanese officials are identified as being open-minded in discussing many issues, including initiatives under APT financial cooperation (Interview with a high-ranking official of BI, May 2012). For the BI official, the Japanese system provided a clear chain of communication from lower-level staff to higher levels of decision making. As a result, all levels of Japanese bureaucracy were aware of any developing issues within such intergovernmental negotiation processes. In Japan's bureaucratic system, most policies are selected bottom-up through coordination processes, instead of top-down (Tsuneki 2012). If BI and BOJ staff are negotiating a particular point, the higher levels of both central banks' management comprehended and committed to the existing agreed points made by the staff. This mechanism secured the continuity of negotiations, even if there was a change of personnel in charge.

Mutual communications with Japanese officials were conducted more frequently when APT financial projects were initiated, facilitated and conducted by Japanese nationals. BOJ and BI worked closely and had regular communication to discuss several important issues related to monetary and financial policies (Interview with a high-ranking official of BOJ, May 2012). Communication between the two authorities was intensified in 2011, when Indonesia and Japan were co-chairs of the APT financial cooperation processes, preparing logistics, administrative affairs and meeting materials. This intensity of communication contributed to develop strong policy coordination between financial authorities in Japan and Indonesia. Vogtle and Martens (2014) argue that communication and exchange of information are essential for transnational policy coordination, particularly in any initiatives in which legally binding agreements were absent. This situation led Indonesia to be more comfortable in working with Japan.

Unsurprisingly, at the outset, Indonesia preferred to approach Japan when it had to pursue its interests in the processes of APT financial initiatives. Indonesia approached Japan first, instead of China, to increase the IMF de-linked portion, as Indonesia assumed Japan would consider its proposal more seriously than if they had approached China. Japan eventually supported the proposal to increase the de-linked portion, having considered the importance of CMIM for Indonesia and also other ASEAN member states.

Further, Japan was also viewed as being more enthusiastic in promoting its ideas or proposals to other APT member countries. Japan is the most passionate Plus Three country (followed by Korea and China respectively) that frequently approaches the FPO to undertake such APT financial projects (Interview with senior official of FPO, July 2012). Japanese enthusiasm was demonstrated when Japan proposed that Yoichi Nemoto stand as the AMRO director candidate. At that time, Japan had sent its candidate in person to approach Indonesian financial authorities and promote his capacity, experience and future work plans. In contrast, China sent its diplomat, assigned to the Chinese embassy in Jakarta, to represent its candidate, Wei Benhua. From this case, the presence of the Japanese candidate in person demonstrated a higher degree of seriousness, commitment and openness—one that could not be expressed by Chinese side.

In contrast, the degree of uncertainty in dealing with Chinese authority was high. A high-ranking official of BI reports an unexpected experience when BI and PBOC were negotiating the extension of the Indonesian-China BSA (Interview, May 2012). After approximately two years, the negotiations were finalised. To follow up on the negotiations, both parties sought approval from their central bank governors. Surprisingly, the Chinese central bank governor, without giving any reasons, was reluctant to sign. This situation was perceived by the BI official as a disappointing moment that reflected a lack of certainty in terms of policy-making process. As a result, the Indonesian financial authority felt less comfortable doing business with its Chinese counterpart. This incident also suggests that the extent to which there is transparency within cooperation arrangements influences the perceptions of Indonesian authorities towards both major powers. In this respect, transparency and accountability in relation to judicial and legal systems are not considered China's strengths (Wanandi 2002, p. 225). Indonesian disappointment with Chinese behaviour also confirms one of the difficulties in shaping regionalism outcomes in East Asia, in that several member countries (including China) do not share universal values of democracy (Terada 2007, p. 18).

Unfavourable perceptions of China on financial issues were also likely to be influenced by Indonesia's unexpected experience when cooperating with China on other issues. One issue that draws public attention was the procurement of Chinese aircraft (MA-60) to support the operation of an Indonesian state-owned airline, *Merpati Nusantara*. Due to many technological defects, discontinuing the procurement was proposed. At the same time, the Indonesian government was seeking financial support from China to realise its extensive electricity project: the 'ten thousand megawatt project' that was expected to deal with the nation's lack of electricity supply. In a nutshell, the MA-60 procurement proposal became controversial not only due to an accident that involved an MA-60 aircraft in the eastern part of Indonesia, in which more than 20 people were killed, but also because the Chinese government used the MA-60 case as a bargaining tool to withhold disbursement of its financing assistance for Indonesia's electricity project. This controversial case eventually became a national issue, triggering negative perceptions of China.

These arrangements suggest that perception is another feature of collaboration between Indonesia and the two major powers in East Asia. Perception can build mutual trust and understanding of cross-cultural sensitivities on both sides. Indonesian financial authorities' positive perceptions of Japan's bureaucratic system, as being more transparent and accommodating than the Chinese, have led them to place high expectations on the policy coordination developed by Indonesia and Japan. In this respect, many Indonesian elites prefer to engage in better communications and develop expanded understandings among policy makers and increasing economic interdependence, as approaches to maintain regional peace and security (Novotny 2010, p. 20). Clearly, the intense communication between officials of Indonesia and Japan has contributed to building a better mutual understanding that was beneficial for stronger cooperation. In contrast, limited communication between Indonesian officials of financial authorities and their Chinese colleagues did not help to lessen Indonesia's negative perceptions of China.

The role of perception in influencing Indonesia's stance towards Japan and China is not new, particularly in security issues. Anwar (1990) argues that leaders' perceptions, especially from the Indonesian military elite, influence Indonesian foreign policy towards China and Japan. She found that Indonesian military leaders perceived direct relations with China carried too much security risk, while there was nothing to fear from Japan's economic or non-economic relations. In line with Anwar, Sukma (2009, p. 600) also argues that China had loomed large in the Indonesian perception of a threat to national security. Deep-rooted sentiment towards, and perceptions of, China pervade both the elite and wider public in Indonesia (Laksmana 2011, p. 31). Therefore, Indonesia remained cautious in dealing with China.

Political-economic interests and perceptions have evidently contributed to shaping Indonesia's position in the regional regulatory governance of APT financial cooperation. Stable political ties, strong economic interdependency and positive perception have played critical roles in fostering collaborative work among Indonesian and Japanese actors. In this respect, the dynamics of bilateral relations have contributed to build either the confidence or the timidity of Indonesia in response to the regulatory governance of APT financial initiatives. The Indonesian-Japanese economic rationale and constructive perceptions have become foundational to building a better environment for regional dialogues.

The following chapter examines Indonesia's responses to the APT regional liquidity support initiative. It particularly applies the features of regulatory regionalism to analyse Indonesia's responses to the governance of CMIM.

NOTES

1. 'One-way' means that only one country is able to withdraw the swap facility, while another country becomes the provider of the swap. In the case of Japan-Indonesia's one-way BSA, Japan is the provider party while Indonesia is the requesting party. Another type of BSA is two-way scheme. In this type of BSA, both parties are eligible to withdraw the swap facility.
2. Ethnic Chinese-Indonesian refers to an Indonesian citizen of Chinese descent.

REFERENCES

Acharya, A. (2011). ASEAN's dilemma: Courting Washington without hurting Beijing. *Asia Pacific Bulletin*, Vol. 133.

Akrasanee, N., & Prasert, A. (2003). The evolution of ASEAN-Japan Economic Cooperation. In *ASEAN-Japan cooperation: A foundation for East Asian community* (pp. 63–74). Tokyo: Japan Center for International Exchange.

Alami, A. N. (2008). Landasan dan prinsip politik luar negeri Indonesia (Foundation and principle of Indonesian foreign politics). In G. Wuryandari (Ed.), *Politik luar negeri Indonesia di tengah pusaran politik domestik (Indonesian foreign politics at the centre of domestic politics)*. Yogyakarta: Pustaka Pelajar.

Alvstam, C. G. (2001). Regionalization still waiting to happen? In M. Schulz, F. Soderbaum, & J. Ojendal (Eds.), *Regionalization in a globalizing world* (pp. 173–195). London and New York: Zed Books.

Amako, S. (2007). *The idea of new international order China is seeking and East Asia Community*. GIARI Working Papers, Vol. 2007, No. 1.

AMRO. (2011). Press release appointment of the AMRO Director, April 6. Retrieved March 10, 2013, from http://www.amro-asia.org/wp-content/uploads/2011/11/AFDM+3-PR-2011-000-20110406-Appointmeent-of-the-AMRO-Director-PR20110503.pdf

Anwar, D. F. (1990). Indonesia's relations with China and Japan: Images, perception and realities. *Contemporary Southeast Asia, 12*(3), 225–246.

ASEAN. (2014). ASEAN+3 Research Group studies. Retrieved October 1, 2014, from http://www.asean.org/news/item/external-relations-asean-3-asean3-research-group-studies

ASEAN Plus Three. (2014). *The joint statement of the 17th ASEAN Plus Three Finance Ministers and Central Bank Governors' Meeting*. Astana: ASEAN Plus Three.

Asian Development Bank. (2008). *Bond financing for infrastructure projects in the ASEAN+3 Region (Financed by the Japan Special Fund)*. Manila: Asian Development Bank.

Bank Indonesia. (2009). Establishment of a bilateral currency swap arrangement between People's Bank of China and Bank Indonesia, March 23. Retrieved May 13, 2014, from http://www.bi.go.id/en/iru/highlight-news/Pages/bilateral%20swap%20agreement%20China%20Indonesia.aspx

Bank of Japan. (2013). *Signing of bilateral swap arrangement between Japan and Indonesia*. Retrieved January 31, 2014, from https://www.boj.or.jp/en/announcements/release_2013/rel131213b.pdf

BBC World Service. (2013). The 2013 BBC country rating pool, May 22. Retrieved October 2, 2014, from http://www.worldpublicopinion.org/pipa/2013%20Country%20Rating%20Poll.pdf

Chongbo, W. (2011). Forging closer Sino-Japanese economic relations and policy suggestions. *Ritsumekan International Affairs, 10*, 119–142.

Chung, C. (2013). China and Japan in 'ASEAN Plus' multilateral arrangements: Raining on the other guy's parade. *Asian Survey, 53*(5), 801.

Daniel, W. (2012). Jepang masih paling rajin kasih utang ke RI (Japan is the most diligent to lend Indonesia), May 22. Retrieved September 1, 2014, from http://news.detik.com/transisipresiden/read/2012/05/22/103916/1921504/4/jepang-masih-paling-rajin-kasih-utang-ke-ri

Emmerson, D. K. (2012). Is Indonesia rising? It depends. In A. Reid (Ed.), *Indonesia rising: The repositioning of Asia's third giant* (pp. 49–76). Singapore: Institute of South Asian Studies.

Hall, D. (2002). Environmental change, protest, and havens of environmental degradation: Evidence from Asia. *Global Environmental Politics, 2*(2), 20–28.

Haswidi, A., & Suharmoko, A. (2009). RI, Japan ink fresh 1.5t yen swap deal. *The Jakarta Post.* Retrieved July 22, 2011, from http://www.thejakartapost.com/news/2009/07/07/ri-japan-ink-fresh-15t-yen-swap-deal.html

He, B., & Inoguchi, T. (2011). Introduction to ideas of Asian regionalism. *Japanese Journal of Political Science, 12*(2), 165–177.

Inoguchi, T. (2011). Japanese ideas of Asian regionalism. *Japanese Journal of Political Science, 12*, 233–249.

Japan External Trade Organisation. (2012). Japan's outward and inward foreign direct investment. Retrieved June 25, 2014, from https://www.jetro.go.jp/en/reports/statistics/

Jayasuriya, K. (2003). Introduction: Governing the Asia Pacific beyond the new regionalism. *Third World Quarterly, 24*(2), 199–215.

Jhaveri, R. (2005). PBOC and Bank Indonesia sign bilateral swap agreement. *Risk.Net.* Retrieved December 19, 2011, from http://www.risk.net/asia-risk/news/1509309/pboc-bank-indonesia-sign-bilateral-swap-agreement

Jiabo, W. (2011). Remarks by His Excellency Wen Jiabao Premier of the People's Republic of China. China-Indonesia Strategic Business Dialogue, Jakarta.

Jize, Q. (2005). Indonesia now a strategic partner. *China Daily.* Retrieved September 17, 2013, from http://www.chinadaily.com.cn/english/doc/2005-04/25/content_437349.htm

Laksmana, E. A. (2011). Variations on a theme: Dimensions of ambivalence in Indonesia-China relations. *Harvard Asia Quarterly, 13*(1), 24–31.

Mietzner, M. (2009). *Military politics, Islam, and the state in Indonesia: From turbulent transition to democratic consolidation.* Singapore: Institute of Southeast Asian Studies.

Ministry of Finance of Japan. (2009). Joint press release on the signing of the agreement on an increase in the maximum amount of the Bilateral Swap Arrangements between Japan and Indonesia under the Chiang Mai Initiative. Retrieved December 17, 2011, from https://www.mof.go.jp/english/international_policy/financial_cooperation_in_asia/cmi/090406press_release.pdf

Ministry of Finance of Japan. (2011). Japan's Bilateral Swap Arrangements (BSAs) under the Chiang Mai Initiative (CMI). Retrieved December 19, 2011, from http://www.mof.go.jp/english/international_policy/financial_cooperation_in_asia/regional_financial_cooperation/pcmie/index.htm

Ministry of Foreign Affairs of Japan. (2008). Joint press statement on the occasion of the entry into force of the Agreement between Japan and the Republic of Indonesia for an Economic Partnership, July 1. Retrieved May 13, 2014, from http://www.mofa.go.jp/region/asia-paci/indonesia/joint0807.html

Ministry of Foreign Affairs of Japan. (2011a). Japan's official development assistance white paper 2010. Retrieved May 13, 2014, from http://www.mofa.go.jp/policy/oda/white/2010/

Ministry of Foreign Affairs of Japan. (2011b). Japan-Indonesia relations. Retrieved July 22, 2011b, from http://www.mofa.go.jp/region/asia-paci/indonesia/index.html

Ministry of Foreign Affairs of Japan. (2012). Japan's ODA: Rolling plan for the Republic of Indonesia. Retrieved May 13, 2014, from http://www.mofa.go.jp/policy/oda/rolling_plans/pdfs/indonesia.pdf

Nomura Research Institute. (2009). *Technical assistance for "promotion of Asian medium Term Note (MTN) program"*. Japan: Nomura Research Institute.

Novotny, D. (2010). *Torn between America and China: Elite perceptions and Indonesian foreign policy*. Singapore: Institute of Southeast Asian Studies.

Pew Research Centre. (2011). Pew Research Global Attitudes Project, July 13. Retrieved July 7, 2012, from http://www.pewglobal.org/2011/07/13/chapter-1-the-global-balance-of-power

Putnam, R. D. (1988). Diplomacy and domestic politics: The logic of two-level games. *International Organization, 42*(3), 427–460.

Rathus, J. (2010). *Affordable delays for the Chiang Mai Initiative?* East Asia Forum. Retrieved May 31, 2012, from http://www.eastasiaforum.org/2010/12/24/affordable-delays-for-the-chiang-mai-initiative/

Saputro, E. (2012). *ASEAN+3 financial cooperation enters a new phase*. East Asia Forum, May 26. Retrieved November 26, 2013, from http://www.eastasiaforum.org/2012/05/26/asean3-financial-cooperation-enters-a-new-phase/

Scott, P. D. (1985). The United States and the overthrow of Sukarno, 1965–1967. *Pacific Affairs, 58*, 239–264.

Shiraishi, T. (1997). Japan and Southeast Asia. In T. Shiraishi & P. J. Katzenstein (Eds.), *Network power: Japan and Asia*. Ithaca: Cornell University Press.

Shiraishi, T., & Katzenstein, P. J. (1997). *Network power: Japan and Asia*. Ithaca: Cornell University Press.

Smith, A. L. (2000). Indonesia's foreign policy under Abdurrahman Wahid: Radical or status quo state? *Contemporary Southeast Asia, 22*(3), 498–526.

Statistics Indonesia. (2011). Perkembangan ekspor dan impor Indonesia April 2011 (The development of Indonesian export-import in April 2011). *Berita Resmi Statistik, 35*(6), 1–11 Retrieved July 22, 2011, from, http://www.bps.go.id/brs_file/exim-01jun11.pdf.

Storey, I. J. (2000). Indonesia's China policy in the new order and beyond: Problems and prospects. *Contemporary Southeast Asia, 22*(1), 145–174.

Sujatmiko. (1999). Japan's role in overcoming the Indonesian economic crisis. *Asia-Pacific Review, 6*(1), 109–131.

Sukma, R. (2009). Indonesia-China relations: The politics of re-engagement. *Asian Survey, 49*(4), 591–608.

Sukma, R. (2012). Domestic politics and international posture: Constraints and possibilities. In A. Reid (Ed.), *Indonesia rising: The repositioning of Asia's third giant* (pp. 77–92). Singapore: Institute of South Asian Studies.

Surbakti, R. (1999). Formal political institutions. In R. W. Baker, H. Soesastro, J. Kristiadi, & D. E. Ramage (Eds.), *Indonesia: The challenge of change.* New York: St. Martin's Press.

Suryadinata, L. (1996). *Indonesia's foreign policy under Suharto: Aspiring to international leadership.* Singapore: Times Academic Press.

Sussangkarn, C. (2010). *The Chiang Mai Initiative Multilateralisation: Origin, development, and outlook.* ADBI Working Paper Series, No. 230.

Terada, T. (2007). *Japan and the evolution of Asian regionalism.* GIARI Working Paper, Vol. 2007-E-3.

Terada, T. (2009). *The rise of China: The impetus behind Japanese regionalism.* East Asia Forum. Retrieved May 29, 2012, from http://www.eastasiaforum. org/2009/07/26/the-rise-of-china-the-impetus-behind-japanese-regionalism/

Tsuneki, A. (2012). Japanese bureaucracy. *Japanese Economy, 39*(3), 49–68.

Vaughn, B. (2007). Indonesia: Domestic politics, strategic dynamics, and American interests. In E. F. McFlynn (Ed.), *Economics and geopolitics of Indonesia* (pp. 79–104). New York: Nova.

Väyrynen, R. (2003). Regionalism: Old and new. *International Studies Review, 5*(1), 25–51.

Vogtle, E. M., & Martens, K. (2014). The Bologna Process as a template for transnational policy oordination. *Policy Studies, 35*(3), 246–263.

Wanandi, J. (2002). The rise of China: A challenge for East Asia. *The Indonesian Quarterly, XXX*(3), 224–233.

Wie, T. K. (1994). Interactions of Japanese aid and direct investment in Indonesia. *Asean Economic Bulletin, 11*(1), 25–35.

Yoshimatsu, H. (2008). Japan and regional governance in East Asia. In N. Thomas (Ed.), *Governance and regionalism in Asia* (pp. 66–88). London: Routledge.

Yoshimatsu, H. (2014). *Comparing institution-building in East Asia: Power politics, governance, and critical junctures.* Palgrave Macmillan.

CHAPTER 6

Indonesia and the CMIM

The regulatory regionalism approach, as advocated in this book, provides a way to examine how Indonesian financial authorities have responded to the Chiang Mai Initiative Multilateralisation (CMIM). In particular, it brings the roles of non-state actors into an analysis of Indonesia's response to the CMIM. It also facilitates the examination of policy coordination networks established by Indonesian financial authorities in response to the initiative. Most importantly, regulatory regionalism can enhance our understanding of the way Indonesian financial authorities have transformed their domestic regulatory system, such that the governance of CMIM can be accommodated.

The establishment of CMIM has stimulated a new mode of regional governance, with three major indicators. The first is the involvement of non-state actors. CMIM comprises the participation of national regulatory bodies and non-state actors at regional and national levels. While it retains state authorities as its main actors, CMIM also engages with International Financial Institutions (IFIs) to form its governance. Regarding this, the participation of regional and global non-state actors has been recognised in existing studies of CMIM. However, national non-state actor participation, including Indonesian, has not been examined in details.

The second indicator is policy coordination. The CMIM has stimulated the emergence of transnational policy coordination between ASEAN Plus Three (APT) member countries and has managed risk governance among financial authorities. The policy coordination includes not only the negotiation process of establishing CMIM but also establishing its operational level. At the national level, Amyx (2004, p. 103) argues that the negotiating process of swap arrangements under APT Cooperation has stimulated the rise of communication networks between central bankers and finance ministers in the region. These were essentially absent during the Asian financial crisis. However, examination of the internal mechanisms for policy coordination between relevant authorities—including the finance ministry and central bank—in response to the APT liquidity support initiative, remain scant in the existing literature.

The third indicator is standardisation. Many elements of CMIM are adopted from International Monetary Fund (IMF) standards. They range from the CMIM contribution size to the decision-making process. CMIM is an example of a regional initiative that builds its governance based on global standards. In this regard, the ways in which the Indonesian financial agencies have adopted CMIM standards and mechanisms have not yet been examined. Such examination may also lead to a determination of whether or not the *de-politicisation* of financial authorities—as has happened to Indonesia's central bank—affects the processes of adopting CMIM governance.

Against this backdrop, this chapter attempts to examine the responses of Indonesian financial authorities to the development of the CMIM as an established regional liquidity support mechanism in East Asia. In this chapter, the participation of Indonesian Ministry of Finance (IMOF) and Bank Indonesia (BI) in CMIM was examined, as these institutions played pivotal roles in the national financial regulatory framework. The chapter argues that Indonesia's responses to the CMIM arise mainly from the state institutions. Indonesian financial authorities have responded positively to the development of the CMIM and intended to transform the national framework to accommodate governance of the regional liquidity support mechanism. As such, the transformation of Indonesia's national regulatory space has proceeded through both 'hard' and 'soft' laws.

As both Indonesian financial bodies are separate entities, and have different ranges of authority, this chapter also examines how the power and mandate of each institution shape their participation in CMIM's governance project. The independence of BI, as Indonesia's central bank, suggests it played a pivotal role in ensuring the transformation of the national space run smoothly.

This chapter is divided into two parts. The first part examines important issues of CMIM governance and its functions as a crisis mitigation mechanism in the region. The second part explores the dynamics of Indonesia's participation in the CMIM process, as well as its responses to the regional liquidity support initiative, particularly regarding the transformation of its national regulatory framework. In this part, de-politicisation of Indonesian financial institutions is also discussed, in relation to the internal transformation process as a response to CMIM governance.

THE CMIM'S EVOLUTION AS A CRISIS COUNTERMEASURE

The establishment of the APT regional pooling fund was basically a response to the inability of individual states in East Asia to deal with the Asian financial crisis. Several APT member countries, including Indonesia, Thailand, Malaysia and South Korea, were severely affected by the crisis. Considering the weak economic conditions due to the deterioration of foreign reserves, the leaders of APT member countries agreed to collaborate in the areas of risk management, corporate governance, the monitoring of capital flows, strengthening of the banking and financial systems, reforming international financial architecture and enhancing self-help mechanisms (APT 1999). This arrangement reflected the needs on regional strength to assist national incapacity. As each state is not able to deal with economic risks individually, the regional supports are expected to form a new space of governance that reduces the effects of risks (Jayasuriya 2010a).

Particularly on the commitment to enhance self-help mechanism, CMIM implicitly emphasised the type of regional cooperation that would be more reliant on regional-owned strengths and resources, rather than international ones. Clearly, it also, to some degree, reflected a protest about the current global financial architecture that always positioned IMF as the lender of the last resort to deal with financial shocks. Soesastro (2006) argues that the regional self-help mechanism can develop an alternative solution for any future financial crises if international lenders refuse to provide financial assistance. Most importantly, the self-help mechanism expresses APT member countries' demands for global—as well as expanded regional—financial governance reforms.

On the operational level, the CMIM manages regional economic risks through monitoring and surveillance of national macroeconomic policies and development. An increasing economic vulnerability demands a type of regulatory governance that can provide some degree of policy harmonisation (Jayasuriya 2003, p. 207). The regional surveillance mechanism is expected not only to monitor the economic status and policies of the APT member countries, but also to anticipate the potential of moral hazards to affect liquidity assistance. Kawai and Houser (2007, p. 19) argue that an effective surveillance mechanism is essential to minimise the moral hazard issue in the application of emergency financial assistance.

Enhancing Transnational Policy Coordination

The CMIM provides an impetus for enhanced transnational policy coordination, particularly as a part of risk-sharing projects that are embedded in the regional self-help mechanism. As such, the CMIM becomes a medium for APT finance ministries and central bank governors to strengthen their policy coordination on liquidity management. There are two types of transnational policy coordination related to the regional liquidity support initiative. The first is policy dialogue among APT financial policy makers. This dialogue is known as the Economic Review and Policy Dialogue (ERPD) that covers five activities: (i) assessing global, regional and national economic conditions; (ii) monitoring regional capital flows and currency markets; (iii) analysing macroeconomic and financial risks; (iv) strengthening banking and financial system conditions; and (v) providing Asian voices in the process of reforming the international financial system (Kawai and Houser 2007; Sussangkarn 2010). In addition, the ERPD provides a peer review mechanism on financial policies among APT member countries. Murase (2007, p. 73) argues that ERPD stimulates peer pressure processes that particularly encourage APT member countries to avoid any inappropriate policies.

While the ERPD has facilitated policy coordination that provided beneficial policy inputs for the member countries, the dialogue has been criticised for its lack of daily surveillance activities. In effect, this means that its capacity to provide early warnings for such unexpected events is limited (Anas and Friawan 2008). The lack of effective surveillance processes also means that the early warning systems are incapable of acting as early crisis countermeasures (Rathus 2012). In response to this weakness, Kawai and Houser (2007) proposed to set up a regional secretariat that allowed ERPD to enhance this effectiveness, especially in exercising a due diligence mechanism during times of economic crisis.

The second is a formal institutionalised regional surveillance process. For Dieter (2000), a monitoring body is indispensable for the establishment of a public regional liquidity fund. The institutionalisation of APT surveillance processes gathered momentum when APT finance ministers agreed to set up an independent surveillance unit that could support CMIM decision-making processes (Saparini 2009). Located in Singapore, as a 'company limited by guarantee', the unit is known as the ASEAN Plus Three Macroeconomic Research Office (AMRO). Since its inception, AMRO has continued to play an important role in shaping new patterns of regional policy coordination on economic surveillance, which has involved the participation of national regulatory bodies, as well as regional and international institutions.[1] Jayasuriya (2010a) argues that the emerging peer review and monitoring systems contribute to a new mode of regional governance in the Asia-Pacific. The establishment of AMRO was the seed for the new mode of regional financial governance in East Asia, where AMRO played a crucial role in transnational policy networks.

AMRO was designed to operate during both peace and crisis times. During peace times, the office carries out monitoring functions to assess macroeconomic conditions and financial robustness, as well as possible macroeconomic and financial threats to the APT member countries. Currently, AMRO's operational capabilities extend to detecting potential risks and vulnerabilities (Azis 2012, p. 328). For the latter function, AMRO contributes to CMIM's decision-making processes following the activation of a swap facility under CMIM (Moon 2012). During times of crisis, the office has a mandate to assess the economic conditions of the crisis-affected country and provide recommendations to the APT financial minister deputies for further responses (Nemoto and Nakagawa 2013). AMRO's comprehensive macroeconomic reports play an influential role in ensuring appropriate countermeasures to potential economic volatilities, especially during crises. There is no doubt that during a crisis, timely and appropriate responses are essential to mitigate any negative impacts on economies in the region. In addition, AMRO is also tasked with monitoring the use of disbursed CMIM funds, to ensure compliance with CMIM agreements.

In general, three important elements play out within AMRO, namely, those of the director, the executive committee and the advisory panel. The director occupies the most strategic and important position in AMRO, with leadership status and responsibility for the management and outcomes of AMRO. As discussed in Chap. 5, Japan and China's interests in occupying this pivotal position have led to a split in the initial tenure of the AMRO director to accommodate the interests of both countries.

AMRO's director has support for analytical responsibilities from groups of economists. The director is responsible to the executive committee. The committee membership includes finance minister and central bank deputies. It has several strategic duties to fulfil, including providing guidance and policy direction to AMRO management, appointing the director and reviewing its performance and AMRO's reports. To support AMRO in terms of strategic, technical and professional guidance, an advisory panel was set up, comprising six nominated individuals: three from the ASEAN bloc and three from the Plus Three bloc. Members of the advisory panel are expected to be highly respected economists who have a comprehensive understanding of the APT regional economy.

The policy coordination function borne by AMRO rests on the way the office conducts surveillance processes. To conduct the surveillance mechanism and to deal with developing data systems, AMRO has established collaboration with other relevant financial institutions, including the IMF and Asian Development Bank (ADB) and has also coordinated with the national surveillance institutions of APT member countries (Siregar and Chabchitrchaidol 2013). The IMF and ADB have engaged with AMRO's operations within a consultancy context, to support the office in specific fields. In this regard, Jayasuriya (2010, p. 104) argues that the regional surveillance and monitoring of national economies is expected to manage the growing risks of future financial turmoil.

As such, the geographic location of AMRO within the hub of the East Asian region means that APT member countries are more likely to receive timely responses and assistance from the regional surveillance unit. Should a potential financial threat arise in the region, AMRO personnel can be deployed immediately to relevant countries (interview with a high-ranking official of AMRO, April 2012). Other IFIs, such as the IMF, which have headquarters outside the region, do not have this quick access capability. Moreover, AMRO's location also provides advantage to monitoring processes that need to be in place during the activation of CMIM's liquidity support. For the member countries, the strategic location of AMRO facilitates timely policy coordination with AMRO's economists as all major cities in APT region have direct flights to Singapore.

Meanwhile, policy coordination with national economic surveillance institutions particularly emerged in the form of a country consultation that included peer review and peer pressure mechanisms. At this stage, AMRO's country consultation shaped a new form of regional policy coordination that shared national and regional responsiveness towards economic risks.

The country consultation also facilitated AMRO in collecting data to produce its surveillance reports. In its current development, AMRO collected data conditional on APT member countries' limited human resource availability (interview with a high-ranking official of AMRO, April 2012). As a result, the validity and overall robustness of AMRO surveillance report analyses might be compromised by limitations in data collection processes. Variations in data quality and presentation between reports further contribute to the challenge of conducting cross-country financial analysis contexts and comparisons (Anas and Atje 2005, p. 14).

Besides limitation in human resource availability, AMRO has also experienced the reluctance of several member countries to disclose macroeconomic data, due to confidentiality. Most ASEAN member countries still considered certain information as sensitive; as such, they did not want to publish their data. The unenthusiastic responses in providing requested data have eventually limited the capacity of the monitoring system to deliver productive outcomes. Functioning as an early warning system, secure and comprehensive data collection processes play a key role in making policy responses more effective (Ito et al. 2005). With its status as a private company, AMRO had no mandate or power to push APT member countries to provide economic data. Therefore, the coordination between AMRO and state agencies was more reliant on voluntary cooperation. Kawai and Takagi (2012) argue that regional policy coordination will further strengthen if AMRO is able to enforce conditionality during crises.

Regarding legal issues, AMRO had a legal constraint that ensured the office could not work impartially, as it was subject to Singaporean financial rules and regulations. This condition impacts on issues of independence and accountability (Rathus 2012). Such legal immunities were absent from AMRO's current status as a private company. To deal with the limitations due to AMRO's legal status, APT finance ministers agreed to shift the status of AMRO from a company limited by guarantee to an international organisation.[2] This new status as an international organisation is expected to facilitate AMRO's function as an objective and independent surveillance unit in the region. Moreover, the new status is also understood to enhance country consultation mechanisms, as well as the quality of AMRO reports. AMRO's status as an international organisation will mean it has greater authority to gather relevant data and information. The new status will likely force APT member countries into new arrangements that are binding in their requirement that member countries must provide existing, or produce, any data requested by AMRO. In addition, having an international organisation status will also assist AMRO to achieve better data-sharing arrangements with other international institutions, such as the IMF (Nemoto and Nakagawa 2013). Without having status as an international organisation, AMRO was difficult to get support data from IFIs as their internal regulations restricted data sharing with non-international organisations.

In its early development, AMRO produced country surveillance and regional reports. AMRO's individual country reports are circulated during the finance minister deputies' March and November meetings. These reports complement those produced by ERPD as the existing institution with responsibility for operations of financial surveillance processes in the region (Siregar and Chabchitrchaidol 2013). For individual country surveillance reports, AMRO produces two reports per country per year, with a focus on particular short-term risks and vulnerabilities of member countries (Nemoto and Nakagawa 2013). In comparison, the IMF surveillance report is produced annually. With respect to discussion on the 'whole of region' surveillance report—formally termed 'AMRO Regional Economic Monitoring' (AREM)—AMRO examines the entire regional economy against a global background. A leading economist of AMRO claimed that from the time the AMRO reports were produced, finance minister deputy discussions began to focus more on the AMRO reports, even though member countries still produced their own ERPD reports (Nemoto and Nakagawa 2013). This indicates that financial authorities are placing more trust in AMRO's economic surveillance. The surveillance mechanism facilitates policy coordination in the form of exchange of views and experiences among member countries. As monitoring the national economy is no longer solely managed by national bodies, the emergence of transnational policy coordination is indispensable, due to the involvement of numerous regional and global actors. However, from the perspective of establishing transparency and openness, the AMRO reports remain confidential, thus protecting the content of AMRO's surveillance reports from public scrutiny and possible criticism. This arrangement raises the issue of AMRO reports' credibility.

Regional Initiatives with Global Standards

The establishment of CMIM as a regional liquidity support arrangement includes regional standard-setting processes. Despite producing new standards for regional governance, CMIM standards are predominantly adopted from international standards, which basically follow IMF standards on safety net mechanisms. In CMIM, IMF standards dominate (Grimes 2011, p. 131). Many CMIM elements, ranging from the distribution of country contribution to decision-making processes, are adopted from the IMF. Siregar (2011, p. 252) argues that CMIM is actually a proxy for many IMF facilities. This arrangement reflects the CMIM's function as a supplement to the existing international financial arrangement, re-emphasising the role of IMF as lender of last resort. For Walter (2008), the adoption of international standards for financial governance in East Asia was part of major developed countries' responses to the Asian financial crisis, and the need to reform global financial architecture. This phenomenon is viewed by Jayasuriya (2004, p. 494) as a system of meta-governance that connects international organisations with regional entities and various national or even sub-national entities.

In a more obvious arrangement with IMF, the CMIM is still equipped with bridging conditionality through the 'IMF-linked portion'. The CMIM-IMF-linked portion means that IMF procedures and conditionality will be enforced once the APT member countries intend to withdraw the IMF-linked portion. The existence of the IMF-linked portion is understood as the reason behind the USA's non-objection stance towards the establishment of CMIM (Yoshimatsu 2014, p. 87). Initially, the IMF-linked portion was set at 80 per cent of the maximum swap amount; it had been reduced to 70 per cent, following the establishment of AMRO. This means that if the APT member countries want to draw CMIM support assistance of more than 30 per cent of their maximum swap amount, they should engage in an IMF arrangement.

The establishment of the IMF-linked portion engenders questions about CMIM's origins. This link presents a significant challenge to maintaining the spirit of the self-help mechanism, whereby the CMIM was set up as a critique of the IMF's financial assistance programme, and its conditionality (Azis 2012, p. 327). While establishing the IMF-linked portion may secure the use of the CMIM fund, it can be viewed as subverting the idea of a regional self-help mechanism, as CMIM is reliant to other IFIs (Grimes 2011, p. 87). The IMF-linked portion may also potentially gain opposition from APT member countries, especially for those that suffered from the IMF's application of an incorrect formula during the Asian financial crisis.

The negative stigma surrounding IMF financing policies still exists within these member countries. In Indonesia, resistance towards the IMF remained strong, even after the IMF argued that it had already transformed its operations and reformed its governance. On this basis, the reduction of the IMF-linked portion could be viewed as a progressive action that is parallel with the spirit of CMIM to limit member countries' dependency on international assistance programmes, while maintaining IMF's authority to address absences in credible regional financial surveillance mechanisms.

Moreover, CMIM divided its total size to reflect APT member countries' contributions and voting power, by imitating IMF members' quotas and voting power. As illustrated in Table 6.1, the Plus Three bloc holds 80 per cent of contribution, with almost 76 per cent of the total voting power. Reflecting on the country contribution, it is clear that ASEAN states are positioned as potential recipients, rather than potential donors, with the exception of Singapore and Brunei Darussalam.

Therefore, CMIM is more likely to support ASEAN member countries than the Plus Three countries. Based on the current configuration of CMIM purchasing multiples, ASEAN countries have larger purchasing multiples compared to the Plus Three countries.[3] Although the ASEAN countries have made fewer contributions to CMIM, their purchasing multiples are more than Plus Three countries that only have purchasing multiples not more than once. As a result, ASEAN countries have access to larger amounts of the pooling fund—up to five times of their contribution. Moon (2012) argues that the CMIM was designed to function more for the benefit of ASEAN countries rather than the Plus Three countries. Neither China nor Japan needs US dollars, due to their massive foreign reserves (Amyx 2004, p. 101). For Korea, it can easily tap US dollars from the US Federal Reserve Bank as it has very close financial relations with the USA. In short, CMIM has become a medium through which Japan and China in particular can demonstrate their leadership in the region, rather than a source of funds.

Regarding the distribution of voting powers within CMIM, the larger contribution of the Plus Three countries means these countries' member representatives hold sway over decision-making processes. It means that the voting powers of Japan, China and Korea are enough to block any decisions related to swap requests in CMIM decision-making processes that require at least two-thirds of effective votes.[4] While the concept of voting power based on contributions is generally accepted by regional or international institutions, the distribution of voting power in CMIM potentially outstrips the voice of small contributors in 'critical situation'

Table 6.1 CMIM contribution, purchasing multiple and voting power

Countries		Financial contribution (billion US$)		Share (%)		Purchasing multiple	Maximum swap amount (billion US$)	Basic votes	Votes based on contribution	Total voting power	%
Plus Three		**192.00**		**80.00**			**117.30**	**9.60**	**192.00**	**201.60**	**71.59**
China	China (Exc. Hong Kong)	76.80	68.40	32.0	28.50	0.5	34.20	3.20	68.40	71.60	25.43
	Hong Kong	8.40		3.50		2.5	6.30	0.00	8.40	8.40	2.98
Japan		76.80		32.00		0.5	38.40	3.20	76.80	80.00	28.41
Korea		38.40		16.00		1	38.40	3.20	38.40	41.60	14.77
ASEAN		**48.00**		**20.00**			**126.20**	**32.00**	**48.00**	**80.00**	**28.41**
Indonesia		9.104		3.793		2.5	22.76	3.20	9.104	12.304	4.369
Thailand		9.104		3.793		2.5	22.76	3.20	9.104	12.304	4.369
Malaysia		9.104		3.793		2.5	22.76	3.20	9.104	12.304	4.369
Singapore		9.104		3.793		2.5	22.76	3.20	9.104	12.304	4.369
Philippines		9.104		3.793		2.5	22.76	3.20	9.104	12.304	4.369
Vietnam		2.00		0.833		5	10.00	3.20	2.00	5.20	1.847
Cambodia		0.24		0.100		5	1.20	3.20	0.24	3.44	1.222
Myanmar		0.12		0.050		5	0.60	3.20	0.12	3.32	1.179
Brunei		0.06		0.025		5	0.30	3.20	0.06	3.26	1.158
Lao PDR		0.06		0.025		5	0.30	3.20	0.06	3.26	1.158
Total		**240.00**		**100.00**			**243.50**	**41.60**	**240.00**	**281.60**	**100.00**

Source: The joint statement of the 15th APT Finance Ministers and Central Bank Governors' Meeting, 2012

instances, in which smaller contributors may face disproportionate risks. For example, with only 4.3 per cent of total voting rights, Indonesia has very limited powers within CMIM and, as such, faces the possibility of being overridden in important decisions by other larger contributors. In this case, ASEAN member countries' dependency on the Plus Three countries—given they are likely to be potential swap recipients of the Plus Three—remains larger. Moreover, the bigger contributors are also able to establish additional conditionality, as the small contributors rely on their supports. Such voting power imbalances in CMIM decision-making processes introduce ineffective outcomes, especially for smaller contributors.

Further, CMIM has also adopted IMF's decision-making bodies. Reflecting the IMF board of governors and executive directors, CMIM established two-level decision-making bodies, namely, the ministerial-level decision-making body (MLDMB) and the executive-level decision-making body (ELDMB) (APT 2010). The structure and operation of these bodies are based on the types of issues they have and the authority to manage. The MLDMB is authorised to make decisions regarding fundamental issues, such as the size of each party's contribution, the maximum swap amounts for drawings and renewals, terms of participation, terms of reinstatement for any members that propose to reinstall or other matters agreed as fundamental. The MLDMB membership is comprised of the 13 finance ministers of the APT member countries. In 2013, APT central bank governors were invited into the MLDMB, in an attempt to shore up more accurate and comprehensive decision-making processes.

In practice, all decisions facing the MLDMB must be reached through consensus. This condition means that any decision taken by the MLDMB needs unanimous approval from the members, as there is no voting mechanism within the MLDMB. To avoid delays or stagnation in MLDMB's decision-making processes, any fundamental issues should undergo prior consultation with the ELDMB, as the CMIM's operational-level decision-making body.

As indicated above, executive (operational)-level decision-making responsibility is held by the ELDMB. In this respect, executive issues are more related to issues like the approval of drawings, approval of drawing renewals, the waiver of any conditions, the declaration of default events and approval of escape.[5] The ELDMB membership comprises the 13 finance minister representatives of the APT member countries, plus 14 central bank representatives of the APT member countries, including Hong Kong. To operate its mandate, the ELDMB can exercise a voting mechanism in addition to using consensus-style decision-making processes. In this respect, any decision at the executive level requires that at least two-thirds of the ELDMB membership's effective votes reach agreement (APT 2010). Effective votes mean the voting rights of each CMIM party, based on its contribution, minus the number of votes of any escaping CMIM party and the swap requesting party. 'Requesting party' refers to any party that makes a request to purchase US dollar under the CMIM arrangement.

The relatively large numbers of CMIM contributors potentially introduces increased complexity into the decision-making process. With 13 members eligible to vote, lengthy delays in the decision-making process are likely. Obviously, the more players, the more complicated a process is. If such delays are not managed efficiently, CMIM's activities may be severely curtailed. In such eventualities, a requesting country may seek alternative funding sources that can provide immediate assistance. In this case, someone may question whether the CMIM can be fully implemented as a high-functioning, efficient and effective body considering the inherent complexities within CMIM's operations. If that happens, the CMIM may be perceived as operationally ineffective (Azis 2012).

Regarding surveillance processes, IMF standards have also (more or less) influenced the CMIM surveillance mechanism. In establishing AMRO, it was assumed that this new institution would replace the role of the IMF in regional surveillance processes (Samboh 2011). However, a senior official of AMRO argued that the purpose and scope of CMIM was distinctively different from that of the IMF, a key point:

> AMRO is not [a] surveillance institution with very broad scope. It is focusing really on the most needed area that should attract more attention from authorities, for example the financial sector, short-term capital flow, and liquidity in the country. (Interview, April 2012)

However, taking an opposing view, Saputro (2011) considers AMRO functions to supplement the IMF's role in the region, rather than compete with it. As a relatively new regional institution, AMRO lacked the data collection standards that made it distinct from the IMF model. AMRO has not yet established region-wide data collection standards (Grimes 2011). There was no such standard that might facilitate advanced data collection within regional financial surveillance processes. As a result, the CMIM was not sufficiently confident with its own surveillance mechanism. For instance, the CMIM-Precautionary Line's (CMIM-PL: see below) decision-making process was to be based on country-specific economic reports and a combination of analyses produced by AMRO, ADB and the IMF (Saputro 2012). For the near future, Abimanyu (2011b, p. 256) suggests that AMRO should also comprise macroeconomic and financial experts, and retain its independence from the IMF.

The latest attempt to bring IMF standards into CMIM elements was the introduction of IMF crisis prevention facilities. While the CMIM was initially set up as crisis resolution facility, APT member countries agreed to establish a new function as a crisis prevention facility in 2012. As a sign of its more advanced progress, the CMIM was equipped to carry out a new crisis prevention function, in the form of the CMIM-PL (Azis 2012). The CMIM-PL's operating procedure merely adopted the IMF's precautionary credit line (PCL) function, as APT finance ministers agreed to engage with the IMF's financial safety net arrangement. Saputro (2012) argues that there are two similarities between the schemes. First, there is the possibility of applying ex-post conditionality for accessing the CMIM-PL, which is also applied to the PCL scheme. Second, the CMIM-PL's qualification criteria imitate those of the IMF.

Interestingly, the CMIM-PL scheme was introduced at the same time as the decision to reduce the IMF-linked portion was taken, a decision that might also be seen as reducing the United States' (USA's) influence in East Asia. In this case, the APT member countries, particularly Japan, attempted to maintain their relationships with the US carefully. This was done to avoid any strong interference in the progress of CMIM, as had occurred in the drawing up of the AMF proposal. A senior Japanese representative for Indonesia argues that the region has to establish a positive and constructive cooperative relationship with the IMF to further develop the APT structure (Interview, April 2012). This assertion implies that the involvement of the IMF should concur with the development of APT financial cooperation. The assertion could also be perceived as suggesting that the Japanese disagreed with any attempts by APT member countries to decelerate dramatically IMF's role in the region. Jayasuriya (2008) argues that state actors in core regional states often provide a pathway through which regional governance is linked to institutions of global governance. Therefore, in the short term, APT financial cooperation will likely still be determined by an international institution, such as the IMF.

Broadening Participation

The CMIM was initiated by state actors in response to possible future financial crises. Nonetheless, the participation of non-state actors has also emerged. Jayasuriya (2003), Jones (2010) and Hameiri (2009) argue that regulatory regionalism underlines the importance of the roles and relations between state and non-state actors in shaping regional governance. In this respect, the CMIM has become the medium for state and non-state actors in shaping regional governance for liquidity support arrangement.

Non-state actors in particular have played significant roles in assisting policymakers to develop APT regional liquidity support. In the initial development of the Chiang Mai Initiative (CMI), several research institutes, such as the Institute for International Monetary Affairs (IIMA), the Korea Institute for International Economic Policy (KIEP) and Danareksa Research Institute (DRI), made concrete proposals on institutional designs for liquidity assistance and policy dialogue (Yoshimatsu 2014, p. 74). The suggestions and recommendations of research institutes have also contributed to shape CMI into a multilateral institution.

The complexity of financial issues has led to the further involvement of non-state actors in CMIM processes. While state agencies have economists and dedicated staff, the professional insights and experiences of non-state actors in dealing with financial affairs were needed to enhance regional initiatives. A broad range of financial complexities has led organisations, such as international rating agencies or accountancy standards organisations, to direct involvement in regional or global governance (Jayasuriya 2004). Therefore, in addition to APT member countries, regional bodies and IFIs, such as the ADB and IMF, were also invited to join CMIM processes. Having the ADB and IMF during the ERPD sessions facilitated an exchange of views not only among APT member countries, but also between state agencies and non-state actors.

Further, the non-state actors have also been involved in the early development of the CMIM surveillance unit. Before the independent surveillance unit was established, the APT finance ministers agreed to have an interim surveillance unit in place, under the control of ADB and the ASEAN Secretariat (ASEC). While this role was temporary, the involvement of the interim surveillance unit reflects another crucial role of non-state actors for the development of regional surveillance mechanisms.

De-politicising Regional Assistance

CMIM governance has led to de-politicisation for two reasons. First, the establishment of AMRO, as a surveillance unit of CMIM, has marked the de-contextualisation of regional institutions from economic authorities. As an independent regional surveillance unit, AMRO is expected to provide analysis and recommendation that is more 'responsible' to the people's interests, rather than to the economic power usually held by state authorities. In this regard, AMRO should reflect independence in any of its operations, for the sake of regional economic stability. One may question the way that AMRO personnel avoid their countries' interests. Grimes (2011) argues that it might be difficult to expect government-affiliated economists to be an individual who remains unconnected to the policy preferences of their home countries. This is a challenge for AMRO to prove to the public that it can work professionally and be independent. However, while the impartiality of AMRO has not been tested yet (as no party of CMIM has activated the swap facility), the existence of AMRO has already reflected the de-politicisation of APT regional initiatives on liquidity support assistance.

The second reason is that the decision-making procedures of CMIM have, more or less, reduced the power of financial authorities within APT member countries to determine the provision of liquidity support assistance. The rigid steps of CMIM decision-making processes, including conducting a surveillance process for macroeconomic and relevant conditions, indicate the efforts of APT member countries to create a more rule-based form of governance (for regional crisis counter mechanism), rather than heightening the discretion of policy makers to deal with such economic shocks. In relation to this, the introduction of voting mechanisms has also, to some extent, contributed to reducing the power of financial authorities in CMIM decision-making processes, by securing the majority of voices to determine a decision. This process is absent if a consensus mechanism is applied. This phenomenon is different from the provision of liquidity support assistance under a bilateral commitment that is usually disbursed based on the discretion of financial authorities, after gaining approval from the head of state.

FULLY SUPPORTING THE CMIM

For Indonesia, deeper regional cooperation and integration offered potential benefits and opportunities. Especially in relation to finance, a former Indonesian finance minister emphasised that APT Cooperation has proven an important medium in its effective response to the global financial crisis and globalisation, through its regional self-help mechanism (Indrawati 2007). This outcome gives confidence to Indonesia to further support the CMIM.

Reaping Benefits for the Indonesian Economy

Over a decade after the Asian financial crisis, Indonesia has developed its economy to gain a better status. According to the World Bank (WB), as can be seen in Fig. 6.1, Indonesian gross domestic product (GDP) increased steadily from around US$140 billion in 1999 to US$846.83 billion in 2011, indicating a growth rate of 5.5 per cent on average during the same period. This data points to Indonesia's expanding economy, which reveals its growing economic size. In addition, the 2012 IMF Article IV consultation also suggests that Indonesia's economy has performed impressively, as reflected in the sharp decline in both the inflation rate and public debt, to under 25 per cent of GDP (IMF 2012). These overall improvements in economic performance mean that Indonesia has successfully developed resilience to the global financial crisis, particularly, in relation to high domestic demand.

Notwithstanding its success in surviving the crises, Indonesia still often experienced pressures, especially from investment, export and

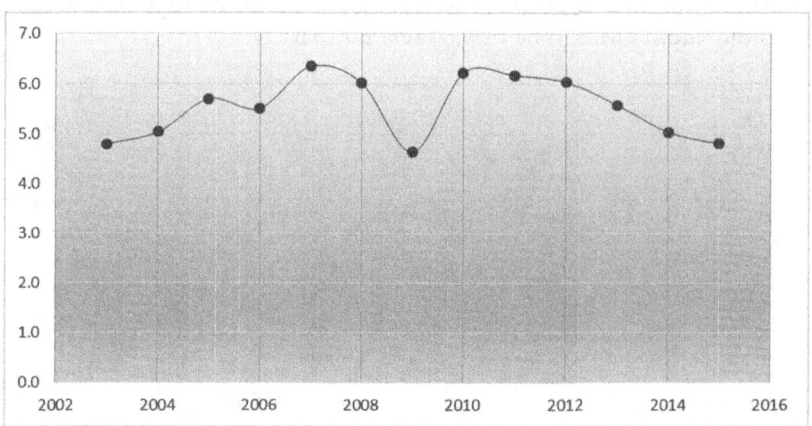

Fig. 6.1 Indonesian GDP. Source: Generated from World Bank's *World Development Indicators* (WB 2013)

consumption. A historical lesson was the difficulties experienced by the Indonesian Stock Exchange (IDX) during 2008, following the decline of other stock markets. As illustrated in Fig. 6.2, the Jakarta Composite Index (JCI) went down by up to 1300 basis points by December 2008, following a sharp decline in the Dow Jones.

Moreover, it is reported that more than 67 per cent of investors in the Indonesian stock market are foreigners (Krismantari 2009). While foreign investors contribute to Indonesia's portfolio capital, the big portion of foreign investors can become quite critical if they withdraw their portfolio investments from the Indonesian Stock Exchange (IDX) simultaneously. The sudden withdrawal of foreign capital from Indonesia is always possible, as Indonesia—as an emerging market—is more risky than developed markets (Marulitua 2008).

The establishment of CMIM has been perceived positively by Indonesian authorities as an additional means to deal with any future financial crisis. A high-ranking official of BI perceived the establishment of CMIM as a 'second line of defence' (Interview, April 2012). For the official, the main support should be from the country's own resources, usually understood to make available from Indonesia's international reserves. This perspective reflected the Indonesian principle that self-reliance on its own capacity was still the best option, rather than relying on foreign supports. From a broader perspective, a middle-ranking official of the IMOF, who was in charge in the APT process, also admitted that CMIM represented an important initiative to protect the nation, as well as the region, from wide economic fluctuations. The official related that:

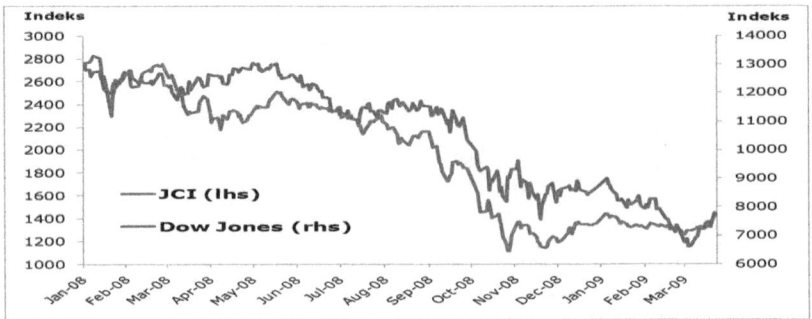

Fig. 6.2   Indonesian stock market. Source: Generated from Bloomberg <www.bloomberg.com> (2013)

Learning from the development of global economy, from the 1997/1998 Asian economic crisis to recent economic crisis, we recognise that CMIM is really important to protect individual country and the region from the economic fluctuation. (Interview, April 2012)

This response suggests that the CMIM matters for domestic and regional stability. As the region becomes more integrated in terms of the economy, any domestic economic problems will flow to other countries. Under an integrated and open economic regime, risks from external economic shocks are increasing. The Asian financial crisis has provided a lesson learnt, in which the seed of a crisis was initially discovered in Thailand and spread quickly to its neighbours, including Indonesia.

Besides the economic benefits of dealing with short-term liquidity problems, the CMIM has also offered Indonesia an opportunity to demonstrate its economic strength. In turn, this means that potentially Indonesia can be a CMIM providing party. As presented in Fig. 6.3, Indonesia's foreign reserve had experienced a positive trend from October 2008 to October 2012. With its robust international reserves, Indonesia sent a message to the market that its economy was restored and strong enough to assist other countries, particularly those ASEAN new member states, in dealing with short-term liquidity problems.

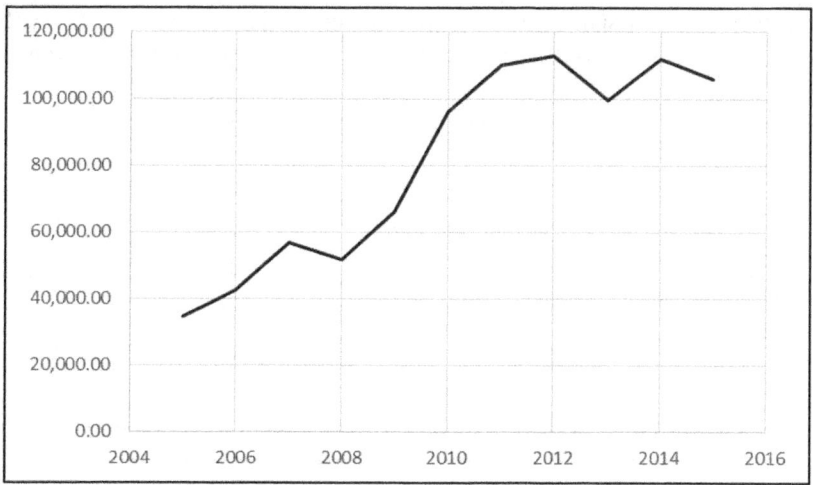

Fig. 6.3 Indonesian foreign reserves (in million US$). Source: Generated from BI official website <www.bi.go.id> (2016)

Indonesia's contribution to CMIM can be viewed as a significant effort by the Indonesian government to realise the formation of a regional self-help mechanism. This is despite it creating an additional burden for Indonesian foreign reserves. In the early establishment of CMIM, the Indonesian foreign reserves amounted to approximately US$64.5 billion. If Indonesia's initial contribution to the CMIM was US$4.77 billion, then it would mean that Indonesia's contribution would represent approximately eight per cent of Indonesia's foreign reserves. As illustrated in Fig. 6.4, compared to the other ASEAN-5 members (Singapore, Thailand, Malaysia, Philippines), the level of Indonesian foreign reserves during the establishment of CMIM was ranked at number four, slightly higher than the Philippines. In this case, Indonesia boldly equalled that of Singapore, Thailand and Malaysia in CMIM individual contributions, although the level of its international reserve was lower than the three other ASEAN-5 countries.[6]

In addition, as a victim of the IMF's inaccurate economic formula applied during the Asian financial crisis, the Indonesian government also views CMIM as a tool to reform the IMF as an existing international support fund institution (Rahmi 2009). A former IMOF deputy minister argues that the IMF often applies double standards in evaluating developing countries' economic conditions, which limits the region's countries access to IMF financial assistance (Abimanyu 2011, p. 231). Developing countries in the Asian region often received unfair assessments from the IMF, even if these countries have made efforts to transform and reform

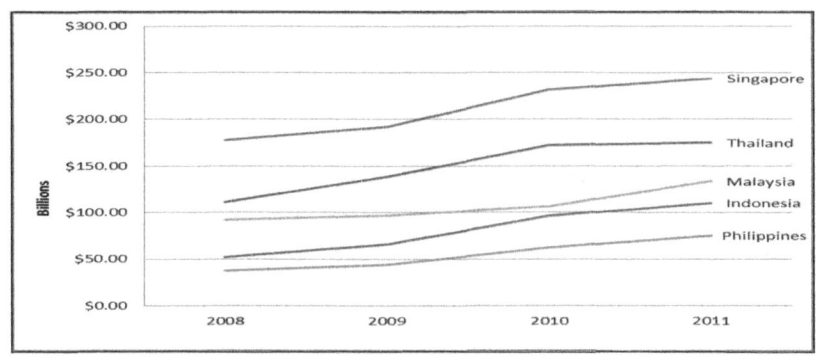

Fig. 6.4 ASEAN-5 foreign reserves. Source: Generated from World Bank's *World Development Indicators* (WB 2013)

many areas of their economies. By joining the CMIM, Indonesia sent a strong message to the IMF that it intended to reduce its dependency on IMF facilities, by being more reliant on regional strengths.

Nonetheless, the economic benefits of CMIM for Indonesia remain vague. With its current contribution to CMIM, Indonesia is able to purchase up to US$22.75 billion.[7] This amount is larger than for any previous maximum swap for Indonesia, in which Indonesia had lower borrowing limits compared to the limits of its Bilateral Swap Arrangements (BSAs) (Kawai 2010, p. 53). However, this swap amount is relatively small compared to the amount of Indonesia's national debt during the Asian financial crisis; this was approximately US$135 billion (Saparini 2009, p. 4). With its negative regard for the IMF, it is likely that Indonesia will not withdraw the maximum borrowing amount, to avoid any IMF programmes—that entails in CMIM-linked portion—that may potentially be opposed by its own public. In other words, Indonesia may only withdraw up to US$6.8 billion, or 30 per cent of its maximum borrowing limit. If this scenario is taken by the Indonesian government, the real potential swap of CMIM for Indonesia is basically smaller than the amount provided by the IMF to support Indonesia in dealing with Asian financial crisis in 1998. At that time, Indonesia received US$20 billion. The amount of the Indonesian potential swap is also smaller compared to the value of reserves, amounting to US$10 billion, which Indonesia had used to stabilise its currency during the global financial crisis in 2008 (Abimanyu 2011, p. 254).

A middle-ranking official of the IMOF agreed that the economic benefits of CMIM remained vague and difficult to quantify. However, the official argued that as the main goal of the CMIM initiative is to maintain economic stability, any amount of financial assistance was important. The official suggested that:

> If we talk about crisis, any amount [of financial assistance] matters and significant in limited liquidity condition. Beyond that, [liquidity shortage] is about psychological matter, meaning that state and region should be aware towards [crisis] that perhaps cannot be predicted. [In this regard], Indonesia is trying to equip its economy by making bilateral and multi-lateral swap [arrangements to show] that Indonesia is ready. (Interview, April 2012)

Indonesia may not gain any direct economic benefit from CMIM, due to the limited size of the available funds. However, the CMIM has the potential to boost market confidence and create positive perceptions in the eyes of investors (Nemoto and Nakagawa 2013). Market stability is often disturbed by misperceptions and low market confidence in a government's own capacity to stabilise its domestic market. Therefore, market players always seek assurances to avoid capital loss. In this respect, the CMIM is expected to provide reassurance for market players that the Indonesian financial authorities have alternative support in place for any future economic shocks. By joining the CMIM, Indonesia also demonstrates to market players that it has additional alternative source of funds to maintain its international reserves and boost market confidence in the midst of global uncertainties. Strong market confidence is expected to generate increased capital inflow and investment to Indonesia (Dalla 2012, p. 9).

The intensity of Indonesia's support for CMIM is reflected in the way Indonesia has strengthened the size of CMIM's pooling fund. Indonesian positive stance towards the doubling of CMIM's pooled funds, from US$120 billion to US$240 billion, was a significant indicator of the country's strong support. Indonesia assumed that the maximum drawing limit of CMIM was insufficient to deal with any future financial crisis (Indrawati 2008). In this context, the APT member countries, particularly from the ASEAN bloc, generally need greater liquidity support, as they mostly have weak economic status.

The idea of establishing a larger funding base also catalysed Indonesia's insistence on increasing the IMF's de-linked portion. BI reportedly proposed to increase the de-linked portion up to 100 per cent (interview with a low-ranking official at Japanese Ministry of Finance (JMOF), May 2012). In this respect, Indonesia expected that CMIM's liquidity support funds could be fully accessed, without the imposition of any IMF conditions. To bring this idea to fruition, Indonesia sought the support of Japan, through Japan's more powerful voice in the APT financial cooperation (Interview with a high-ranking official of BI, May 2012). Eventually, Indonesia successfully convinced its Japanese colleagues, even though Japan did not embrace the proposal in its entirety. Japan's backing of Indonesia's idea to increase the IMF de-linked portion took place in the context of a gradual agreement process. The approach taken by Japan was from its position as potential creditor, who naturally did not want to lose its international reserve easily, but at the same time also understood the importance of CMIM for countries like Indonesia.

As it turned out, not all members of APT financial cooperation agreed to the idea of increasing the IMF de-linked portion. Initially, China, Singapore and Brunei opposed the proposal. A low-ranking official from

JMOF argued that China's and Singapore's opposition to the initial proposal was due to their self-confident as potential creditors within CMIM processes, and that they were unlikely to activate CMIM's swap facility (Interview, May 2012). For both countries, opposing the proposal would also reduce the possible risks of losing their funds under CMIM's less developed functions and operations. By rejecting the idea of increasing the IMF de-linked portion, China in particular implicitly encouraged a potential swap requesting party to seek financial assistance from the IMF—in which China has deposited a larger contribution. In a similar vein, Rathus (2011, p. 124) argues that Chinese efforts to keep the IMF under CMIM governance—by way of retaining a larger IMF-linked portion—are intended to limit Japan's ability to lead the regional cooperation. If the IMF has no influence in the operations of the mechanism, then this would mean the US would also be voiceless. Consequently, Japan would take full control of the CMIM. On another front, Singapore's stance was in opposition to that of Indonesia's and the other ASEAN member states', who posited themselves as potential recipients of CMIM due to their weaker economic status. Singapore's already significant accumulation of foreign exchange reserves meant that Singapore was likely to have little enthusiasm for the progress of CMIM (Amyx 2004, p. 100).

Limited Participation of Non-state Actors

Indonesia's responses to CMIM as a regional pooling fund have predominantly come from state institutions. In this case, IMOF and BI became the main actors in dealing with CMIM regional governance. This observation supports Komori's (2009, p. 338) summation, and that of Murray (2010, p. 313), who both find that governments remain primary actors in the new East Asia and Asia-Pacific region regional architecture. Following MacDonald and Woolcock's (2007, p. 64) classification of state actor, the Indonesian state actors controlling CMIM process are classified as members of the government executive branch including ministries, bureaucracies and independent regulatory agencies.

The contribution of Indonesian non-state actors to CMIM-related activities was limited. Although Indonesian economists within national research institutes have published opinion pieces in the public media, such publicity has not directly influenced the internal regulatory transformation aimed at facilitating CMIM governance. The limited participation of Indonesian non-state actors in CMIM processes at a national level demonstrates that for specific financial issues, the role of state actors is irreplaceable.

There are two important factors that shape the dominant roles of Indonesian state actors in CMIM processes. The first relates to sovereignty matters. As economic policies are at the core of sovereignty, public actors, including state and monetary authorities, are the most relevant stakeholders (Blizkovsky 2013, p. 79). The integrity of state sovereignty is understood as the main factor that pressures Indonesian financial authorities to adopt all CMIM's processes. As the adequacy and fluctuation of short-term liquidity are sensitive factors to consider in national stability, the state should be able to fully control the management of foreign reserves. A lesson learnt from the Asian financial crisis is that a sharp decline in national foreign reserves would trigger international intervention in Indonesia. However, any international intervention poses a threat and, as such, may make state sovereignty more vulnerable. Ravenhill (2002, p. 189) argues that international monetary cooperation poses more of a threat to sovereignty than does trade integration.

The demand for a strong state presence in dealing with foreign reserve issues rises as Indonesian non-state actors are assumed to be pivotal players in risking the Indonesian economy. During the Asian financial crisis, private firms—considered as non-state actors—were regarded as having contributed to the loss of Indonesia's foreign reserves, due to their large foreign debt levels (Wie 2012, p. 117). Therefore, the Indonesian government took foreign reserves management as a serious policy issue. For instance, in the wake of the Asian financial crisis, BI was sidelined from the executive power and given a mandate to exclusively manage Indonesian international reserves. The other Indonesian state bodies had no jurisdiction over international reserves. The separation of BI from the executive administration of the Indonesian government was expected to protect the professionalism and independence of the Indonesian monetary authority, and insulate international reserves from any intervention and abuse of power from any parties, including from the Indonesian president or other influential politicians (McLeod 1999). Since then, the BI held more decisive power to shape and determine particular agendas related to the transformation of the national space in response to any international cooperation related to foreign reserve management, including the CMIM.

The second factor that determines the domination of Indonesian state actors in the CMIM is related to the nature of confidentiality within CMIM processes. From its establishment to the present, the CMIM has been discussed behind 'closed doors' among APT member countries. At the national level, the confidentiality of the CMIM was secured to restrict non-state actor involvement in CMIM development. There was, however, no documentary evidence that identified the involvement of Indonesian non-state actors in CMIM preparatory consultations. This situation is consistent with a previous study conducted by Chandra and Hanim (2004) on the responses of Indonesian non-state actors to forms of cooperation related to ASEAN. As one finding, Chandra revealed that Indonesian non-state actors felt they had been excluded from many ASEAN initiatives, due to their limited access to relevant documents and current information (Chandra and Hanim 2004, p. 165). Regarding the CMIM, the IMOF and BI have provided the public with information related to the progress of CMIM's development, through their websites and the mass media. However, this information comprised only general aspects of CMIM negotiation processes, while the initiative's technical arrangements remained confidential.

National Coordination Networks

Operationally, Indonesian involvement in CMIM processes was represented by the IMOF and BI. While the IMOF and BI operated as independent bodies, they have agreed to exercise their mandates and present a unilateral stance when dealing with CMIM's technical negotiations. A participating BI official realised that, although BI was an independent body under Indonesian administrative structures, it could not fully represent Indonesia as a nation in CMIM processes. A political aspect put the Indonesian finance minister in the front line for regional cooperation (interview with a high-ranking official of BI, April 2012). In this respect, BI followed the IMOF's policy on CMIM, on the basis of its functions with international monetary management. This arrangement implies another sign of collaborative processes between the regulatory bodies involved in financial regionalism.

At the technical level, Indonesian participation in APT financial cooperation was managed by the Fiscal Policy Office (FPO/*Badan Kebijakan Fiskal*) of the IMOF and the International Directorate of BI. Figure 6.5 illustrates that under the FPO, issues concerning the CMIM's operations form part of the function of the Centre for Bilateral and Regional Policy (CBRP/*Pusat Kebijakan Regional dan Bilateral*). In general, these functions encompass the responsibility to formulate, analyse and evaluate any

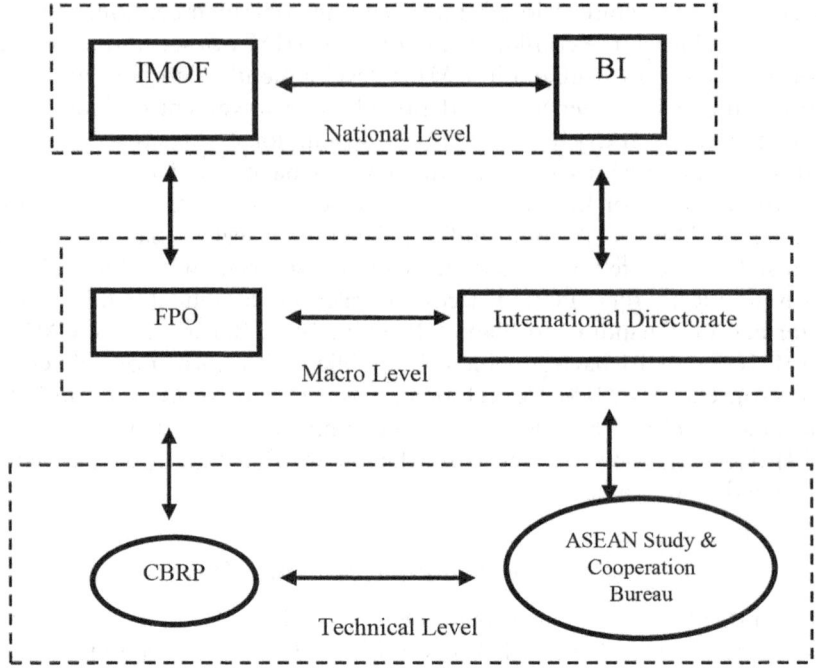

Fig. 6.5 Indonesian policy coordination network regarding CMIM. Source: Author's visualisation

policies related to bilateral and regional cooperation, including those that emerge from the APT financial cooperation. Meanwhile, within the BI International Directorate, CMIM-related issues are managed by the ASEAN Study and Cooperation Bureau (*Biro Kerjasama dan Studi ASEAN*).

The centre consisted of four divisions (*bidang*), and 16 sub-divisions (*sub-bidang*). As such, APT financial issues were under the sub-division of APT and other forums (*sub-bidang Forum APT dan Lainnya*). Within the FPO, CMIM issues were managed solely by the head of the APT and other forum sub-divisions. At the same time, this sub-division had responsibility to manage other APT initiatives such as ABMI and the research group. This arrangement was somewhat ironic, considering the importance of the regional pooling fund for Indonesia as a potential borrower of these funds. In comparison, a low-ranking JMOF official had the sole responsibility for CMIM matters, while for other issues of APT financial initiatives, other officials would take responsibility (interview with a low-ranking official of JMOF, May 2012). This comparison of personnel in charge, between Indonesia and Japan, indicates how the two countries differ in the level of priority they assign to APT financial cooperation. This also reflects how emerging and advanced countries view the significance of such regional initiatives.

Regarding the CMIM, operational policy coordination took place through formal meetings between the IMOF and BI. Although there was no regular meeting schedule in place, both institutions met when a relevant issue arose, and prior to upcoming CMIM meetings. As such, policy coordination between these two bodies was more reactive in style, rather than a well-planned strategic approach. A high-ranking official of BI related that policy coordination activities between BI and the IMOF were more frequently triggered by technical aspects (Interview, April 2012). This brief overview of the nature of IMOF-BI policy coordination on CMIM illustrates that this function is more focused on technical elements, rather than a long-term strategic expectation of the regional pooling fund. Although the synergy between the IMOF and BI was still related to such technical aspects, this arrangement has shown a consistency with the concept of regulatory regionalism as entailing collaboration among national governance bodies.

Further, the IMOF and BI also worked closely to coordinate regional surveillance processes, particularly when gathering fiscal and monetary macroeconomic data. The IMOF managed fiscal data, while BI took responsibility for managing monetary data. In the CMIM context, the policy coordination of surveillance processes resulted from the CMIM agreement that mandated national authorities to coordinate the sharing of information/data with AMRO as the regional surveillance unit. In this respect, policy coordination among surveillance units, at any level, in the form of information production and exchange, makes a significant contribution to the APT framework (Nesadurai 2009, p. 369).

The collaboration between the IMOF and BI on economic surveillance is not new. The collaboration has resulted in the National Surveillance Unit (NSU). This unit was initially established with the intention of responding to the ASP—a process deemed necessary to facilitate collaborative action between the ASEC's Macroeconomic Surveillance Unit and the surveillance contact person, in their monitoring of macroeconomic and financial development in ASEAN member country states (Anas and Atje 2005, p. 7).

The Indonesian NSU consisted of two entities under the IMOF and BI. The entity under the IMOF has dealt with fiscal and real sector developments, while at BI the entity was in charge of monetary and banking sector developments (Anas and Atje 2005, p. 16). The Indonesian NSU was established slowly, as the ASP was inaugurated in 1998. A lack of human resource capacity and infrastructure were probably the major reasons for the delay. In Indonesia, the NSU was not a dedicated institution with a formal secretariat. Rather, it was a part of both the IMOF's and BI's surveillance functions. For a number of reasons, the interdependency between the Indonesian NSU and AMRO was indispensable, as the operation of AMRO in producing regional macroeconomic analyses relied mainly on the provision of data from relevant institutions in APT member countries, including the Indonesian NSU. While AMRO can collect data from any resources, the provision of relevant data from related countries is more reliable (Siregar and Chabchitrchaidol 2013). Indonesia was committed to providing AMRO with timely and valid data, to develop more effective surveillance mechanism. This commitment was demonstrated during AMRO's 'country consultation' visit, in which the IMOF and BI jointly prepared the materials requested by AMRO. An interviewee of the IMOF explains:

> We coordinate with BI in response to any information requested by AMRO. Prior to their visit, we ask the AMRO staff about what they need, so that when they visit us, we are already well prepared (with the requested data). (Interview with a middle-ranking official of FPO, April 2012)

The AMRO's country consultation visit was a pivotal occasion, as it facilitated the exchange of information accounts of experience, in relation to economic policy and development. In this case, the country consultation facilitated discussion on economic and financial policies, as well as risks between AMRO economists, IMOF and BI officials. Such information gathering meant that Indonesia could benefit from the synergies between regional bodies and NSUs.

The tight collaboration developed by AMRO and the Indonesian NSU presents a concern regarding an aspect of regulatory regionalism, on how the government and regional organisations promote cross-border policy coordination. With AMRO, such collaboration is needed to build an effective regional monitoring mechanism, while for Indonesian state agencies, policy coordination with AMRO enables domestic awareness of potential crises that may flag the need for regional action. The AMRO-Indonesian NSU collaboration—through country consultation—facilitates peer review and to some degree peer pressure processes that place regional policies within the Indonesian policy-making area. Jayasuriya (2008, p. 26) refers this process as facilitating the creation of a governance regional space within national policy-making apparatus.

Internal Transformation and De-Politicisation

In order to integrate CMIM agreements into the Indonesian regulatory framework, Indonesian financial authorities mainly transform Indonesian national regulatory frameworks through 'hard law'—using existing governmental power. In CMIM's case, hard law worked through the acceptance process of CMIM agreement. Indonesia accepted the CMIM by signing the Articles of Agreement of CMIM in 2009.

The acceptance was processed by the IMOF, along with BI. As the financial and monetary authorities were legally separated bodies in Indonesia, the legal commitment of the leaders of these two authorities was needed. In practice, the signatures of both the Indonesian finance minister and the governor of BI were required to approve the CMIM agreement. The finance minister's approval was required, as this position held the power in all matters relating to managing the national financial sector. The approval of the BI governor was required, as the governor had the authority to manage Indonesia's international reserves. Sri Mulyani Indrawati, the former Indonesian finance minister, along with Darmin Nasution, the acting governor of BI at that time, signed the CMIM agreement in late December 2009. In August 2010, the adjustment of the Philippines' contribution to CMIM eventually led to contribution adjustments for all other ASEAN member countries. Indonesia's finance minister, Agus D.W. Martowardojo, and BI governor, Darmin Nasution, authorised the amendment of the CMIM agreement.[8]

In the case of Indonesia, the finance minister always signed the CMIM agreement after the BI governor signed it. The sequence of the CMIM agreement signatory process, which sees the governor of BI signing the agreement prior to the Indonesian finance minister, suggests that the *de-politicisation* of BI has affected the internal regulatory transformation processes within Indonesia's jurisdiction. The independence of BI has made the Indonesian central bank psychologically no longer subordinate to the IMOF, so that it was relatively straightforward for the leader of BI to comply with the governance requirements of the regional initiative. The high confidence demonstrated by BI in the process of bringing the CMIM agreement into force was likely due to its exclusive power to manage Indonesian foreign reserves alone. In this process, either the IMOF or Indonesian parliament did not present any intervention to BI. As such, the *de-politicisation* of financial authorities has contributed to ease the implementation of legal procedures.

Further, the exchange of signatory pages between Indonesia and other APT member countries—to bring the CMIM agreement into force—demonstrates a straightforward legal process for such international agreement. In this process, the Indonesian financial authorities did not require an endorsement from either the Indonesian president or parliament. The Indonesian financial authorities neither sought a presidential decree nor a new law to make the CMIM agreement legally effective.

According to Law No. 24/2000 on International Agreement (*Perjanjian Internasional*), such international agreements need to be legalised through Indonesian law, or by presidential decree, to ratify the agreement within Indonesia's judiciary. The six broad groupings related to specific areas of international agreements required to be legally endorsed by the DPR are (i) politics, peace, defence, and national security; (ii) geographical change or determination of Indonesian borders; (iii) national sovereignty; (iv) human rights and environment; (v) formation of new legal principles; and (vi) foreign loans and grants (Article 10, Law No. 24/2000). Some other areas of international agreements only need endorsement by presidential decree. In this case, the legal process is simpler, as it merely proceeds within the executive side. The need for legalisation stands in contrast to general mechanisms of regulatory regionalism that more usually operate through 'soft law' (Jayasuriya 2008, p. 25). However, Jayasuriya clarifies that the use of hard law, such as ratification, is still accepted (personal correspondence, 13 July 2011). For him, ratification is an important step towards regulatory regionalism, which establishes the modes and standards through which the agreement is given effect.

The smooth legal transformation to bring the CMIM agreement into Indonesia's jurisdiction is an intriguing case for Indonesia. It occurred in the absence of a specific regulation that clearly determined or regulated whether currency swaps, as a basis of CMIM operations, were categorised as a loan or not. However, it was found that, regardless of whether the currency swap should be categorised as a loan or not, all relevant laws and regulations supported the option that a new law or presidential decree was not necessarily required to bring CMIM governance into Indonesia's jurisdiction.

According to Article 10, Law No. 24/2000, foreign loans and/or grants sought by the Indonesian government require parliamentary approval. In this case, the specific legal basis of any foreign loans lies within Law No. 1/2004, related to state treasury matters (*Perbendaharaan Negara*). Operationally, the procedures for obtaining foreign loans are regulated by Government Regulation No. 10/2011 on Procedure on Obtaining Foreign Loan and Receiving Grant (*Tata Cara Pengadaan Pinjaman Luar Negeri dan Penerimaan Hibah*). However, Government Regulation No. 10/2011 only covers foreign loans intended for government purposes (including central and local governments, as well as state-owned enterprises), such as for financing the state budget, managing the debt portfolio or financing national institutions' priority activities. Purposes other than those related to liquidity or international reserves come under the authority of BI. Under the law, BI has a right to seek foreign loans to maintain international reserves (Point 3, Article 13, Law No. 23/1999 related to BI). To do so, BI does not need to proceed through a ratification process that would entail the release of a new law or a presidential decree. Therefore, none of these legal bases are applicable to determine whether the CMIM needs a law or a presidential decree to bring the CMIM agreement into force.

Further, if a swap for liquidity purposes is not categorised as loan, then it does not need parliamentary approval, as the swap lies outside the earlier identified six broad groupings of international cooperation areas that require DPR approval. In this regard, a swap can be categorised as a means by which international reserves can be managed. In practice, BI can maintain international reserves through selling, purchasing or allocating its reserves, such as gold and securities, and through seeking foreign loans. All activities related to maintaining international reserves require neither parliamentary approval nor a presidential decree.

To ensure the legal process to accommodate CMIM (that was already taking place with BI), the IMOF coordinated with two other relevant authorities, the Indonesian Ministry of Foreign Affairs (IMOFA) and the Indonesian Ministry of Law and Human Rights (IMOLHR/*Kementerian Hukum dan Hak Asasi Manusia*). It was anticipated that the IMOFA would support the IMOF in dealing with such diplomatic processes, while the IMOLHR was expected to provide legal advice should Indonesia require financial assistance from the CMIM during financial crises.

The involvement of the IMOLHR in the CMIM demonstrates a closer scrutiny of the legalities of the proposed financial assistance, to limit the possibility of conflicts of interest, inconsistencies in interpretation of guidelines and procedures, and domestic law violations. This assurance will also give higher confidence to swap providing countries regarding particular actions. For the Indonesian authorities, by seeking legal advice in advance, the possibility of legal disputes arising in the management of future financial crises—as happened during the last economic shock—could be reduced.

Indonesian financial authorities experienced legal disputes that were mired in economic and political controversies during the 1997/1998 Asian financial crisis and the 2008/2009 global financial crisis. The Indonesia central bank's provision of liquidity support, known as *Bantuan Likuiditas Bank Indonesia* (BLBI), was used to defend the Indonesian banking sector from collapse amidst the Asian financial crisis. The general opinion in Indonesia viewed the provision of BLBI during the Asian financial crisis as unlawful, allegedly involving corruption. In contrast, the former governor of BI, who was in the administration during that period, insisted that the provision of BLBI was legally possible under Article 32 (Point 3) of the Central Bank Act of 1968 and President Instruction on 3 September 1997 (Djiwandono 2004, p. 67).

A similar situation occurred in the midst of the global financial crisis, when Indonesian financial authorities needed to manage the insolvent *Century Bank*, later renamed as *Mutiara Bank*. In order to avoid a flow-on systemic effect of the Century Bank's collapse to the Indonesian financial sector, the financial authorities—consisting of the Indonesian finance minister, the governor of BI and the head of the Indonesia Deposit Insurance Corporation (*Lembaga Penjamin Simpanan*/LPS)—decided to inject IDR 6.7 trillion into the bank, in the form of BI's temporary equity participation (Taufik 2009). In this case, although the authorities claimed that they implemented the policy based on economic practices and guided by existing legal procedures, the decision led to legal and political disputes. The minister of finance was compelled to step down from her office, even though, to date, none of the policy makers related to this case have been found guilty of any wrongdoing.

In addition to the hard law process, the national transformation to accommodate CMIM's governance was also conducted by Indonesian financial authorities through a soft law approach. In this regard, the Indonesian authorities posited CMIM as an alternative mechanism to counter crisis in its national crisis management protocol (CMP). The CMP was set by the IMOF, BI, LPS and Indonesian Financial Service Authority (*Otoritas Jasa Keuangan*/OJK), to provide guidance for the implementation of crisis prevention and mitigation measures nationally (Brodjonegoro 2012). Each of the relevant institutions set the CMP based on their mandate, functions and capacities. In practice, the CMP covered all aspects of the economic surveillance mechanism, including details of the methods used to exchange and share data, the sharing of economic-financial data, meetings among relevant institutions and decision-making processes <www.antaranews.com, 7 June 2012>. The CMP included guidelines for timing announcements to declare a crisis, or any indicators that lead to a crisis, or the end of a crisis. The CMP also contained particular tools or instruments that could be used to deal with the crisis. In the CMP, the CMIM was one of alternative instruments that can be used to manage the crisis.

The establishment of the CMP was another sign of the de-politicisation of Indonesia's economic policy-making processes, especially through the creation of a rule-based form of crisis mitigation mechanism. The CMP provided a framework that limited the power of financial authorities, especially the IMOF and BI, to deal with economic crises, while at the same time, it enhanced transparent governance, to avoid the misuse of power and moral hazards. The involvement of two independent financial authorities—LPS and OJK—in the CMP governance implicitly presented a new Indonesian approach in shaping crisis countermeasures.

In a regional context, the CMP was expected to accord with CMIM procedures. A high-ranking BI official stated that the CMP provided a warning mechanism that informed decision makers about how Indonesia might respond to countries that sought financial assistance or provide about alternative options to secure regional stability:

> The CMP includes how to operate surveillance mechanism, sharing of information, discussion among national institutions, and the decision making process. [It includes] whether we are in crisis, or in direction to crisis, or close to crisis; [and] what kind of tools [or] instruments we use to solve the problem. (Interview, April 2012)

Operationally, under the CMP, each financial authority formulated a set of crisis indicators intended to assess the level of urgency of a particular economic situation (BI 2011). In this regard, several CMP's functions have been parallel to CMIM governance. For instance, the CMIM standards and procedures, such as the requirement to maintain foreign reserves at a level equivalent to three months of imports and to maintain foreign reserves at a level equivalent to more than a three-month period of short-term debt, would be applied as indicators, defining the stresses on Indonesia's balance of payments. Overall, the alignment between the CMP and the CMIM was also expected to create better crisis mitigation processes between national and regional arrangements, which were specifically designed to include the implementation of systematic and simultaneous measures (Interview with a high-ranking official of BI 2012).

The alignment of Indonesian national safety measure with CMIM governance is another form of meta-governance in APT financial regionalism. In this case, CMIM standards operate within the Indonesian anti-crisis policy framework as an alternative measure. This is generally parallel with the notion of regulatory regionalism, in which the new governance works within the existing framework (Jayasuriya 2010, p. 106). In this respect, CMIM governance has already been existing at the regional, started to work in national level. Such parallels between governance at regional and national levels would facilitate the smooth implementation of agreed mechanisms and procedures among member countries.

The formal engagement of Indonesia in the CMIM has also positioned the country within a regional system of financial regulation that facilitated globalised governance of the economy. As the CMIM continues to adopt the rules of global financial governance, such as IMF governance on credit lines, governance in a global context has a presence within the Indonesian domestic regulatory framework (Saputro 2012). The adoption of IMF governance by the CMIM enabled the IMF to keep promoting its programmes to Indonesia even though a majority of Indonesian public objected to the Indonesian government's engagement with the IMF. This mode of governance eased the responsibility of Indonesian financial authorities to maintain alternative sources of financial assistance from international institutions, in the face of domestic public opposition towards the IMF.

To further analyse Indonesia's responses to APT financial regionalism, the following chapter examines the responses of Indonesian financial authorities to an ongoing APT regional initiative in the bond market. The four features of regulatory regionalism are also applied, to confirm the validity of regulatory regionalism as an alternative approach in examining national responses towards financial regionalism in East Asia.

Notes

1. *Company limited by guarantee* is a form of legal status for such associations and other non-profit organisations in Singapore. With this status, AMRO has full capacity to conduct any business or activity or enter into a transaction in the Singaporean jurisdiction boundary. This status was established by APT finance ministers to avoid administrative and legal procedures that could be taken to establish an international organisation status for AMRO, and to expedite the operation of AMRO as a regional surveillance institution.
2. Starting from 19 February 2016, AMRO status has become international organisation.
3. The purchasing multiple is a multiplier number used in the CMIM to determine the maximum drawing amount for each contributor. The bigger purchasing multiple, the more amount can be drawn from CMIM pooling funds.
4. While the agreement of the CMIM is not publicised openly, Sussangkarn (2012) and Hassdorf (2011) reveal that a two-thirds weighted majority vote is required to activate a swap.
5. 'Escape' is a term that refers to withdrawal from participation in providing fund for a requesting party. Any party that elects not to join in decision-making process due to a particular reason as set in the CMIM Agreement is named as the 'escaping party'.
6. The Philippines' initial contribution to the CMIM was a lower contribution than the other ASEAN-5 members, as its gross international reserve (GIR) has not yet reached US$45.5 billion.
7. The term 'purchase in swap mechanism' refers to the purchasing power of US$ by the swap requesting party, in exchange of its sale of local currency to the swap providing party.
8. Sri Mulyani Indrawati was expelled from her office on 20 May 2010. She was replaced by Agus Martowardojo, former CEO of Bank Mandiri, an Indonesian state-owned bank. Darmin Nasution was eventually appointed as governor of BI.

References

Abimanyu, A. (2011). *Refleksi dan gagasan fiskal (Reflection and ideas of fiscal policy)*. Jakarta: Gramedia Pustaka Utama.

Amyx, J. A. (2004). Political dynamics of regional financial cooperation in East Asia. *Japanese Economy, 32*(2), 98–112.

Anas, T., & Atje, R. (2005). *Economic surveillance and policy dialogue in East Asia: Making the ASEAN surveillance process a new*. Jakarta: Centre for Strategic and International Studies.

Anas, T., & Friawan, D. (2008). *The future role of the IMF: Asian perspectives.* Singapore: Friedrich Ebert Stiftung.

ASEAN Plus Three. (1999). *The joint statement on East Asia cooperation.* Manila: ASEAN Plus Three.

ASEAN Plus Three. (2010). *The joint ministerial statement of the 13th ASEAN Plus Three Finance Ministers' Meeting.* Tashkent: ASEAN Plus Three.

Azis, I. J. (2012). Asian financial safety nets? Don't hold your breath. *Public Policy Review, 8*(3), 321–340.

Bank Indonesia. (2011). Special topics. *Financial Stability Review*, No. 17, Jakarta.

Blizkovsky, P. (2013). Stakeholders of economic governance: European perspective. In S. Biscop (Ed.), *Studia Diplomatica LXVI-1* (pp. 71–92). Belgium: Academia Press.

Brodjonegoro, B. (2012). *Indonesian economic outlook and crisis management protocol mechanims.* Paper presented to "Seminar on ASEAN+3 Macroeconomic Research Office (AMRO): Strengthening AMRO for regional surveillance and regional financial arrangement", Jakarta, April 12.

Chandra, A. C., & Hanim, L. (2004). Indonesia's non-state actors in ASEAN: A new regionalism agenda for Southeast Asia? *Contemporary Southeast Asia, 26*(1), 155–174.

Dalla, I. (2012). *East Asian bond markets in 2020: Progress, prospects, and future challenges.* Working Paper.

Dieter, H. (2000). *Monetary regionalism: Regional integration without financial crises.* CSGR Working Paper, No. 52/00, pp. 1–27.

Djiwandono, J. S. (2004). Liquidity support to banks during Indonesia's financial crisis. *Bulletin of Indonesian Economic Studies, 40*(1), 59–75.

Grimes, W. W. (2011). The Asian monetary fund reborn? Implications of Chiang Mai Initiative Multilateralization. *Asia Policy,* (11), 79–104.

Hameiri, S. (2009). Beyond methodological nationalism, but where to for the study of regional governance? *Australian Journal of International Affairs, 63*(3), 430–441.

Hassdorf, W. (2011). Much ado about nothing? Chiang Mai Initiative Multilateralisation and East Asian exchange rate cooperation. *Ritsumeikan Annual Review of International Studies, 10,* 121–142.

Indrawati, S. M. (2007). *"Ten years after the crisis", emerging Asian regionalism.* Paper presented to the 40th Annual Asia Development Bank Meeting of the Board of Governors, Kyoto, Japan, May 2007.

Indrawati, S. M. (2008). *Perspectives on Asian economic integration and cooperation.* Emerging Asian regionalism book launch, 41st Asia Development Bank Annual Meeting of the Board of Governors, Madrid.

International Monetary Fund. (2012). *Indonesia: CPSS-IOSCO recommendations for securities settlement systems—The equity and corporate bonds securities settlement systems.* Washington, DC: International Monetary Fund.

Ito, T., Ogawa, E., Kawai, M., Kawasaki, K., & Murase, T. (2005). *Research papers and policy recommendations on economic surveillance and policy dialogue in East Asia*. Tokyo: Institute for International Monetary Affairs.

Jayasuriya, K. (2003). Introduction: Governing the Asia Pacific beyond the new regionalism. *Third World Quarterly, 24*(2), 199–215.

Jayasuriya, K. (2004). The new regulatory state and relational capacity. *Policy & Politics, 32*(4), 487–501.

Jayasuriya, K. (2008). Regionalising the state: Political topography of regulatory regionalism. *Contemporary Politics, 14*(1), 21–35.

Jayasuriya, K. (2010). The emergence of regulatory regionalism. *Global Asia, 4*(4), 102–107.

Jones, P. (2010). Regulatory regionalism and education: The European Union in central Asia. *Globalisation, Societies and Education, 8*(1), 59–85.

Kawai, M. (2010). *East Asian financial co-operation and the role of the ASEAN+3 Macroeconomic Research Office*. Bonn: German Development Institute.

Kawai, M., & Houser, C. (2007). *Evolving ASEAN+3 ERPD: Toward peer reviews or due diligence?* Tokyo: Asian Development Bank Institute.

Kawai, M., & Takagi, S. (2012). A proposal for exchange rate policy coordination in East Asia. In M. Kawai, P. J. Morgan, & S. Takagi (Eds.), *Monetary and currency policy management in Asia*. Cheltenham: Edward Elgar.

Komori, Y. (2009). Regional governance in East Asia and the Asia-Pacific. *East Asia: An International Quarterly, 26*(4), 321–341.

Krismantari, I. (2009). Foreign investor dominate Indonesia stock market. *Jakarta Post*. Retrieved September 29, 2014, from http://www.thejakartapost.com/news/2009/01/02/foreign-investors-dominate-indonesia-stock-market.html

MacDonald, K., & Woolcock, S. (2007). Non-State actors in economic diplomacy. In N. Bayne & S. Woocock (Eds.), *The new economic diplomacy* (pp. 77–103). London: Ashgate.

Marulitua, R. (2008). *Bursa efek Indonesia masih belum bergairah (Indonesian stock exchange not passionate yet)*. Kompas.com. Retrieved January 15, 2012, from http://bisniskeuangan.kompas.com/read/2008/10/30/07343536/Bursa.Efek.Indonesia.Masih.Belum.Bergairah

McLeod, R. H. (1999). Crisis-driven changes to the banking laws and regulations. *Bulletin of Indonesian Economic Studies, 35*(2), 147–154.

Moon, W. (2012). The G20 and Asian monetary cooperation. In J. Park, T. J. Pempel, & G. Xiao (Eds.), *Asian responses to the global financial crisis: The impact of regionalism and the role of the G20* (pp. 104–119). Cheltenham: Edward Elgar.

Murase, T. (2007). Economic surveillance in East Asia and prospective issues. *The Kyoto Economic Review, 76*(1), 67–101.

Murray, P. (2010). Comparative regional integration in the EU and East Asia: Moving beyond integration snobbery. *International Politics, 47*(3/4), 308–323.

Nemoto, Y., & Nakagawa, S. (2013). Regional financial cooperation in East Asia: Development and challenges. In T. Shiraishi & T. Kojima (Eds.), *ASEAN-Japan Relations* (pp. 184–206). Singapore: Institute of Southeast Asia Studies.

Nesadurai, H. S. (2009). Economic surveillance as a new mode of regional governance: Contested knowledge and the politics of risk management in East Asia. *Australian Journal of International Affairs, 63*(3), 361–375.

Rahmi, M. (2009). *Asean Plus 3 tinggalkan ketergantungan pada IMF (ASEAN Plus Three leaves its dependency on IMF)*. Retrieved December 19, 2011, from http://economy.okezone.com/read/2009/05/06/277/217032/asean-plus-3-tinggalkan-ketergantungan-pada-imf

Rathus, J. (2011). *Japan, China, and networked regionalism in East Asia, Critical Studies of the Asia Pacific Series*. Hampshire: Palgrave Macmillan.

Rathus, J. (2012). *ASEAN's Macroeconomic Research Office: Open for business*. East Asia Forum. Retrieved August 26, 2012, from http://www.eastasiaforum.org/2012/05/23/aseans-macroeconomic-research-office-open-for-business/

Ravenhill, J. (2002). A three Bloc World? The new East Asian regionalism. *International Relations of the Asia-Pacific, 2*, 167–195.

Samboh, E. (2011). ASEAN's AMRO may 'replace' IMF financial role. *The Jakarta Post*, April 8. Retrieved July 7, 2011, from http://www.thejakartapost.com/news/2011/04/08/asean%E2%80%99s-amro-may-%E2%80%98replace%E2%80%99-imf-financial-role.html

Saparini, H. (2009). *Policy response to overcome crisis: A lesson from Indonesian case*. Paper presented to International conference on "Re-regulating global finance in the light of the global crisis", Beijing, China.

Saputro, E. (2011). *Where to for ASEAN+3's macroeconomic research office?* East Asia Forum, June 18. Retrieved June 29, 2011, from http://www.eastasiaforum.org/2011/06/18/where-to-for-asean3-s-macroeconomic-research-office/

Saputro, E. (2012). *ASEAN+3 financial cooperation enters a new phase*. East Asia Forum, May 26. Retrieved November 26, 2013, from http://www.eastasiaforum.org/2012/05/26/asean3-financial-cooperation-enters-a-new-phase/

Siregar, M. (2011). Indonesia's structural reform. *The Indonesian Quarterly, 39*(3), 249–255.

Siregar, R., & Chabchitrchaidol, A. (2013). *Enhancing the effectiveness of CMIM and AMRO: Selected immediate challenges and tasks*. ADBI Working Paper 403. Tokyo: Asian Development Bank Institute.

Soesastro, H. (2006). Regional integration in East Asia: Achievements and future prospects. *Asian Economic Policy Review, 1*(2), 215–234.

Sussangkarn, C. (2010). *The Chiang Mai Initiative Multilateralisation: Origin, development, and outlook*. ADBI Working Paper Series, No. 230.

Sussangkarn, C. (2012). *Toward a functional Chiang Mai Initiative*. East Asia Forum. Retrieved July 26, 2013, from http://www.eastasiaforum.org/2012/05/15/toward-a-functional-chiang-mai-initiative/

Taufik, S. (2009). Kronologi aliran Rp 6,7 triliun ke Bank Century (The cronology of IDR 6.7 trillion injection to Century Bank). *Tempo Interaktif.* Retrieved February 12, 2014, from http://www.tempo.co/read/news/2009/11/14/063208353/Kronologi-Aliran-Rp-67-Triliun-ke-Bank-Century

Walter, A. (2008). *Governing finance: East Asia's adoption of international standards, Cornell Studies in Money.* Ithaca: Cornell University Press.

World Development Indicators. (2013). Washington, DC: World Bank.

Wie, T. K. (2012). *Indonesia's economy since independence.* Singapore: Institute of Southeast Asian Studies.

Yoshimatsu, H. (2014). *Comparing institution-building in East Asia: Power politics, governance, and critical junctures.* Palgrave Macmillan.

CHAPTER 7

Indonesia and the ABMI

Despite its progress on developing the technical and operational elements of bond markets, Asian Bond Market Initiatives (ABMI) has shaped a new regional governance in financial cooperation. The new governance includes changes in existing bond market regulations and best practices that entail collaborative action between regulators and other parties within domestic bond markets. Such collaboration has also created a complex policy network in the region that has led to various reactions from member countries.

The central objective of this chapter is to delve deeper into Indonesia's responses to ASEAN Plus Three (APT) bond market initiatives, in the light of recent empirical developments within the Indonesian bond market. In this regard, the regulatory regionalism approach provides a way to understand the involvement of Indonesian state and non-state actors in the regional bond market development. It also helps to disentangle the policy coordination between Indonesian bond market-related authorities, as well as policy coordination between Indonesian state agencies and non-state actors in the bond market. In particular, the regulatory regionalism approach also assists in analysing the reactions of Indonesian financial authorities towards ABMI's project on standardisation.

In ABMI, while state agencies remain primary actors in negotiation processes, there is a growing participation of non-state actors. The participation of market players, for instance, is increasingly essential, as they

© The Author(s) 2017
E. Saputro, *Indonesia and ASEAN Plus Three Financial Cooperation*,
DOI 10.1007/978-981-10-3029-1_7

hold first-hand experiences of market operations. Capling and Low (2010, p. 5) argue that most governments lack both the research capacity and commercial intelligence; thus, governments often depend on the private sector for market information.

The participation of market players in addition to state agencies in the development of ABMI has also stimulated the establishment of policy coordination mechanisms that comprised state and non-state actors at national and regional levels. In this respect, the policy coordination process between state and non-state actors is dynamic, as both actors understandably have similar and different objectives and interests. However, the national policy coordination in response to ABMI has not been examined in detail.

With regard to standardisation, ABMI attempted to foster the integration of bond markets in the region through a regional standard-setting project on market practices and harmonisation of regulations. ABMI particularly promoted the establishment of common bond market standards, to facilitate the formation of regional benchmarks. It also encouraged APT member countries to harmonise bond market regulations, to minimise regulatory gaps and to limit regulatory obstacles for cross-border transactions. As standardisation and harmonisation deal with various existing market practices and regulations, examination of the responses of regulators and market participants is required to envisage the degree of internal transformation conducted by member countries.

Further, current ABMI projects have also marked the de-politicisation of regional financial arrangements. The establishment of the Credit Guarantee and Investment Facility (CGIF) and ASEAN Plus Three Bond Market Forum (ABMF), for instance, indicates a new mode of regional governance that moves from a full state power of governance into a more rule-based form of governance. This arrangement has lessened the discretionary power of state regulatory agencies involved in ABMI projects.

This chapter argues that while Indonesia actively participated in the development processes of ABMI, the Indonesian bond market regulatory agencies were disinclined to transform the national regulatory framework to facilitate bond market projects under the auspices of APT financial cooperation. As ABMI projects led to market liberalisation, particularly standardisation and harmonisation, the financial authorities considered the Indonesian bond market as not ready to compete with other bond markets in East Asia. As such, they attempted to avoid the negative effects of these projects.

This chapter is divided into two sections. The first section examines the development of APT bond market initiatives. This examination pays exclusive attention to the governance of two bond market projects—CGIF and ABMF—as both are relatively more advanced, compared to other projects under ABMI. The second section examines the responses of relevant organisations under the Indonesian Ministry of Finance (IMOF), as well as Indonesian non-state actors, to APT regional bond market projects.

APT Bond Market Initiatives

ABMI's progress was considered long-winded before the implementation of the New ABMI roadmap. Under this roadmap, the work of ABMI Task Forces (TFs) has been accelerated, and has resulted in significantly advanced progress. The most concrete outcome of ABMI's efforts is the launch of CGIF by APT finance ministers at their thirteenth meeting in Tashkent (APT 2010b). In a later development, ABMI also succeeded in creating a novel project—namely, ABMF—with an intention to foster the standardisation of market practices and the greater harmonisation of regulations for cross-border bond transactions.

The CGIF

Among ABMI initiatives, CGIF is the most prominent and concrete project that can be regarded as the first successful APT corporate bond-oriented initiative. Initially, this was referred to as the Credit Guarantee and Investment Mechanism (CGIM), before the 13th APT Finance Ministers' meeting (AFMM+3) agreed to rename it as CGIF. As reflected in its name, CGIF aims to provide regional support for both credit guarantee services and investment provisions. As an initial step, the CGIF only focused on providing credit guarantees. The investment facility would be established once the guarantee mechanism was running effectively. Technically, the guarantee mechanism of CGIF operates through the provision of credit enhancement for corporate bonds in the region, which are denominated in local currencies (Kurihara 2012). By gaining credit enhancement from CGIF, any corporate bond in the APT region will have more opportunity to gain market access, as their bond rating will increase due to the CGIF guarantee.

The initial total fund of the CGIF was US$700 million (APT 2010a). This size comprised contributions from the Japan Bank for International

Cooperation (JBIC) that represented the Government of Japan (US$200 million), China (US$200 million), South Korea (US$100 million), Asian Development Bank (ADB) (US$130 million) and ASEAN's combined contribution of US$70 million (ADB 2010). These contributors have ownership rights in the form of shareholdings and decision-making power, proportional to their respective contributions. In particular, the participations of ADB and JBIC in CGIF indicate that the issue of sovereignty is less critical in the processes of APT bond market initiatives. It is a major breakthrough in the midst of the high-level sensitivity over economic sovereignty that remains strong in other APT financial cooperation bodies, such as Chiang Mai Initiative Multilateralisation (CMIM), in which it still fully acknowledges its contributors as sovereign entities.

CGIF provides credit guarantees to bond issuers. In return, CGIF will receive guarantee fees from the bond issuer, while the bond issuer will receive cash from investors or agents. Until the end of 2013, two private companies were already receiving credit guarantees from CGIF: Noble Group Limited (listed in Singapore) and an Indonesian-based corporation, PT BCA Finance (CGIF 2013). The Noble Group issued corporate bonds denominated in Thai *baht*, whereas PT BCA Finance issued its bonds denominated in Indonesian *rupiah*.

The ABMF

Another advanced initiative under the auspices of ABMI is ABMF. Established in 2010, ABMI was expected to be a common platform to standardise market practices and to harmonise regulations related to cross-border bond transactions (APT 2010b). The establishment of ABMF was triggered by cross-border bond transactions that faced numerous regulations, various legal systems and different market practices within APT member countries. The various regulations and best practice applicable to each market of the APT member countries are crucial considerations for cross-border investments and settlements. However, Asian investors have limited knowledge on investing in Asian bond markets, due to multiple requirements (Wong 2012). ABMF was expected to respond to this problem. Initially, ABMF was to focus on government bonds, as they grew at a faster rate than corporate bonds, and have become major instruments used by many Asian authorities to seek fiscal expansion. In a later development, the focus was not only on government bonds, but also on covering corporate bonds.

There are two major market barriers: *settlement barriers*, such as messaging standards, settlement cycles and physical certificates; and *regulatory barriers*, including foreign investor registration, currency exchange controls, cash controls and legal frameworks (Yamadera et al. 2010). The barriers not only hinder cross-border issuance, but also simultaneously discourage cross-border investment. The limited and opaque information regarding local bond issuers, unusual messaging and high tax rates are some of the barriers that inhibit cross-border investment. Every decision on cross-border bond investment is made based on the expected rate of return and risks. Put simply, foreign entities may not invest into such markets if they cannot obtain accurate and sufficient information related to bond products and relevant regulations, to avoid potential losses.

Some APT member countries, such as Japan, China and South Korea, have attempted to reduce bond market barriers to facilitate cross-border issuance, particularly related to regulatory constraints on bond market development. These countries have facilitated the ability of foreign entities to issue bonds denominated in the local currency of Plus Three countries in their markets (Hyun 2011, p. 4). For example, Japan has introduced the *Samurai Bond*, South Korea the *Arirang Bond* and China the *Panda Bond*. However, other APT member countries remain unable to deal with settlement and regulatory barriers.

Operationally, ABMF divided its functions into two 'sub-forums' (SF) namely SF-1 and SF-2. SF-1 collected information on regulations and market practices, whereas SF-2 enhances regional Straight-Through Processing (STP) (Yamadera 2011, p. 21). Yamadera (2011) explains that SF-1 is responsible for collecting data related to regulations, including issuance procedures, trading rules and investment rules for domestic investors, while SF-2 deals with the identification of custodian procedures and all transaction procedures. Each SF consists of *national members*, *national experts* and *international experts*, who have relevant experience and knowledge in bond-related issues. While the national members are expected to represent domestic market opinions, national experts are expected to contribute to the resolution of particular domestic issues. Meanwhile, international experts are expected to contribute to the development of cross-border transactions (Yamadera et al. 2010, p. 103). To deal with administrative and documentation issues, ADB was appointed as the Secretariat of ABMF. With various players from different institutions, the structure of ABMF was quite novel for regional financial cooperation. Prior to the establishment of ABMF, the APT Cooperation did not have a regional arrangement that could synchronise the activities of different actors in forming procedures or regulations.

In 2012, ADB released the first ABMF product, known as the ASEAN Plus Three Bond Market Guide (ABMG). The report identified and provided analysis on key elements of bond market infrastructure and regulations, such as private placement, requirements of investors and beneficial owners, and the details of public offerings in APT member countries (ADB 2012a). The ABMG was expected to be the first reference point for potential investors before they explored further information about bond markets in particular APT member countries. Besides this, the report could also be used as a reference for financial authorities, particularly capital market regulators, to create improvements in operating their domestic bond markets. ABMG provided comparative analyses that were useful for related authorities to understand their level of development, particularly on issues that dealt with market infrastructure and regulatory frameworks, and compared themselves with other markets in the region. As stated in the ABMG, there was still room for improvement, especially in areas of legal and regulatory uncertainty, as well as in establishing transparent rules (ADB 2012a, p. 3).

Non-state Actors in Bond Market Projects

ABMI projects have embraced the participation of non-state actors, including market players, research institutes and scholars. Several multinational financial institutions (i.e., ADB, IMF and World Bank/WB), research centres (i.e., Nomura Research Institute, Centre for International and Strategic Studies/CSIS), financial institutions (i.e., Citibank, JP Morgan) and universities in APT member countries have been asked to provide support, mainly in the form of research studies on particular areas of projects. A Japanese senior economist refers to ABMI as a public-private collaborative forum for promoting regional financial integration (Shimizu 2013). This perspective reflects a new arrangement in the East Asian regional cooperation, in opposition to traditional diplomatic patterns that usually position state actors as the sole players for any regional arrangements. Rethel (2010, p. 505) argues that the new regional arrangement in East Asian economic arrangements is another step towards a shift from a 'developmental state' to a 'market state', in which the market increasingly determines the direction of capital movement. This phenomenon confirms one regulatory regionalism feature that indicates the movement from state to non-state. Private or non-state actors have played a growing role in public regulatory functions in the region (Jayasuriya 2009, p. 343). In this regard, non-state actors were no longer passive actors that only follow market regulations; they were instead regarded as active players. For non-state actors, ABMI was an alternative medium to put pressure on the current domestic regulatory system.

Among the non-state actors, ADB has made a significant contribution towards the development of ABMI. Besides taking part as a CGIF contributor, the bank has provided policy advice through technical assistance, has supplied regular information related to the development of each APT member's bond market through the ABO and Asian Bond Monitor (ABM), and has also promoted national and regional bond market development by issuing ADB bonds denominated in local currencies (Bhattacharyay 2013, p. 127). In a more crucial role, ADB was given a mandate as the trustee of CGIF. As a trustee, ADB holds and manages CGIF funds and assets (APT 2010b). With advanced technical expertise, high operational experiences and wider market coverage, ADB has the capacity to manage commercial funds better than APT member countries. The involvement of the ADB in CGIF suggests that APT member countries have delegated their policy-making function and responsibility for managing public funds, which would usually be undertaken by state actors, to a non-state actor. The delegation of APT member countries' authorities to ADB was conducted through 'hard law', in which all APT member countries declared the position and responsibility of ADB in the CGIF agreement as agreed and approved by all parties.

Another sign of non-state actor participation in the development of ABMI was the involvement of market players in ABMF. Various bond market institutions in the APT member countries, such as the Japan Securities Dealers Association, Nomura Securities Co. Ltd., Korea Capital Market Institute, Philippine Dealing System Holding and Thai Bond Market Association, have engaged in ABMF's series of meetings. The participation of private institutions in ABMF was due to its coverage area, which comprised not only government bonds, but also corporate bonds. To create a better understanding of both types of bonds, market participants' perspectives were necessary. Therefore, ABMF included market participants and bond market experts, to supplement the participation of government officials or market regulators. For regional bond market development, more precisely, the participation of market players in ABMF helped identify characteristics, barriers and impediments of regional bond market development. Hyun (2014, p. 2) argues that ABMF is a public-private entity with a practical goal. On this basis, ABMF strengthens the roles of non-state actors to set standards and common practices that were previously absent from many markets in East Asia (ADB 2012a). ABMF generated inputs from first-hand experience, representing market expectations.

The establishment of ABMF as a platform for collaboration between bond market regulators and market players indicates the formation of *accountability communities* in APT financial regionalism. As Jayasuriya (2010b) argues, accountability communities operate through deliberative forums. The characteristic of ABMF—which provided equal opportunity for regulators and market players to deliberatively express their perspectives, knowledge and interests, to enhance bond market development—has laid the foundation for accountability communities in the East Asian regional bond market.

Standardisation and Harmonisation Projects

Regional standard setting was another ABMI project. The character of ABMI, which serves to place pressure on domestic actors, has brought local markets up to regional standards (Amyx 2004). The standard-setting project was initiated in response to different levels of bond market development among member countries, perceived as the most challenging issue faced by the APT member countries. This challenge was particularly identified as the biggest constraint to cross-border bond market transactions. Grimes (2008) argues that the ABMI implicitly reflects regional acceptance of global financial standards. In this respect, the global financial standards are still perceived by many Asian countries as the values of global financial institutions. As Asian state financial authorities normally are active in both international and regional forums, they mediate between the international and domestic levels. Rethel (2010, p. 506) argues that the financial authorities participate in international forums of bond markets and financial system development, while at the same time adapting international norms and best practices for their domestic markets.

To develop better regional bond markets, APT member countries asked ADB to review policies, practices and regulatory standards of bond issuance in the member countries, including the possibility of harmonising regulations, standards and practises for further bond market development in the region (Lee 2008, p. 1). Following the request, the ADB conducted a study focusing on the harmonisation of regulation and the standardisation of best practices of government and corporate bond management in APT member countries. The study also covered the prospect of private sectors supporting the harmonisation process—a prospect that became a consideration in the APT finance ministers' deliberations over the development of cross-border transaction and settlement processes (APT 2009).

The ADB's study findings on bond market development were published in late 2010. The reported findings emphasised the need to harmonise regulations and standards of bond markets in the APT region. In its report, ADB argued that harmonisation was necessary to reduce transaction costs in both primary and secondary markets (Yamadera et al. 2010, pp. 2–3). The harmonisation of regulations was also expected to facilitate cross-border capital flows and to establish improved financial integration. In relation to investments, harmonisation strategies have the potential to reduce investment costs for establishing adequate infrastructure. Finally, ADB's study findings became a cornerstone for standardisation and harmonisation projects within the APT bond market initiative. To progress the proposed standardisation and harmonisation projects, ADB recommended the establishment of ABMF.

Varied market conditions, and differences in regulatory systems, have created different approaches in dealing with standardisation and harmonisation related to bond markets. There are basically two approaches of harmonisation and standardisation: *bottom-up* and *top-down*. The bottom-up approach refers to mutual recognition of regulations among member countries, while the top-down approach deals with creating common rules and standards for all member countries (ADB 2012a). Yamadera et al. (2010, p. 70) argue that standardisation of best practice and harmonisation of regulations can only be conducted through the bottom-up approach, in which market practices and regulations should be standardised and harmonised one by one, step by step, for every single member country. While the procedures involved in this approach are acceptable, their implementation is time consuming and costly, considering different economic developments among the APT member countries. Alternatively, Yamadera et al. (2010, p. 74) also propose another approach, which is top-down, that can be an option to facilitate standardisation and harmonisation throughout the Asian offshore market, and thus avoid conflict in national laws and regulations between APT member countries. By taking this approach, APT financial cooperation can produce common standards and apply them to the offshore market. The top-down approach is relatively more difficult to conduct, as it may significantly change market practices and regulations that have been in place in the domestic bond market for many years.

Accordingly, the process of a regional standard-setting project under the auspices of APT bond market initiative remains debatable. Amyx (2004, p. 107) argues that APT financial cooperation intends to set a regional benchmark for formulating and enacting regulations and best management practices for bond markets, rather than extending existing national bond market arrangements at the regional level. In contrast, APT financial cooperation is likely to maintain existing standards that have already been implemented in APT member countries, rather than produce new standards for all members (Interview with middle-ranking official of Debt Management Office/DMO, May 2012). The steps taken by ABMF to identify barriers to, and similarities between, regulations and practices among markets in the region imply that ABMF intends to build regional benchmarks based on existing regulations and practices.

Another sign of standardisation was demonstrated in CGIF governance. In this respect, CGIF operational standards were expected to be parallel with ADB standards, as the trustee of CGIF. Within CGIF, all operations should comply with ADB operational policies (Point 2, Article 6, CGIF Articles of Agreement). Operationally, once a corporation met 'minimum standards', ADB would further assess the eligibility of the corporate bond issuer to gain credit enhancement. This arrangement demonstrated the wider scope of the regional standard project in financial issues, not only covering macroeconomic subjects such as economic growth or financial stability, but also encompassing economic micro-aspects. The increasing harmonisation of standards and codes, such as in macro- or microeconomic governance, is a critical point in the new regional governance (Jayasuriya 2003).

In a particular case, however, the minimum standard applied by ADB did not reflect the fundamental idea of credit enhancement. For example, to gain CGIF's guarantee, a corporation should have at least an investment grade (BBB−) rating from the local rating agency. This requirement was problematic, as such corporations were unlikely to have any difficulties in accessing capital from the market. If a credit rating reflects a credit guarantee agency's opinion of how likely it is that a bond issuer will repay a particular debt or financial obligation (Darbellay 2013), it then reflects as worthy or not worthy if investors place their money into a bond issuer. An investment grade in credit rating terms means that such issuers have passed a minimum level of creditworthiness for investment. Therefore, if such a corporation holds an investment grade rating, it should be relatively easy to seek capital from the market as it is worthy to invest on the corporation. In other words, the credit enhancement provided by CGIF will not provide maximum benefits for the corporation to gain capital. The CGIF credit guarantee will only generate optimum benefits if the guarantee is provided for non-investment grade corporate bonds. The nature of CGIF as a commercial institution, as well as the contributors' concerns about potential losses, are likely to be the main reasons behind the determination of holding of an investment grade as minimum requirement. This phenomenon suggests that a particular issue of standardisation remains hotly contested, in the sense that it may distort the main objective of CGIF.

Enhancing Collaborative Work

ABMI has led to enhanced policy coordination among financial markets of the APT member countries. There are at least three factors that stimulate the enhanced policy coordination in ABMI. First, there are numerous programmes under the auspices of ABMI TF. Kurihara's (2012) work provides the progress of each TF of ABMI. TF 1 of ABMI, for example, has been working on developing a deep and liquid local currency and regional bond market, to promote economic development and a more resilient financial market. TF 1 has introduced CGIF and the Asian MTN, and has also been working on bond financing for infrastructure projects. On technical progress, TF 2 of ABMI has created an Asian Bond Online (ABO) that provided timely information on bond market developments in APT member countries. TF 2 has also worked on enhancing the investment environment, particularly in relation to institutional investors, through several programmes, such as the Asian bond market summit and an institutional investor survey. The advanced progress of ABMI was accelerated by TF 3 actions that initiated the establishment of ABMF. Meanwhile, TF 4 initiated discussions on the possibility of establishing a regional settlement intermediary (RSI), as a means to reduce settlement risks for regional bond transactions. These programmes required a high level of collaborative action and effective policy coordination among relevant parties of ABMI. Such policy coordination was necessary, not only to conceptualise specific ABMI programmes, but also to ensure that the programme could be run properly. To coordinate these various programmes, the APT member countries set a steering group within ABMI to consolidate the progress of all ABMI programmes.

Second, there were various levels of domestic bond market development for APT member countries. The development of APT member countries' domestic bond markets ranged from the advanced bond markets, such as in Japan or South Korea, to the non-existence of bond markets, such as in Cambodia. This condition provided impetus for the establishment of effective policy coordination, in the sense that ABMI should facilitate peer review process and sharing of experience among diverse bond market regulators and players. In practice, the APT member countries used ABMI forums as a medium for each bond market authority to present the movement and progress of their domestic bond markets through 'self-assessment' mechanism (Grimes 2008). The presentation included exchange information regarding the current development of and policies implemented on domestic bond markets, and mutual reviews from member countries.

Third, there was growing participation of various actors in several ABMI projects. Particularly in relation to diverse actors in ABMI (state and non-state), the demand to enhance policy coordination also increased with the increased participation of various actors in ABMI. Such policy coordination was necessary to facilitate the sharing process of professional knowledge and experience of non-state actors on bond market, against the interests of state financial authorities. In this regard, ABMI provided a basis for policy coordination not only among regulators, but also between the regulators and market players.

Limiting Political Aims

The progress of ABMI has also sparked the de-politicisation of APT bond market projects, which tends to reduce political intervention of member countries. The first evidence of this phenomenon is related to CGIF governance. This is particularly due to the function of CGIF that operates as a commercial entity, although it is a product of intergovernmental cooperation. CGIF's business processes were set up to avoid state intervention or any discretion from contributors. In this regard, the CGIF articles of agreement indicate that a key function of CGIF is to undertake commercial activities covering four areas of business. Point 2, Article 2, of the CGIF agreement states that the functions of CGIF include guaranteeing bonds that are denominated in local currencies, guaranteeing bonds that are not denominated in local currencies, making investments for the development of bond markets and undertaking other such activities or services that are consistent with CGIF objectives. As guarantor, CGIF is 'forced' to have prudent operations, to ensure that its guarantee meets market expectations and reflects the real conditions of the guaranteed bond. To achieve this objective, all of CGIF's decisions should be free from any political intervention that could potentially influence CGIF operations.

A further sign of the de-politicisation of CGIF was the participation of JBIC as a CGIF contributor, and the appointment of ADB as a trustee of CGIF. The Japanese government's decision to ask JBIC to be its representative in CGIF, instead of the Japanese Ministry of Finance (JMOF), can be viewed as the intention of Japan to lessen its political intervention. By instigating JBIC here, which relatively had less political power, Japan presented a scenario to let the CGIF operate as commercial entity, working on a professional basis to achieve maximum profits. Similarly, the decision to provide ADB with a mandate as a trustee of CGIF suggests that the rule-based mechanism of CGIF is to avoid any disruptions as a result of political interference from APT member countries. Clearly, the CGIF's operational philosophy suggests the movement of East Asian regional arrangements from a discretionary approach to a governance-based operation.

Moreover, de-politicisation also occurred in the current development of ABMF. ABMF meetings over the standardisation of market practices and harmonisation of bond market regulations that involved market players indicated the attempt to create more market-oriented rules, by promoting perspectives and roles from actors external to state authorities. ABMF is the pathway to develop autonomous regional regulatory institutions that are expected to be immune from political opportunisms.

INDONESIA'S COMPLICATED STANCE ON THE ABMI

Before examining Indonesia's responses to ABMI projects, it is worthwhile to understand the structure of the Indonesian bond market and identify several actors in that market. During this study, the bond market was part of Indonesia's capital market; as such, it was under the IMOF control. Three organisations under the IMOF had relevant mandates to carry out functions related to the regulatory governance of APT bond market projects. These state authorities were represented by the Fiscal Policy Office (FPO), the Capital Market and Financial Institution Supervisory Body (hereinafter referred to as Bapepam-LK) and DMO.

As mentioned in Chap. 6, the FPO was in charge of general regional cooperation within the IMOF, including ABMI. In addition, the Bapepam-LK and the DMO also played substantive roles in negotiation processes of ABMI, as the operations of the Indonesian bond market remained under their authority. These two state agencies under the IMOF were also in the front line within any ABMI processes.

Bapepam-LK was a key financial agency that had authority to regulate and develop Indonesian capital market, as well as to develop policies related to financial institutions (excluding the banking sector, which was under BI's authority). Bapepam-LK was equipped with the authority to formulate standards, norms, criteria and procedures related to financial institution's operations (Article 1485, Finance Minister Regulation No. 184/2010). This was an important state regulatory agency that determined the regulatory framework in the Indonesian bond market. However, since December 2012, Bapepam-LK's authority has been transferred to *Otoritas Jasa Keuangan* (OJK)—a new Indonesian financial service authority (Wibawa 2012). Since that time on, the OJK has had the power to regulate and monitor any activities related to the banking sector, capital market, insurance, pension funds, financing institutions and other types of financial services. According to Article 5, Law No. 21/2011 on Financial Service Authority, the OJK was established to conduct an integrated regulatory and supervisory system for all financial activities in Indonesia, taking over several functions of IMOF and BI. In this book, the roles of OJK in APT financial regionalism are not discussed further, as this institution was still in the power transition period during data collection.

Further, another key institution under the IMOF was DMO. This directorate general was responsible for formulating any policies related to debt management, including government bonds (Article 1308, the Finance Minister Regulation No. 184/2010). It is understood that DMO was established in connection to IMF recommendations to address alleged mismanagement issues related to Indonesia's huge debts. Before DMO was established, Indonesia's massive debts were ironically managed only by a unit equal to echelon III.[1] Therefore, further institutional development was needed to manage Indonesia's debt situation (Indrawati 2001, p. 79). The DMO was set up not only to deal with managing outstanding debts but also to procure alternative budget financing sources. In regard to bond issuance management, the DMO only focused on government bonds, while corporate bonds were regulated by the Bapepam-LK, as a part of the broader capital market.

In general, Indonesian financial authorities supported the development of APT regional bond market initiatives. For Indonesian financial authorities, ABMI became a conduit for knowledge sharing. Indonesian financial authorities admitted that ABMI has facilitated their learning from advanced member countries' experiences, even though many ABMI projects have not yet been accomplished (Interview with high-ranking official of IMOF, April 2012). In addition, Indonesia could observe other member market conditions and built better policy awareness (Interview with middle-ranking official of FPO, April 2012). A similar response was also presented by the Indonesian Stock Exchange (IDX) authority, which viewed ABMI projects, particularly ABMF, as representing valuable efforts, from which the Indonesian capital market institutions could learn more (Interview with a director of IDX, October 2013). These developments implicitly exhibit the character of APT financial cooperation as a source of knowledge and experience sharing among member countries. Soesastro (2007) argues that sharing policy experiences within regional cooperation can assist member countries to improve their national capacity for policy development and implementation. The positive perspectives of Indonesian financial authorities on the learning process embedded in APT financial cooperation reflect the authorities' intention to adopt new policies or best practices of the bond market from other parties beyond their national territory.

To demonstrate its positive response towards ABMI, the government of Indonesia supported the establishment of CGIF. Following the signing of the CGIF agreement in Tashkent, in May 2010, Indonesia contributed US$12.6 million to the scheme (Suharmoko 2010). This contribution was equal to that contributed by other ASEAN-5 member states, even though the Indonesian corporate bond market remained underdeveloped. Indonesia's contribution to CGIF suggests the demand of Indonesia's bond market to have larger support for its corporate bond market.

On the issue of credit guarantees, while the majority of Indonesian corporate bond issuers have gained an investment grade from a local credit rating agency, they continued to face challenges in accessing market investment flows, particularly those from foreign investors. As illustrated in Fig. 7.1, until 2008, 84 per cent of total issuers have gained an investment grade from the local credit rating agency (PEFINDO). However, Indonesia's corporate bond issuances remained small in comparison to its neighbours, such as Singapore or Malaysia. The small issuance of Indonesian corporate bonds provided evidence of limited access to the

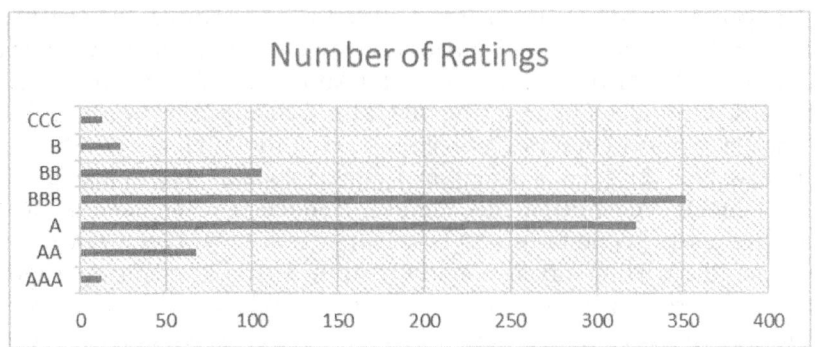

Fig. 7.1   The number of Indonesian corporate bonds. Source: Generated from PEFINDO official website <www.pefindo.com> (2010)

market. Thus, the establishment of CGIF became an alternative means for Indonesian corporate bond issuers to broaden their potential investment sources.

Indonesia has also indicated further expectations of CGIF, particularly regarding investment facilities. While investment has not been part of CGIF's business, BI, whose authority over capital reserve, was encouraged to use Indonesian reserves to further contribute to CGIF as a long-term investment (Antique and Latif 2011). This recommendation expresses the confidence of Indonesian economists in the future prospects of CGIF, not only for the benefit of the corporate market, but also for state financial agencies.

Growing Participation of Non-state Actors

Positive responses to CGIF were also demonstrated by Indonesia's private sector. Within this sector, CGIF was perceived as a facility that could boost investor confidence and decrease the level of risks (Darmawan 2011). This expectation reflects the role of regional arrangements in maintaining risk, due to intensified global interdependence (Jayasuriya 2008). Credit enhancement provided by CGIF reduced the potential of risks normally borne by investors. Investors might have a higher degree of confidence in putting their investments into a corporate bond that has gained guarantee from CGIF, compared to the issuer having no guarantee at all. Having a guarantee from recognised institutions, such as CGIF—that are backed up by state actors—indicates that the issued bond is relatively less risky, as other institutions are prepared to support the issuer. For example, the Indonesian corporation PT BCA Finance, which gained credit enhancement from CGIF, has successfully accessed a Japanese investor for the first time. This success story not only suggests that CGIF is welcomed by the Indonesian private sector to assist corporate bond issuances, but it also implies that CGIF's function to reduce potential risks works properly.

To support the current mechanism of ABMI, Indonesian financial authorities welcomed the participation of non-state actors in any ABMI projects. The authorities have never challenged the participation of non-state actors at a regional level, such as ADB or research institutes, in managing or contributing to ABMI regional projects. Indonesia had no issues with the presence of ADB as the trustee of CGIF, although Indonesia's contribution to CGIF was allocated from the national budget (public funds), which should normally be managed by a sovereign entity. According to the senior official of the FPO, Indonesia realised that ADB had the experience to deal with multilateral cooperation, and the technical skills to deal with the operational issues of such financial projects (Interview, July 2012). Given the technical complexities usually embedded in such initiatives, APT member countries may face difficulties if they have to deliver the daily operations of these initiatives. This possibility suggests that Indonesia had been supporting the existing governance of ABMI, including the participation of non-state actors.

Further, there were three Indonesian Self-Regulatory Organisations (SROs)—namely, the Central Securities Depository (*Kustodian Sentral Efek Indonesia*/KSEI), the Indonesian Stock Exchange *(Bursa Efek Indonesia*/IDX) and the Indonesian Clearing and Guarantee Corporation (*Kliring Penjaminan Efek Indonesia*/KPEI)—that had participated in ABMF processes. These organisations were basically private companies, but they had been granted business licences and a mandate to conduct certain functions in capital markets. The SROs had been given certain rights by state financial authorities to regulate themselves and to set rules for their members in any activities related to capital markets (Balfas 2012, p. 399). As previously illustrated in Fig. 7.1, the three SROs were located in the Indonesian capital market structure, with various functions. In short, KSEI had the responsibility to provide security depositories and settlement services to secure investors' investment portfolios. At the same time, it provided timely information for market transactions. IDX facilitated capital market transactions, including corporate bonds, whereas

KPEI provided clearing and guarantee services for stock exchange settlements (IMF 2012).

The participation of Indonesian SROs indicates that financial regionalism in East Asia involves participation of not only international or regional non-state actors, as represented by IFIs, but also non-state actors at the national level. The rise of non-state actor participation (from emerging countries) is relatively new in regional arrangements, while the movement of political authority from public institutions to various privatised institutions has been identified as an essential trend in regional governance (Jayasuriya 2010a, p. 107). In most cases, including in ABMI processes, active non-state actors were mainly from advanced member countries, while the number of non-state actors from smaller countries remained limited.

Moreover, participation of national non-state actors also indicates the shift in regional arrangements from *state-based* decision-making processes to *state and non-state partnership-based* decision-making processes. Jayasuriya in Jones (2010, p. 62) argues that the combination of public and private organisations has the capacity to perform legislative, monitoring and compliance activities in relation to specific functions within and beyond national boundaries, and to shape the formation of accountability communities.

In Indonesia's context, the prominent role of Indonesian non-state actors has emerged in the area of compliance activities, whereby they engaged in standardising the best practices of bond markets. In practice, the three Indonesian SROs represented Indonesia as national members of ABMF. They worked alongside Indonesian financial state authorities in ABMF. This arrangement was intriguing, as both Indonesian state and non-state actors together had become national members of ABMF (ADB 2012a). None of these actors were national or international experts.

The participation of Indonesian non-state actors in ABMF also raised a conflict of interest issue. This particularly related to the question of how to identify the dividing line between state and non-state authorities. Despite its contribution towards the development of a regional bond market, the existence of a private actor in ABMF could generate conflict between national and corporate interests (Interview with high-ranking official of Bapepam-LK, April 2012). For instance, while the government, as regulator, should consider many aspects of the financial sector such as tax, national income and the business climate in dealing with intergovernmental arrangement, the private sector merely focused on commercial interests, as opposed to public interests.

This situation puts pressure on the question of democratic account-ability. It is simply because the preferences or interests of non-state actors potentially influence and undermine the process of regionalism. As non-state actors usually act based on pragmatic or economic motivations, the transformation of the national regulatory space may face serious con-flicts of interest that disturb the adoption of regional governance. In this respect, legitimacy becomes a serious question in relation to the involve-ment of national non-state actors in the regionalism of bond markets. However, the assertion of Indonesian financial authorities also implies that Indonesian state actors attempt to minimise the involvement of Indonesian non-state actors for the public interest. In relation to this type of government position, Grimes (2008, p. 24) argues that a number of economies are not yet willing to fully yield control of financial sectors to market forces.

Complex Policy Coordination

The Indonesian national policy coordination network on ABMI processes included not only state agencies, but also non-state actors. As illustrated in Fig. 7.2, operationally the *Pusat Kebijakan Regional dan Bilateral* (Centre for Bilateral and Regional Policy/CBRP) of FPO was in charge

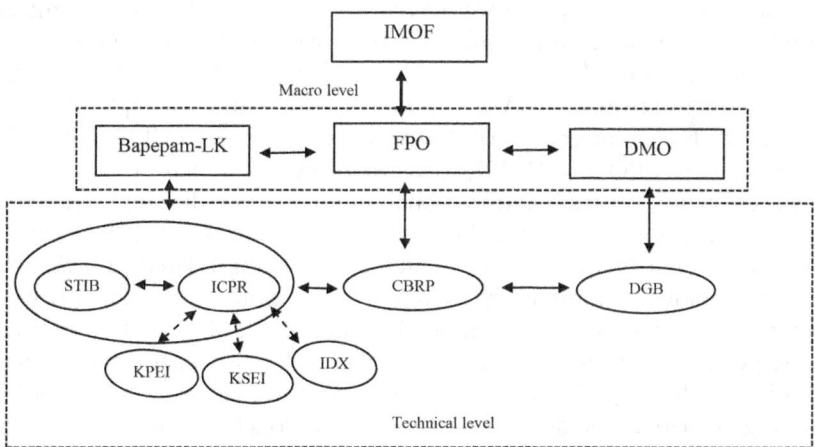

Fig. 7.2 National policy network in response to ABMI. Source: Author's own visualisation

of the national coordination of ABMI projects. To deal with technical issues, CBRP worked closely with several divisions under Bapepam-LK and DMO.

Within Bapepam-LK, the International Cooperation and Public Relations (ICPR) division became the focal point for internal coordination processes. Therefore, in many ABMI initiatives, the ICPR division cooperated with CBRP. The ICPR division of Bapepam-LK also coordinated with other directorates or divisions of Bapepam-LK, to deal with technical issues related to the bond market. On many occasions, the *Biro Transaksi dan Lembaga Efek* (Securities Transaction and Institution Bureau/STIB) provided materials, opinion and analysis. The role of this bureau was critical, as it conducted vital functions by formulating regulatory frameworks for capital market transactions, including procedures, standards and market mechanisms (Article 1610, the Finance Minister Regulation No. 184/2010). Any transformation of the capital market regulatory system was formulated by this bureau. Meanwhile, CBRP also coordinated with the *Direktorat Surat Utang Negara* (Directorate of Government Bonds/DGB) of DMO. This directorate formulated and implemented any policies and operating standards related to government bonds, including norms, standards, procedures and their criteria (Article 1353, the Finance Minister Regulation No. 184/2010). In ABMI, officials from the government bond directorate involved in CGIF and ABMF meetings. For Jayasuriya (2009, p. 340), connections between domestic regulatory agencies create regulatory webs that lead to policy networks.

Indonesian macro-level policy coordination, which only included state actors in response to ABMI projects, was relatively simple. All state regulatory bodies in charge of ABMI were under the IMOF. Although Bapepam-LK, FPO and DMO, to varying degrees, function well in their dealings with domestic and regional bond market development, they performed simple policy coordination. Craswell and Davis (1994) argue that policy coordination can be achieved by forcing related programmes together under one minister. In this respect, policy coordination does not trigger any competition in shaping national policy that may occur more generally within intragovernmental coordination at the macro-level. Woolcock (2007, p. 27) argues that the institutional structures of policy making determine the degree to which negotiators have autonomy. As the three Indonesian state agencies were part of the same national institution, they coordinated based on their own departmental functions and mandates. With this simple arrangement, the state could easily maintain any potential tensions that might emerge as a consequence of regional standard-setting projects. This type of coordination differed from national policy coordination in response to APT regional liquidity initiative, as it included two separated agencies, IMOF and BI.

The policy coordination regarding ABMI processes among relevant actors within the IMOF was more concerned with technical matters. In this regard, the policy coordination related more to responding to technical issues, rather than determining a clear path for Indonesia's strategic position in ABMI (Interview with high-ranking official of Bapepam-LK, April 2012). The policy coordination was only limited to responding to the previous outcomes of ABMI technical meetings, and to prepare materials for upcoming meetings. In another words, the policy coordination to determine a strategic position in ABMI remained scant.

In contrast to policy coordination among state actors, policy coordination between state and non-state actors in Indonesia was relatively weak. While the participation of Indonesian non-state actors clearly shaped new patterns of policy coordination, Indonesia's policy coordination mechanism had not fully facilitated active communication between regulators and the private sector, in response to the development of the regional bond market. Policy coordination between Bapepam-LK and the SROs remained limited. The SROs appeared to coordinate sporadically with Bapepam-LK as there did not appear to be a regular coordination mechanism between the two bodies. In fact, there was only a meeting with Bapepam-LK at the beginning of the ABMF series of meetings (Interview with a director of Indonesian Stock Exchange/IDX, October 2013). In a similar vein, another interviewee mentioned that coordination meetings between IMOF and SROs were only held at the initial stages of ABMF development (Interview with a director of KSEI, October 2013). This situation resulted in a lack of information related to the progress of ABMF and confirmed Hamilton-Hart's (2007) finding that several groups of the business sector have been left out of the policy process in Indonesia.

Weak policy coordination between national regulatory bodies and non-state actors in Indonesia potentially leads to increased vulnerability in the process of regionalism on APT bond market projects. If regulatory regionalism requires the development of new forms of multi-level governance (Jayasuriya 2009, p. 340), then weak policy coordination contributes to challenge the regionalism development. That is because multi-level governance only operates properly when robust policy coordination that conveys standards and mechanisms across levels of governance exists. The sustainability of coordination processes among various actors with different purposes and objectives is one distinctive feature of regional governance (Yoshimatsu 2010, p. 231). In this regard, the regionalism process of APT bond market initiatives faces critical questions to do with how national regulatory agencies shape proper policy coordination with non-state actors to transform national regulatory framework. This is particularly so in a country with a relatively strong state-based decision-making system, such as in Indonesia. The regulator's unwillingness to accept the participation of national non-state actors in the process of ABMI contributes to the perceived lack of policy coordination processes.

Mixed Responses to Standardisation and Harmonisation

While, in general, Indonesia expressed its support for the development of ABMI, Indonesian state and non-state actors generally showed unenthusiastic responses, especially to ABMI's efforts to achieve standardisation and harmonisation. However, they also presented supportive views of these processes. These mixed responses emerged primarily due to financial institutions' different interests and authorities. The DMO, as the issuer of Indonesian government bonds, viewed standardisation and harmonisation projects as a potential way to tap into capital from the wider market. The DMO perceived standardisation and harmonisation as less harmful projects. Such projects did not contradict the current Indonesian regulatory system and had the potentials to broaden Indonesia's market size. A middle-ranking official of DMO argued that:

> Like or dislike, we have to join (standardisation and harmonisation) as we have committed to do it. We view that, at least, there is no contradiction between existing regulations and proposed cross-border transaction as a core objective of harmonisation and standardisation ... and they will be beneficial since regional saving can be used as a source of financing in the region. (Interview, May 2012)

The assertion of the DMO official reflected confidence in the recent positive progress of Indonesian government bonds. The Indonesian bond market has been dominated by government bonds. As illustrated in Fig. 7.3, until mid-December 2012, government bonds has occupied the Indonesian market, with 82.89 per cent of total market share, while corporate bonds represented only 17.11 per cent.

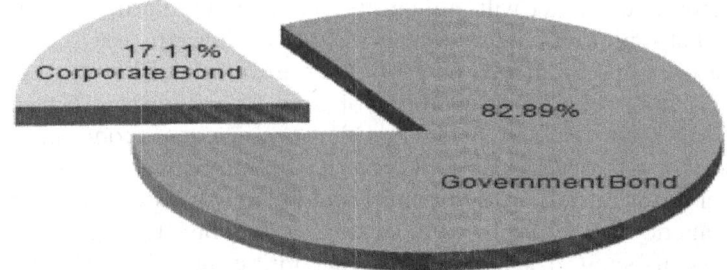

Fig. 7.3 Outstanding 2012 bonds in Indonesia. Source: Generated from Bapepam-LK official website <www.bapepam.go.id> (2012)

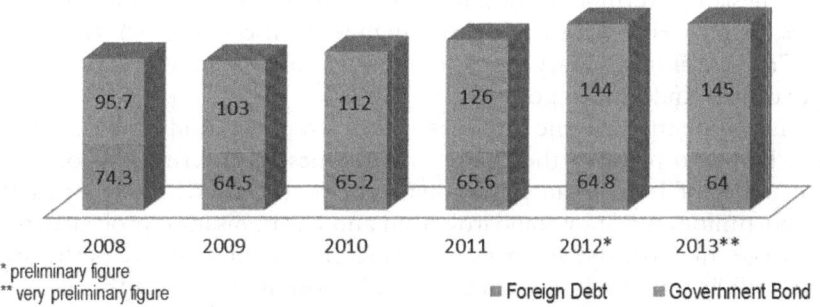

Fig. 7.4 Indonesian government debts (in US$ billion). Source: Generated from DMO official website <www.dmo.or.id> (2013)

Initially issued to deal with bank recapitalisation costs, Indonesian government bond became an important instrument for fiscal deficit. In recent years, Indonesian government bonds have taken over the role of foreign assistance in supporting Indonesia's national budget. The data presented in Fig. 7.4 demonstrates that the size of Indonesian government bonds has been increasing, while, at the same time, the size of internationally sourced loans (foreign debt) has been declining.

According to a middle-ranking official of DMO, since 2004, government bonds constituted the main financial instrument for managing the national budget (Interview, May 2012). Beyond economic calculations, establishing the government bond market in Indonesia can also be perceived as an attempt to demonstrate its economic sovereignty over foreign assistance. For Sharma (2001, p. 1416), a well-developed local currency bond market will mitigate the vulnerability within the financial sector that might arise from an over-reliance on foreign debt.

In a later development, the Indonesian government bond market has gained a high level of acceptance not only from domestic players, but also from foreign investors. The significant progress in economic growth and sound macroeconomic indicators has attracted foreign investors to channel funds into the government bond market. In late 2011, the Fitch rating agency raised the Indonesian sovereign debt rating to BBB— after 14 years of being at a BB+ level. Other rating agencies—Moody's and Standard & Poor—also followed the upgrading in 2012. For Indonesia, this rating trend has assisted the government to convince global investors that Indonesia was a less risky prospect for bond market investment. The Indonesian government bond market continued to attract foreign investors, as its yields were among the highest in the region (ADB 2012b, p. 75). Up until January 2013, foreign investors held approximately 33 per cent of Indonesian government bonds.

The potentials of the Indonesian government bond had stimulated the DMO to broaden the market for Indonesian government bonds. As the issuer of Indonesian government bonds, the DMO viewed that the opportunities made by standardisation and harmonisation projects would be larger than the threats that might emerge as a consequence of the projects. While standardisation and harmonisation might pose a threat to the Indonesian economy, the capital inflow potential from the broader market was still necessary as a source of finance. Thus, in the context of government bonds, Indonesian financial authorities were more confident in the standardisation of market practices, and the harmonisation of bond market regulation.

In contrast, Bapepam-LK as a capital market regulator, tended to take a cautious stance towards standardisation and harmonisation, particularly when associated with corporate bonds. The state agency viewed the ABMF standardisation and harmonisation project as an invisible 'menace' that potentially hindered the development of the Indonesian domestic bond market. Bapepam-LK had a cautious attitude towards standardisation and harmonisation for two reasons. The first was related to the less developed market infrastructure. In terms of infrastructure, Indonesia's bond market infrastructure was relatively less developed compared to other major APT member countries, including ASEAN-5 <www.koran.tempo.co, 1 April 2014>. As presented in Table 7.1, Fabella and Madhur (2003, p. 7) revealed that Indonesia had the lowest ranking of East Asian countries in

Table 7.1 Indicators of financial infrastructure quality (0 to 10, poor to excellent)

	Delivery and settlement	Benchmark yield curve	Public issuance modality	Private issuance modality	Average score	Ranking of East Asian countries
Hong Kong, China	8	8	8	8	8	1
Singapore	8	8	8	8	8	1
Taipei, China	8	4	8	8	7	2
Korean Republic	6	6	8	6	6.5	3
Malaysia	6	4	6	6	5.5	4
Thailand	4	4	4	4	4	5
PRC	2	0	2	0	2	6
Philippines	2	0	4	0	1.5	7
Indonesia	2	0	2	0	1	8
USA	10	10	10	10	10	–

Source: Fabella and Madhur (2003)

terms of financial market infrastructure. They emphasised that Indonesia did not have adequate infrastructure for bond trading and has an under-developed information dissemination system and a non-integrated settle-ment system.

In addition, Dalla (2003) also argues that several areas of the Indonesian bond market, such as the inter-dealer market, benchmarking, investor base coverage and clearing and settlement systems, needed to be further developed. Especially in relation to settlement systems, currently BI has facili-tated settlement processes together with KSEI. While BI had the official mandate to facilitate the clearing and settlement process for government bonds, KSEI was also processing settlements, particularly for retail bonds and corporate bonds (Dalla 2003). According to the Bapepam-LK's 2010–2014 Master Plan, an integrated clearing and settlement system was needed to enhance the efficiency of post-trade transactions (Bapepam-LK 2010, p. 97).

Indonesian financial market infrastructure quality was relatively low, particularly in terms of common standards. A participating respondent of KSEI admitted that Indonesia had not yet implemented the SWIFT format, and only relied on its own security identification number, a specific code for a particular security product, produced by IDX (Interview, October

2013). Another example was related to investor categorisation. While most APT advanced member countries, such as Japan, Korea, Malaysia, Singapore and Thailand, already have standards for qualified *institutional* and *professional* investors—as several of their bonds are intentionally developed for cross-border purposes—Indonesia has not defined these types of investors in the Indonesian bond market (ADB 2012a). These situations made the Indonesian market difficult to integrate with other regional markets in the future. A high-ranking official of Bapepam-LK argued that Indonesia's less developed market infrastructure was a major problem that hindered the readiness of Indonesia to further engage with APT bond market projects. The official stated that:

> There are many offers to set integration, linkage, and so on. For countries that have sound infrastructure, [the offers] are beneficial. [In this respect] we still have many fractions. If we talk about bond market, for instance, [in fact] we do not have an infrastructure yet. (Interview, April 2012)

These views uncover the Indonesian financial authority's concerns about the inability of the Indonesian domestic market infrastructure to compete with other major countries. The awareness of the Bapepam-LK official also confirmed Levinger's (2014, p. 13) argument that the Indonesian market was isolated from, and less integrated with, other Asian markets. Only a market with a well-developed infrastructure could gain maximum benefits from market integration, as projected by APT financial cooperation. This situation suggests that domestic bond market infrastructure emerges as a pivotal factor for Indonesia to deal with ABMI standardisation and harmonisation projects. As regionalism in East Asia is also more or less driven by the market (Katzenstein 2000), any domestic market fragility or vulnerability will weaken state institutions in regional integration. On this basis, standardisation and harmonisation projects would expose Indonesia's 'immature' bond market to potential external threats, as they had to fill the gap to achieve regional benchmarks. For this reason, the Indonesian private sector was likely to avoid the APT standardisation and harmonisation projects.

To further develop market infrastructure, the Bapepam-LK had conducted several programmes. The programmes were initiated in 2006 to enhance the Indonesian bond market, by focusing on three main issues (Bapepam 2006). The first was creating a primary dealer system to boost the performance of government bonds in the primary market. This system was also expected to operate as a common base for market organisation and access harmonisation. The second was the formation of a price discovery mechanism to support the function of the bond-pricing agency, in providing fair value for bonds, independently and objectively. Third, Bapepam-LK intended to complete the Electronic Trading Platform (ETP) to facilitate retail bond trading. Gray et al. (2014) reported that electronic platforms for Indonesian government and corporate bond transactions already existed, but were rarely used. In 2012, Bapepam-LK was in the middle of improving the capital market infrastructure, including the processing structure system, Single Investor Identity (SID), and data warehousing (Interview with low-ranking official of Bapepam-LK, April 2012). However, the extent to which progress had been made on these efforts remained unclear.

The second reason for Indonesia's cautious stance towards standardisation and harmonisation projects was the lack of domestic player capacity. In bond markets, there are three major key players: issuers, underwriters and investors. In this regard, the capacity of Indonesian domestic players to compete was relatively less than for foreign players (Dalla 2003). Therefore, if Indonesia joined the regional bond market standardisation and harmonisation, it meant that Indonesian domestic players had to play in the same field, with the same best practices and under the same regulation with other players from the region. This condition potentially generated disadvantages for Indonesian bond market players, as they had less capacity compared to market players in other advanced APT member countries. For example, according to a participating interviewee from IDX, almost all investment banks used foreign underwriters to promote their products in international markets (Interview, October 2013). As the experience and networks of the Indonesian market players were limited compared to neighbouring markets, investment banks were more confident about using foreign human resources that generally had more experience in creating international networks. Thus, in addition to market infrastructure, market player capacity could be understood as another important factor for Indonesia when dealing with APT financial regionalism.

In response to the lack of capacity of the Indonesian market players, Bapepam-LK had made special assistance available to the domestic market. The authority created local initiatives as a strategy to protect local players, without controlling access by foreign players (Interview with high-ranking official of IMOF, April 2012). The strategy was conducted through several programmes, including enhancing internal controls and improving human resource capacity. This strategy was regarded as reasonable; prohibiting foreign players might result in adverse outcomes for domestic players, should foreign markets adopt similarly exclusionary treatment towards their foreign (including Indonesian) players. Moreover, to assist players in Indonesia's capital market, Bapepam-LK and IDX planned to establish the Investor Protection Fund to deal with broker insolvency (Citibank 2013).

Mixed perspectives in response to standardisation and harmonisation were also evident in Indonesian non-state actors. Parallel with DMO's view, an interviewee of IDX claimed that standardisation and harmonisation might assist the Indonesian government and corporate bonds to access wider markets (Interview, October 2013). As standardisation and harmonisation potentially provided wider market access, it was expected that Indonesian bonds would readily attract supplementary investors from other APT markets, as Indonesian bond yields were relatively high compared to those of other countries, such as Malaysia, the Philippines or Thailand (Kusumaningtyas and Theo 2012). In this regard, standardisation was perceived as a means to broaden market access, particularly for government bonds.

However, a different perspective was presented by a participating respondent from KSEI, who argued that standardisation and harmonisation had positive and negative sides regarding settlement processes, as the core business of KSEI. The interviewee stated that:

> [With harmonisation and standardisation], central depositories (in the APT region) can open their accounts one to another, in order to complete [settlement process] smoothly. For instance, Singapore's central depository can open accounts in Indonesia. [If we follow standardisation], I am afraid that foreign players will not need [a] central custodian in Indonesia as they can directly open [an] account in Singapore. However, [on the] positive side, Indonesian players do not need to open accounts … overseas if they want to invest in foreign market. They only need to open an account in KSEI. (Interview, October 2013)

The concern of the KSEI official about the impact of standardisation and harmonisation on the settlement process was plausible, as regional bond markets need well-organised clearing and settlement processes to provide an efficient transfer of ownership. In practice, the clearing and settlement processes need cross-border access to different markets, as well as allowing for interactions between different systems (Park and Park 2004, p. 205).

Therefore, once the clearing and settlement authorities among APT countries were harmonised in terms of legal and administration matters, and standardised in terms of operational systems, then investors might easily find the best service with the lowest cost for their bond transactions. This expectation was usually associated with a well-developed market infrastructure. Considering the current market infrastructure, the Indonesian clearing and settlement agency potentially lost its investors if all market mechanisms and practices were standardised and harmonised.

Further, Indonesian non-state actors also viewed that the harmonisation of bond market regulations was a challenging task, although it was not an impossible project. A participating respondent from IDX considered that several elements of the bond market, such as corporate issuance, level of service and disclosure matters, were potentially to be standardised (Interview, October 2013). However, there were also several issues related to bond markets that were difficult to be harmonised. One of these was tax law. As each country imposed different taxes for bond transactions, harmonising tax laws would be a difficult process. On this issue, all respondents representing Indonesian non-state actors shared a similar view that harmonising tax law was a difficult task, although it was a pivotal aspect in the development of regional bond markets. Amyx (2004, p. 107) argues that changes in tax law are required to achieve a well-functioning bond market. For Indonesia, the government has gradually imposed income tax on the interest earned on bond transactions.[2] If the Indonesian government was forced to raise income tax levels for the harmonisation of bond market regulation, the process might take time and involve a tough negotiation process, as changing tax laws would involve parliamentary engagement and affected national interests, including national revenue.

In the face of liberalising bond markets, Indonesian bond market players expressed their sceptical views about a one-size-fits-all standard, as they could jeopardise domestic players' business. Standardisation and harmonisation were still perceived by Indonesian market players as a threat, rather than a potential. Following standardisation means constraining national behaviour and, at the same time, fostering a general convergence towards regulatory regimes (Walter 2008). Simply, standardisation can also be perceived as sacrificing domestic privilege for the sake of broader market efficiency. On this point, APT standardisation project faced a challenge from Indonesian domestic market players.

Clearly, in an area where Indonesia was relatively more advanced or ready enough to compete, such as in government bonds, it presented positive responses to standardisation of the bond market. Walter (2008, p. 33) defines this phenomenon as *standard compliance based on material incentives* that usually dominate the compliance outcomes by public or private actors in the short to medium term. In this regard, potential material benefits gained from bond market standardisation were perceived by Indonesian financial authorities as higher than the potential costs that should be borne. In contrast, when the potential benefits of bond market standardisation were lower than the potential costs that could emerge due to inefficient domestic market operations, such as in the corporate bond market, Indonesia tended to resist, at least passively, the standardisation project.

The policy options taken by Indonesia reflect its position towards economic liberalisation, including financial markets, that is always driven by pragmatism. For instance, as mentioned in Chap. 4, Indonesia allowed foreign investors to hold 99 per cent of the total stock of Indonesian local banks. This policy was issued in order to generate investment to save the Indonesian banking sector that suffered due to financial crisis. Another example is the October 1988 Package (Pakto 88), which was implemented when Indonesia suffered a serious balance of payments crisis. The package provided a larger opportunity for investors to set up new banks with minimal capital and allowed foreign banks to open branches outside Jakarta.

Market liberalisation was more about political issue in Indonesia. It was a sensitive issue that could generate political instability. It was sensitive as the Indonesian constitution stipulated that any economic resources should be used to maximise the wealth of the Indonesian people, not foreigners. To avoid political complexity, Indonesian administrations never made any great efforts to undertake liberalisation. They tended to treat liberalisation as a last option and made it subject to economic conditions. Indonesian regimes have been reluctant to liberalise financial markets, especially the banking sector and capital markets, to protect their business cronies who support the regime (Pepinsky 2010). Soeharto, for instance, took the business lobby seriously because it supported his regime's developmentalist projects.

The spirit of anti-liberalisation as stipulated in the Constitution has encouraged Indonesian financial authorities to protect domestic market. Therefore, by nature, the private sector in Indonesia tended to follow this spirit as it provided more benefits to the interests of Indonesian business. In this context, joining the standardisation and harmonisation projects was not a good option as it would expose the Indonesian private sector to broader competition. As a result, the Indonesian private sector tended to be a passive player in regional projects such as these.

While there were pros and cons regarding standardisation and harmonisation projects on bond market development, Indonesia was expected to follow the progress of the projects, but under a different pattern. A low-ranking official of Bapepam-LK, who had been in charge as a national member of ABMF, argued that Indonesia could still follow the standardisation process to narrow the gap between the Indonesian and advanced bond markets; however, its pace was unlikely to be as fast as other member countries (Interview, April 2012). In addition, the senior official of FPO viewed that while harmonisation of regulation was needed, it should not be developed as a rigid and binding commitment (Interview, July 2012). The expectation for step-by-step and non-binding commitments on the harmonisation of bond market regulations suggested that Indonesia needed to ensure that harmonisation would not hinder the progress of its own domestic bond market. In this respect, any initiatives that potentially threaten to weaken Indonesian domestic market competitiveness, including standardisation and harmonisation, would be opposed. The pattern of standardisation and harmonisation proposed by Indonesian financial authorities suggests that regional standardisation and harmonisation projects should not dramatically change Indonesian domestic regulatory frameworks, but rather provide principles that can be adopted by Indonesian state or non-state actors when they have to revise their regulatory regime. This arrangement reflects an aspect of regulatory regionalism in which the national systems may retain elements of their own national regulatory architecture, while adopting regional standards (Jayasuriya 2010b).

As an alternative to the cross-border governance process, Indonesian financial authorities considered a mutual recognition approach, instead of standardisation and harmonisation. In mutual recognition, each member country retains its own regulations and practices, while mutually accepting other members' regulations and practices (Chen and Mattoo 2008). Mutual recognition can be perceived as an implicit acceptance of different technical regulations and standards that are applied in each country; simply, it is a different way of achieving the same regulatory objective (Pacheco 2006, p. 2). In other words, there is no need to change or adjust existing regulations or practices, as required by standardisation and harmonisation. A high-ranking official of Bapepam-LK argued that considering different levels of market development, it was more workable if the cross-border bond market transactions within East Asia were facilitated through mutual recognition, rather than through standardisation and harmonisation (Interview, April 2012). This type of regulatory governance was more compatible with the status of the Indonesian bond market, which needed more protection from financial authorities.

The proposed mutual recognition approach presents an opposing attitude to challenge the ongoing process of regional regulatory governance, as it does not involve transformation projects within the national space of member countries. The proposed approach also suggests that a contentious regulatory regime exists in the regionalism process of APT bond market initiatives. In Indonesia's context, the ongoing APT regional standard-setting projects should face competition with an international standard regime, as represented by International Organisation of Securities Commissions (IOSCO). As a member of IOSCO, Indonesia should follow IOSCO's objectives and principles of securities regulation to formulate bond-related regulations and to establish market practices (Dalla 2003). In this respect, the existing Indonesian bond market standards that were built upon international standard regimes were expected to contend the development of regional standards.

Proposing a mutual recognition mechanism implied that Indonesia, in general, had not been ready to join regional standardisation projects on bond markets, as it still focused largely on protecting its domestic market. Consequently, there was a gulf between the Indonesian domestic bond market regime and the APT regional governance regime that led to the politics of regionalism of bond markets. For Jayasuriya (2009, p. 337), this is the difficult part of regionalism that ensures implementation is distant from a simple functional process. As a result, compliance with any progress on APT regional bond market governance was relatively slow.

In addition, the mixed responses demonstrated by Indonesian financial authorities, as well as Indonesian market players, implied that regional financial standard setting was a contested project in East Asian financial regionalism. It might gain either support or opposition from national actors. If He and Inoguchi (2011, p. 172) argue that many domestic factors play significant roles in shaping Asian regionalism, then in the Indonesian bond market context, the authorities and interests of the state and non-state actors emerged as important factors in regional standard-setting projects. The different views of Indonesian domestic actors on the standardisation project of ABMI confirmed Hameiri and Jayasuriya's (2011) argument that 'regulatory conflict' between regional and national projects occurs within the state; not outside the state.

Minimal Effects of De-politicisation

There were at least two signs of de-politicisation of financial institutions in Indonesia. The first was the establishment of SROs. As institutions that held powers to regulate several aspects of the bond market, SROs had potential to be far from a democratically elected office. In this respect, the institutional power of bond market management, especially corporate, was de-politicised to achieve fair and efficient transactions (Balfas 2012). In a regional context, one might expect that the de-politicisation would stimulate SROs to have an independent stance when participating in regional bond market development. ABMF, for instance, provided opportunities for Indonesian market players to be active and deliberative in expressing their views, which might be different from the governments' perspective. However, the empirical evidence showed that the stance of Indonesian SROs in ABMF was rather vague, as they restricted themselves from expressing their own views deliberatively. According to a respondent from KSEI, the stance in ABMF was always the same as the position taken by Indonesia's capital market authority, although they were never asked to follow the authority (Interview, October 2013). A participating respondent from IDX argued that IDX could not propose a different view, as it is basically 'an extension' of a government body (Interview, October 2013). As an extension of a government body, IDX could not offer a response that differed from the state authority. They simply did not want to trigger any misunderstanding with the Indonesian financial authorities by taking different views or positions on the ABMF, which had the potential to hurt their business. Having the same stance means protecting their business. Therefore, while the SROs had autonomous power at the domestic level, they remained under the shadow of the bond market regulator's authority at the regional level.

This situation was in contrast to the core function of ABMF: that it was expected to enhance dialogue between private sector and regulators to develop bond markets in the region and promote harmonisation, standardisation and integration (ADB 2012a). This type of participation by

Indonesian SROs still followed the traditional mode of non-state actors' engagement, in which they lobbied national regulatory agencies in the expectation that their preferred position will be incorporated, along with national interests as represented by state actors in international forums (MacDonald and Woolcock 2007, p. 78). There was a risk in following this type of participation in which there was no guarantee that the government would follow the policy preference that non-state actors proposed, while the real voice of non-state actors did not get heard in regional forums.

Beside these psychological and institutional barriers, as an 'extension' of the financial authorities, Indonesian SROs were trapped in a 'membership snare' as they were allocated to the same group as national members in the ABMF. While having the same membership meant holding the same authority, it also meant that Indonesian financial authorities could monitor, and to some extent control, the stance or position of the SROs in every single discussion of the ABMF. This situation could be different if the SROs were working for different types of membership, in which they might have more freedom to express their stance. Therefore, at this stage, de-politicisation at the regional level was unlikely to help push autonomous financial institutions, such as SROs, to challenge regional arrangements.

The second sign of de-politicisation of financial institutions in Indonesia was the establishment of OJK. Set up as an independent body, and not as part of the executive branch, OJK was designed to be free from any intervention in delivering its mandates (Article 2, Law No. 21/2011 on Financial Service Authority). On this basis, OJK could also be expected to be free from political intervention. Put simply, OJK was an example of the de-politicised financial authority placed beyond the control of Indonesia's elected government. In regard to OJK, this new financial institution had limited engagement with regional financial processes, including ABMI. It had remained absent from any ABMI processes during this study's fieldwork. Therefore, the effects of de-politicisation on OJK's responses to the development of APT financial initiatives could not be examined or determined by this study.

The next chapter will conclude the overall discussion and analysis of this study. It articulates the important findings, the contribution of this study to the literature and the directions of future studies related to East Asian financial regionalism.

Notes

1. In Indonesian ministerial structure, echelon III refers to a unit led by a deputy director. The upper level of this unit is echelon II, which is led by a director; the highest is echelon I, which is led by a director-general.
2. The Government Regulation No. 16/2009 on Income Tax on the Income gained from Bond Interests states that the income tax at zero per cent should be imposed by 2009 to 2010; five per cent by 2011 to 2013; and 15 per cent by 2014 onward. However, the enforcement tax rate at 15 per cent by 2014 has been deferred until 2015 to give an incentive for domestic players to participate more in the market.

References

Amyx, J. A. (2004). Political dynamics of regional financial cooperation in East Asia. *Japanese Economy, 32*(2), 98–112.

Antique & Latif, S. (2011). Anggito: BI tak perlu intervensi rupiah. *VivaNews*. Retrieved December 19, 2011, from http://us.fokus.vivanews.com/news/read/196636-anggito--bi-tak-perlu-lagi-intervensi-rupiah

ASEAN Plus Three. (2009). *The joint media statement of the special AFMM Plus Three, action plan to restore economic and financial stability of the Asian region.* Retrieved December 12, 2011, from http://www.asean.org/22158.htm

ASEAN Plus Three. (2010a). *Articles of agreement of Credit Guarantee and Investment Facility.* Retrieved February 25, 2013, from http://www.cgif-abmi.org/cgif/pdf/CGIF_Articles_of_Agreement.pdf.

ASEAN Plus Three. (2010b). *The joint ministerial statement of the 13th ASEAN Plus Three Finance Ministers' Meeting.* Tashkent: ASEAN Plus Three.

Asian Development Bank. (2010). ADB to contribute to ASEAN+3 Credit Guarantee Facility, April 14. Retrieved March 11, 2013, from http://www.adb.org/news/adb-contribute-asean3-credit-guarantee-facility

Asian Development Bank. (2012a). *ASEAN+3 Bond Market Guide.* Manila: Asian Development Bank.

Asian Development Bank. (2012b). *Asia Bond Monitor.* Manila: Asian Development Bank.

Balfas, H. M. (2012). *Hukum pasar modal Indonesia (Indonesian capital market law).* Jakarta: Tatanusa.

Bapepam. (2006). Siaran Pers akhir tahun 2006 (the 2006 end of year press release). Retrieved May 12, 2014, from www.bapepam.go.id/bapepamlk/siaran_pers

Bapepam-LK. (2010). *The capital market and non-bank financial industry master plan 2010–2014.* Jakarta: Bapepam-LK.

Bhattacharyay, B. N. (2013). Determinants of bond market development in Asia. *Journal of Asian Economics, 24*, 124–137.

Capling, A., & Low, P. (2010). The domestic politics of trade policy-making: State and non-state actor interactions and forum choice. In A. Capling & P. Low (Eds.), *Governments, non-state actors and trade policy-making* (pp. 4–28). Cambridge: Cambridge University Press.

Chen, M. X., & Mattoo, A. (2008). Regionalism in standards: Good or bad for trade? *The Canadian Journal of Economics, 41*(3), 838–863.

Citibank. (2013). Market infrastructure developments impacting equities markets: Insights for institutional clients. Retrieved October 30, 2014, from http://www.citibank.es/transactionservices/home/about_us/articles/docs/market_infrastructure_equaties_110713.pdf

CGIF/Credit Guarantee and Investment Facility. (2013). Progress report 2013. Retrieved December 28, 2014, from http://www.cgif-abmi.org

Craswell, E., & Davis, G. (1994). The search for policy coordination: Ministerial and bureaucratic perceptions of agency amalgamations in a federal parliamentary system. *Policy Studies Journal, 22*(1), 59–73.

Dalla, I. (2003). *Harmonization of bond market rules and regulations in selected APEC economies.* Manila: Asian Development Bank.

Darbellay, A. (2013). *Regulating credit rating agencies.* Elgar Financial Law Series. Edward Elgar Publishing.

Darmawan, A. D. (2011). Credit guarantee encourages issuance of corporate bonds. *Indonesia Finance Today.* Retrieved December 19, 2011, from http://en.indonesiafinancetoday.com/read/4197/Credit-Guarantee-Encourages-Issuance-of-Corporate-Bonds

Fabella, R., & Madhur, S. (2003). *Bond market development in East Asia: Issues and challenges.* Retrieved February 11, 2013, from http://www.adb.org/sites/default/files/publication/28182/wp035.pdf

Gray, S., Felman, J., Carvajal, A., & Jobst, A. A. (2014). Developing ASEAN-5 Bond markets: What needs to be done? *Asian-Pacific Economic Literature, 28*(1), 76–95.

Grimes, W. W. (2008). *Political economy of bond market initiatives in East Asia.* Paper presented to American Political Science Association 2008 Annual Meeting, Boston, MA, August 28.

Hamilton-Hart, N. (2007). Government and private business: Rents, representation and collective action. In R. H. McLeod & A. J. MacIntyre (Eds.), *Indonesia: Democracy and the promise of good governance* (pp. 63–114). Singapore: Institute of Southeast Asian Studies.

Hameiri, S., & Jayasuriya, K. (2011). Regulatory regionalism and the dynamics of territorial politics: The case of the Asia-Pacific region. *Political Studies, 59*(1), 20–37.

He, B., & Inoguchi, T. (2011). Introduction to ideas of Asian regionalism. *Japanese Journal of Political Science, 12*(2), 165–177.

Hyun, S. (2011). *The Asian Bond Markets Initiative and the Yen, Yuan, and Won*. Korean Capital Market Institute. Retrieved October 7, 2014, from http://www.kcmi.re.kr/eng/periodical/opinion_list.asp?syear=2014&pg=16&zno=375

Hyun, S. (2014). *ABMF and standardisation of the Asian bond market*. Korean Capital Market Institute. Retrieved December 31, 2014, from www.kcmi.re.kr/common/downloadw.asp?fid=17008&fgu=002001

Indrawati, S. M. (2001). Fiscal issues and decentralization. In A. L. Smith (Ed.), *Gus Dur and the Indonesian economy* (pp. 77–82). Singapore: Institute of Southeast Asian Studies.

International Monetary Fund. (2012). *2012 Article IV Consultation: Indonesia*, No. 12/277. Washington, DC: International Monetary Fund.

Jayasuriya, K. (2003). Introduction: Governing the Asia Pacific beyond the new regionalism. *Third World Quarterly, 24*(2), 199–215.

Jayasuriya, K. (2008). Regionalising the state: Political topography of regulatory regionalism. *Contemporary Politics, 14*(1), 21–35.

Jayasuriya, K. (2009). Regulatory regionalism in the Asia-Pacific: Drivers, instruments and actors. *Australian Journal of International Affairs, 63*(3), 335–347.

Jayasuriya, K. (2010a). The emergence of regulatory regionalism. *Global Asia, 4*(4), 102–107.

Jayasuriya, K. (2010b). Learning by the market: Regulatory regionalism, Bologna, and accountability communities. *Globalisation, Societies and Education, 8*(1), 7–22.

Jones, P. (2010). Regulatory regionalism and education: The European Union in central Asia. *Globalisation, Societies and Education, 8*(1), 59–85.

Katzenstein, P. J. (2000). Regionalism and Asia. *New Political Economy, 5*(3), 353–368.

Kurihara, T. (2012). *Achievements of Asian Bond Markets Initiative (ABMI) in the last decade and future challenges*. Paper presented to OECD-ADBI 12th Roundtable on Capital Market Reform in Asia, Tokyo, February 7.

Kusumaningtyas, D. A., & Theo, R. (2012). *Yield obligasi Indonesia terseksi di Asia Tenggara (Indonesia government bond's yield is the sexiest in Southeast Asia)*. Kontan. Retrieved October 10, 2014, from http://investasi.kontan.co.id/news/yield-obligasi-indonesia-terseksi-di-asia-tenggara

Lee, J. W. (2008). *Harmonization of bond standards in ASEAN+3*. Manila: Asian Development Bank.

Levinger, H. (2014). *What's behind recent trends in Asian corporate bond markets?* Frankfurt: Deutsche Bank Research.

MacDonald, K., & Woolcock, S. (2007). Non-State actors in economic diplomacy. In N. Bayne & S. Woocock (Eds.), *The new economic diplomacy* (pp. 77–103). London: Ashgate.

Pacheco, A. A. (2006). *Mutual recognition agreements and trade diversion: Consequences for developing nations.* Geneva: Geneva Graduate Institute.

Park, D., & Park, Y. C. (2004). Toward developing regional bond markets in East Asia. *Asian Economic Papers, 3*(2), 183–209.

Pepinsky, T. B. (2010). *Openness without liberalization: Why bankers in developing countries support financial internationalization.* Paper presented at APSA 2010 Annual Meeting, September 2–5, 2010, Washington, DC.

Rethel, L. (2010). The new financial development paradigm and Asian bond markets. *New Political Economy, 15*(4), 493–517.

Sharma, K. (2001). The underlying constraints on corporate bond market development in Southest Asia. *World Development, 29*(8), 1405–1419.

Shimizu, S. (2013). *Japan's bilateral financial cooperation with ASEAN members progressing.* Retrieved April 16, 2014, from http://ajw.asahi.com/article/views/opinion/AJ201309250045

Soesastro, H. (2007). Macroeconomic policy reform strategy for regional cooperation. *The Indonesian Quarterly, 35*(2), 167–173.

Suharmoko, A. (2010). ASEAN+3 backs firms with $700m credit guarantee. *Jakarta Post*, April 15. Retrieved December 19, 2011, from http://www.thejakartapost.com/news/2010/04/15/asean3-backs-firms-with-700m-credit-guarantee.html

Walter, A. (2008). *Governing finance: East Asia's adoption of international standards, Cornell Studies in Money.* Ithaca: Cornell University Press.

Wibawa, A. A. (2012). *Bapepam-LK resmi beralih tangan ke OJK (Bapapem-LK formally hand overed to OJK).* Kontan, December 28. Retrieved December 29, 2014, from http://keuangan.kontan.co.id/news/bapepam-lk-resmi-beralih-tangan-ke-ojk

Wong, C. M. (2012). Asean+3 to mimic EU's common currency bond issuance. *Asiamoney, 23*(9), 55.

Woolcock, S. (2007). Theoritical analysis of economic diplomacy. In N. Bayne & S. Woolcock (Eds.), *The new economic diplomacy: Decision-making and negotiation in international economic relations.* Aldershot: Ashgate.

Yamadera, S. (2011). *Harmonization of bond standards: ASEAN+3 Bond Market Forum (ABMF).* Paper presented to FSD CoP Seminar, September 1. Retrieved November 15, 2012, from http://www.aric.adb.org/pdf/FSD_CoP_Seminar_1Sept2011.pdf

Yamadera, S., Hahm, J. H., & Hyun, S. (2010). *Harmonization of bond standards in ASEAN+3: Report to the Task Force 3 of the Asian Bond Market Initiative.* Manila: Asian Development Bank.

Yoshimatsu, H. (2010). Understanding regulatory governance in Northeast Asia: Environmental and technological cooperation among China, Japan and Korea. *Asian Journal of Political Science, 18*(3), 227–247.

CHAPTER 8

Conclusion

As a central focus, this study argued that the Indonesian financial authorities generally responded positively to regional initiatives under the auspices of ASEAN Plus Three (APT) financial cooperation. However, these authorities responded less enthusiastically to particular APT financial initiatives that could potentially hinder Indonesia's national interests. In this respect, the domestic political economy became a determinant in forming the Indonesian state agencies' behaviours and policy options towards regional arrangements.

Under the democratic administration, Indonesian participation in APT financial cooperation was led by the Indonesian Ministry of Finance (IMOF) and Bank Indonesia (BI). These two state agencies held the mandate and function to deal with APT financial initiatives. In addition, Indonesian non-state actors have also begun to participate in East Asian financial regionalism, in the wake of Indonesia's political transition.

Indonesia's responses to APT financial cooperation have been reflected in the internal regulatory transformation that was largely influenced by the institutional changes and policy coordination within Indonesia's financial regulatory agencies. The major institutional change related to the Indonesian financial sector was the distribution of power over the financial sector, to meet a 'check and balance' mechanism. In this regard, the most evident power distribution was the separation of the central bank from the executive power of the government.

© The Author(s) 2017   207
E. Saputro, *Indonesia and ASEAN Plus Three Financial Cooperation*,
DOI 10.1007/978-981-10-3029-1_8

Policy coordination among Indonesian actors also influenced Indonesia's international regulatory transformation. The policy coordination was mainly concerned with technical, rather than strategic, issues. The policy coordination among Indonesian actors was also characterised by limited opportunities for effective collaboration in relation to regular face-to-face meetings, limited sharing of information and infrequent communication.

The transformation of Indonesia's regulatory space occurred through both soft and hard law approaches. In the context of regulatory regionalism, the process of adopting regional standards and mechanisms was usually settled through soft law, by which state regulatory agencies attempted to align national governance with regional arrangements. However, empirical evidence demonstrated that Indonesian financial authorities also used hard law to introduce regional regulatory governance to the national framework.

FACTORS AFFECTING INDONESIA'S RESPONSES

Drawing on an assessment of empirical development in Indonesia, this thesis revealed several major factors that influenced Indonesia's responses to APT financial cooperation, including the domestic political economy, bilateral interdependence and perception, the nature of policy coordination and the de-politicisation of regulatory agencies (as visualised in Fig. 8.1).

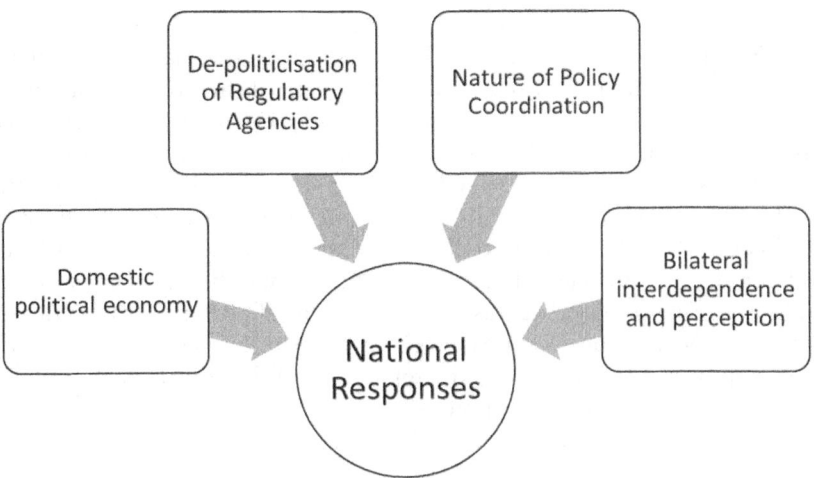

Fig. 8.1 Factors affecting Indonesian responses. Source: author's own visualisation

The Domestic Political Economy

Domestic politics had influenced Indonesia's commitment to regional cooperation. The change in domestic politics had influenced Indonesian financial authorities' responses to regional initiatives. In the context of a regulatory regionalism process, there were similarities and differences between Indonesian non-democratic and democratic administrations, in response to financial regionalism in East Asia. A key similarity was that both non-democratic and democratic administrations intended to engage with financial regionalism in East Asia, and were willing to transform the national regulatory framework to accommodate a regional arrangement.

Significant differences were apparent in the purposes of regional engagement and in the scope of participation. The shift from a non-democratic to democratic government administration had been marked by the intention of democratic administrations to reap economic benefits from regional arrangements and moved away from the political stability purpose previously expected by non-democratic administrations. Indonesian democratic administrations started to perceive regional cooperation as an alternative forum to recover and sustain the domestic economy in the wake of the Asian financial crisis.

In terms of participation, the change in domestic politics that brought democratic values to the Indonesian political system had contributed to configure a new pattern of Indonesian participation in regional financial cooperation. Democratisation had offered greater opportunities for actors other than state agencies to participate in the process of financial regionalism in East Asia. As democratisation demanded more transparency and public engagement, Indonesian non-state actors started to engage in APT financial cooperation, through research study projects and knowledge sharing forums.

Following shifts in the domestic political system, Indonesia's institutional power over the financial sector has also been modified. In the process, this led to shifts in the structures and mandates of financial authorities. These changes have not only modified power divisions within the financial sector but, as a consequence, have also shaped a new pattern of policy-making processes. Indonesian financial policy making became complex, mainly because the number of actors dealing with financial sector-related issues increased. The policy-making process often took time considering internal governance, functions and mandates within relevant authorities.

In the context of regional arrangements, the institutional changes have influenced the capability of Indonesian state authorities to determine their stance over regional initiatives. Under the current regime, almost all Indonesian financial authorities had potential to represent Indonesia in bilateral, regional or international forums. With different degrees of representation, Indonesian financial authorities could create policy networks and collaborate on concrete cooperation with their colleagues in the region, on behalf of Indonesian interests.

Meanwhile, Indonesia's economic conditions also influenced the Indonesian financial authorities' responses. The authorities considered current indicators of macroeconomics and domestic market conditions as the base from which to respond to any initiatives related to APT financial cooperation. This pragmatic approach led the Indonesian financial authorities to respond differently to various initiatives under the auspices of APT financial cooperation.

The combination of positive economic growth trends, an accumulation of foreign reserves and the trauma of the region's financial shocks provided impetus to the Indonesian government to join the APT financial initiative on regional liquidity support arrangements. For Indonesia, the Chiang Mai Initiative Multilateralisation (CMIM) was viewed as the second line of defence to deal with economic crises, after its own capacities. To demonstrate their support for the regional initiative, the Indonesian financial authorities created a space in the national framework, by bringing the CMIM agreement into Indonesia's jurisdiction. The intention to support CMIM has also been progressed through the adoption of several CMIM standards and mechanisms into Indonesia's regulatory framework.

In contrast, the weak market infrastructure and relatively incapable market players have led to Indonesia's unenthusiastic response towards regional bond market development. The current status of the domestic bond market has determined that the Indonesian financial authorities provided only half-hearted support to the process of several projects under the auspices of Asian Bond Market Initiative (ABMI). For Indonesia, ABMI projects, particularly the standardisation of market practices and the harmonisation of market regulation, had potentially hampered the developing Indonesian corporate bond market. Indonesia's financial authorities perceived the progress of standardisation and harmonisation as an opportunity for APT advanced member countries to gain more benefits from the Indonesian bond market, rather than as an opportunity for Indonesia to reap more capital from broader market transactions.

The De-politicisation of Regulatory Agencies

This study has suggested that de-politicisation over state financial agencies, as occurred with the Indonesian central bank, contributed to shape Indonesia's responses to regional arrangements. The role of de-politicisation in shaping Indonesia's responses to APT financial governance was visible from the way Indonesian financial authorities brought CMIM governance into Indonesia's regulatory system. In this respect, the mandate and independence of BI to manage monetary policy had helped the authority to transform Indonesia's regulatory system into a less complicated process. The legalisation of the CMIM agreement was proceeded by the financial authorities through a hard law approach, in the form of an exchange of signatory documents, without further legal procedures involving the Indonesian parliament. This legal process was made possible as BI, an independent financial authority, had a mandate to manage international reserves solely and to make international arrangements without any intervention from the executive (IMOF), or from the legislative body (*Dewan Perwakilan Rakyat*/DPR). Although the approval of the DPR was not necessarily obtained, the legal procedure for bringing CMIM governance into the Indonesian regulatory framework can be categorised as a hard law process, as the 'acceptance' of the CMIM agreement was a part of formal governmental legislation.

Moreover, the de-politicisation that occurred at the regional level has also influenced Indonesia's responses to APT financial cooperation. On the one hand, the existence of ABMF as a 'de-politicised entity' in APT financial cooperation has stimulated the participation of Indonesian non-actors. Although the participation remained limited, the de-politicisation of APT regional regulatory bodies has already empowered Indonesian non-state actors to express their perspectives on regional governance setting. In contrast, the ABMF has triggered cautious reactions from Indonesian financial authorities towards the conflicting interests that potentially emerge, due to the involvement of private players in designing the governance of regional bond markets. All this indicates that de-politicisation at national and regional levels affects Indonesia's responses to the development of APT financial cooperation, although they have different degrees of influence.

Internal Policy Coordination

Policy coordination has also contributed to shape Indonesia's responses to regional financial arrangements under the auspices of APT Cooperation.

There were three types of Indonesian policy coordination in response to APT financial regionalism found in this study: internal policy coordination between units within a state actor; policy coordination between state actors; and policy coordination between state and non-state actors.

Internal policy coordination within a state actor was relatively simple, in the sense that the policy coordination was conducted as part of the technical functions of a unit within a state actor. A more complex process appeared when policy coordination involved two or more Indonesian state actors responding to regional arrangements that entailed a common national stance. The policy coordination processes became much more complicated when Indonesian non-state actors were involved. This was due to the difficulty of determining the 'dividing line' separating public over private interests. The Indonesian regulatory agencies seemed disinclined to build a sound policy coordination involving non-state actors to avoid the conflict of interests that potentially occurred if non-state actors were involved in regulatory governance-making. In a country like Indonesia, where a state-based decision-making system remains strong, policy coordination was only robust among state actors.

Policy coordination among Indonesian national actors, which predominantly occurred at a technical level, has led to shape responses more on technical matters related to current APT financial projects, rather than to long-term strategic regional governance. Even for regional projects that entailed responses from different financial regulatory agencies, such as CMIM or Economic Review and Policy Dialogue (ERPD), Indonesian financial authorities were mainly concerned with technical issues.

Internal policy coordination in Indonesia was generally weak in the sense that there were no formal and regular coordinating events. As a result, Indonesia's financial authorities tended to produce 'fragmented' responses. This means that the responses produced by the Indonesian agencies were not always unified, while they were still expected to form similar (if not a single) responses representing Indonesia's stance. Each agency had limited perspectives of other agencies that made them consider only their own internal interests. In this study, this phenomenon was demonstrated by the varying reactions of Bapepam-LK and Debt Management Office (DMO), the two regulatory agencies related to bond markets, in response to regional bond market standardisation, although both agencies were under the Indonesian Ministry of Finance (IMOF).

However, similar effects were not found in transnational policy coordination. Transnational policy coordination had limited effect on

Indonesia's responses to APT financial cooperation. The transnational policy coordination, in the context of APT financial cooperation (in the form of regional surveillance mechanisms or meetings between regulators and players of bond markets), did not influence Indonesia's responses. Rather, they were merely perceived as practical processes that should be followed by Indonesian actors to proceed regional initiatives.

Bilateral Interdependence and Perceptions

Indonesian financial authorities' responses towards APT financial cooperation have also been influenced by relations between Indonesia and the two biggest powerhouses in East Asia, Japan and China. While Japan and China were important countries in the progress of APT financial cooperation, they also had essential roles to play in Indonesia's national development. Indonesia's responses to regional arrangements were marked not primarily by competition between regional power houses. Sino-Japanese power rivalry had limited influence on Indonesia's responses to APT financial cooperation. Rather, the responses were influenced by bilateral ties between Indonesia and the two East Asian powerhouses.

Notwithstanding growing Sino-Indonesian bilateral relations, in practice, Indonesia preferred to work closely with Japan for two main reasons. Firstly, in terms of a bilateral political economy, Indonesian-Japanese relations encompassed higher economic advantages, with fewer political controversies. For Indonesia, Japan provided not only economic opportunities in the area of trade, investment and finance, but it also offered assistances anytime Indonesia faced economic difficulties. Secondly, Indonesia had a positive regard for the internal mechanisms and the bureaucratic culture within Japan's financial authorities; this initiated a reliable process of cooperation. For Indonesian officials, internal processes within Japan's bureaucracy appeared relatively transparent and predicable, thus shaping certain expectations. In this respect, wide-ranging Indonesian-Japanese bilateral cooperation in the financial sector has facilitated intense communication processes that have promoted positive perceptions and trusts. The robust bilateral political economies between Indonesia and Japan, as well as Indonesian officials' positive perceptions about their Japanese counterparts, have encouraged Indonesian financial authorities to propose support for Japanese-led initiatives under the auspices of APT financial cooperation.

THEORETICAL CONTRIBUTION AND REFINEMENT

This section summarises the contribution and refinement of regulatory regionalism. As a relatively new approach, regulatory regionalism has not been applied to financial regionalism. In this study, there are two major contributions of the regulatory regionalism approach.

First, the regulatory regionalism approach was useful to examine regional-national interaction in the financial regionalism process. While the approach emphasised active participation of domestic actors and processes within a state, regulatory regionalism did not exclude regional-level dynamics from the analysis. This study found that regulatory regionalism was able to cover financial regionalism processes from both levels of analysis. This could help explain the new model of regional governance on financial issues in East Asia, which have moved beyond traditional models of intergovernmental arrangement, while at the same time disentangling domestic 'variables' that usually become the foundation for national commitments to regional cooperation. These have not been revealed by existing approaches to regionalism. The 'cover both sides' ability of regulatory regionalism benefits researchers by setting an 'inter-mestic' analysis of the current regionalism process.

Second, the regulatory regionalism approach could provide an analytical framework that accounts for the complexity of national regulatory transformation, institutional interactions and political commitments in response to regional arrangements. The strong attention of regulatory regionalism on domestic dynamics was beneficial to comprehend the way state regulatory agencies attempted to bring regional arrangements into force in the national space. It has also revealed interactions among state regulatory agencies in policy-making processes related to regional arrangements that were previously missing from discussions on regionalism. Again, regulatory regionalism has helped to disentangle domestic potentials and constraints that led to the dynamics of national positions in the regionalism process.

Despite its contribution as an alternative framework to understand national response towards financial regionalism, regulatory regionalism still leaves room for improvement. There are four proposals of refinement for regulatory regionalism drawn from this study. The first is related to the emerging model of regional governance conceptualised in the regulatory regionalism literature. Jayasuriya (2009) argues that the current mode of regional governance is more reliant on the active participation of state regulatory agencies, rather than formal international treaties or regional organisations. According to this study, this conception of the new mode of regional governance is partly true. The empirical findings have demonstrated that the roles of formal international treaties or regional organisations remained influential in the current development of regional governance in financial sectors. The establishment of CMIM agreements, as well as Credit Guarantee and Investment Facility (CGIF) agreements that bound APT member countries, suggests that formal international treaties are still important to govern East Asian financial regionalism. In this respect, the commitments of Indonesia and other APT member countries to CMIM were mainly reflected in their legal acceptance of the CMIM agreement. A similar process occurred with CGIF.

Further, the APT agreements construct a supra-national authority for policy making for regional financial cooperation. With CMIM, the agreement provides authority to ASEAN Plus Three Macroeconomic Research Office (AMRO) to 'judge' the economic condition of particular member countries, as well as the region, in the context of regional economic stabilisation. Meanwhile, the CGIF agreement provides authority to CGIF as a supra-national entity to determine the 'quality' of corporate bonds issued in the APT member countries. These arrangements suggest that active participation of state regulatory agencies has not replaced the existing form of regional governance that is still reliant on the formal legal commitment and operations of regional organisation. Rather than becoming a new mode of regional governance, the active participation of state regulatory agencies, particularly in financial cooperation, may only become a new feature of regional governance.

The first proposal of refinement has led to the second proposal, which is *the use of soft law*. Jayasuriya (2004, 2008, 2009, 2010a) argues that the current regional governance relies on soft law, rather than hard law. This study challenges such arguments. According to this study, the implementation of regional governance at national level still largely involved hard law, through the acceptance of international treaties. The governance of CMIM came into force in Indonesia's jurisdiction because of the CMIM agreement's legal process. Although Indonesian financial authorities have also adopted several standards of CMIM into their crisis management mechanisms—as a reflection of the soft law approach—the legalisation of CMIM governance became the most important part of the enforcement stage. The hard law process made regional governance of the liquidity support facility operated in Indonesia's regulatory system. Indeed, this does not mean that using soft law is irrelevant. The standardisation and harmonisation projects under the auspices of ABMF certainly showed this trend. However, while any forms of soft law, such as standardisation and harmonisation, have emerged in the current regional governance, hard law remained. Simply, the new mode of regional governance relies on both methods with flexible applications.

The third proposal is related to factors affecting the transformation of the national space. While the regulatory regionalism has emphasised the importance of internal transformation of the state in the new mode of regional governance (Jayasuriya 2009), it has provided insufficient analytical tools to explain the process. According to this study, institutional interests and actor capacity are two influential factors that can be used to explain internal transformation. This study suggests that the two factors have stimulated, as well as limited, the actors' participation in transforming national space for those actors' interests. The interests of Bapepam-LK and DMO over bond market regulations have contributed to shape diverse reactions towards internal transformation, to accommodate regional standard-setting projects. As discussed in Chap. 7, Bapepam-LK resisted, while DMO welcomed standardisation. This variation reflected the institutional interests of the two state agencies. It certainly affected their intention to provide space to accommodate regional standards of bond markets. Moreover, the internal transformation also depended on the way the actors perceived their own capacity. The capacity of Indonesian market players to face bond market liberalisation, which was relatively weaker than other market players in the region, has forced them to resist any attempts to transform domestic regulatory environments related to the bond market. This situation may generate problems, particularly in relation to the process of 'domestication' of regional standards.

The last proposal of refinement concerns internal policy coordination. Jayasuriya (2010) emphasised the importance of policy coordination in the process of regionalism. However, there was limited information on the operational elements of policy coordination, especially at a national level. The discussion over internal policy coordination has not been developed well, although coordination was basically at the centre of the regulatory regionalism process. Rather, the existing studies on regulatory regionalism put more stress on transnational policy networks that only reflect the collaboration between national regulatory agencies from different states.

According this study, the internal policy coordination among various actors (not only state but also non-state actors) played a significant role in the sense that this process defined national responses to regional governance. This includes whether or not, and to what degree, the national actors transform regulatory space within the state. In this study, the intense communication and collaboration between IMOF and BI helped the financial authorities to shape their stance over regional liquidity support arrangements and contributed to the process of adopting regional crisis countermeasure standards. In this regard, while Jayasuriya's summation of transnational policy coordination networks is important as a feature of the new mode of regional governance, the domestic level of policy coordination should receive equal emphasis to gain a more comprehensive analysis.

DIRECTIONS FOR FURTHER RESEARCH

Based on the findings, discussions and analyses provided in this study, I propose anticipated directions for three elements: Indonesia's future responses to East Asia financial regionalism, the prospect of East Asian financial regionalism and the potential research on East Asian financial regionalism.

Indonesia's Policy Options

Indonesia has been a proponent of financial regionalism in East Asia. Considering its democratic political system and open-market economy, Indonesia is predicted to further embrace regionalism in the financial sector. The democratic values of transparency and accountability tend to ease the way for Indonesian financial authorities and institutions in responding to further regional standard-setting processes in financial areas. Meanwhile, the open-market economy has driven Indonesia to welcome foreign economic players and, at the same time, engage with foreign markets to enhance its economic opportunities. In this respect, compliance with financial regionalism processes, including regional standards, has become an important process to deal with cross-border economic transactions.

In a regulatory context, the posture of Indonesian financial regulatory agencies suggested that in the future, Indonesian financial policy-making processes will be shaped by the active participation of de-politicised institutions, such as BI and the OJK. As these two institutions have mandates to regulate and govern the financial sector in Indonesia, they have the potentials to shape the regulatory governance of Indonesia's financial sector.

It is also within their capacity and willingness to adopt or comply with regional standards and mechanisms. Currently, OJK has now been starting to engage more deeply in regional financial arrangements. Whether OJK will be an effective financial regulatory agency needs to be studied further. The further study may include the effects of de-politicisation on OJK's policy and responses, as well as Indonesia's general stance, to the development of APT financial cooperation.

Further, the IMOF will continue to represent Indonesia in regional forums on financial affairs. However, due to the transfer of its mandate to OJK in financial policies, as covered by its mandate and function, the ministry should create a new pattern of policy coordination with other financial regulatory bodies, especially BI and OJK. A new pattern of policy coordination among financial regulatory bodies is expected to determine the future of transformation processes in Indonesia's internal regulatory framework.

The participation of Indonesian non-state actors is likely to be enhanced, along with the wider scope of financial cooperation. While the current participation is only related to capital and bond market-related issues, the expanded scope of APT financial cooperation that covers infrastructure financing and disaster insurance (APT 2014) could extend the future participation of Indonesian non-state actors in regional arrangements. However, the involvement of Indonesian non-state actors may still be limited to dealing with technical issues based on their expertise, or to analytical activities limited to an individual country study. For cross-country analytical studies, research institutions from the Plus Three countries and international organisations will still dominate.

The absence of a grand strategy in the area of international foreign policy, particularly in finance, will require Indonesia to take prudent action to shore up its responses to future financial regionalism in East Asia. Indonesian financial authorities will continue to base their future responses on current domestic interests and conditions, instead of on potential prospects for financial initiatives. Put simply, Indonesia will remain in a defensive position, rather than take an expansive stance on regional financial arrangements.

The Direction of East Asian Financial Regionalism

As regulatory improvements in financial sector are critical for many emerging economies in the East Asian region, the regional standard-setting project will remain at the centre of East Asian financial regionalism. Many East Asian countries, particularly the ASEAN countries, are still improving their capital markets. Countries like Cambodia, Lao PDR and Myanmar are just starting to develop their stock markets. At the same time, some member countries need to enhance their financial regulations. The fragility of financial systems in several APT member countries such as Indonesia, Thailand and the Philippines concerning external economic shocks implies that these countries need better regulatory systems to govern their domestic financial sectors. Under these conditions, regional standard-setting projects remain critical.

In particular, the ongoing market integration within ASEAN will provide a catalyst for further regional standard projects in East Asia. The ASEAN Economic Community (AEC), in particular, has fostered the standardisation of market practices and harmonisation of regulation to facilitate cross-border economic transactions among ASEAN member states. In the future, the development of standard setting in ASEAN will determine the progress of regional standard-setting processes throughout the broader Asian region. ASEAN offers potential markets, reliable supply of materials and competitive labour costs. Therefore, any regional projects in ASEAN will affect other regional arrangements in Asia.

Further, the influence of International Financial Institutions (IFIs) in the process of regional standard setting will continue to exist. The outcomes of regional standard-setting projects will also be determined by inputs from existing IFIs, such as the International Monetary Fund (IMF), the World Bank (WB) and the Asian Development Bank (ADB), as they will continue to be involved in regional regulatory governance processes. In this respect, international regimes can either restrain or promote regional standard-setting processes. They may assist and accelerate regional standards, but they can also restrain the transformation of national regulatory frameworks. The emergence of an IMF linkage portion in the operational mechanism of CMIM suggests how international regimes can become entangled in regional standard-setting processes. In a more practical way, the intention of APT finance ministers and central bank governors to use IFIs as a benchmark for AMRO operations demonstrates that international regimes place their interests in regional standards and mechanism processes. While it is possible to single out the participation of IFIs from any regional standard-setting projects in East Asia, it may not be worthwhile for East Asian countries to exclude IFIs standards from the reference lists of regional standard-setting processes.

Moreover, as national non-state actors' participation in East Asian financial regionalism will continue to rise, it is predicted that regional standard-setting projects will consider domestic circumstances more seriously. In this regard, finding similarities between such regulations, or best practices between APT member countries, will constitute a basic step for further standardisation and harmonisation projects. In contrast, setting up a new regional standard will not be the first option, considering various market practices within the member countries. For APT member countries, compatibilities between regional and domestic standards will continually determine the internal transformation processes. For instance, Japan, China and Thailand will face a slightly more complicated process in transforming their best practices in bond markets if the regional standards use the Latin alphabet, as they usually use their own language characters. On this basis, the viability of a future regional standard-setting project will also be determined by calculating the costs of compliance with such standards.

Implications for Further Research

There are two areas of future research that can be drawn from this book. The first relates to the scope of the study on the national responses to regional financial cooperation. While this study has focused on a single country, comparative studies would allow researchers to unearth general domestic features in the process of financial regionalism, helping to determine various constraints in every member country. A comparative perspective will also assist in constructing more acceptable governance on financial affairs for member countries in the region.

The second area is related to national responses to standard-setting projects. This study has highlighted that standardisation gained different responses from Indonesian financial authorities. This study also revealed that APT financial cooperation has adopted global standards, and also potentially formed regional standards based on national standards. This phenomenon suggests that research on the national acceptance of different sources of standards needs to be undertaken. Such research is important to understand the pattern of national regulatory agencies' expectations, and to what degree international actors influence national responses towards financial standard-setting projects.

REFERENCES

ASEAN Plus Three. (2014). *The joint statement of the 17th ASEAN Plus Three Finance Ministers and Central Bank Governors' Meeting.* Astana: ASEAN Plus Three.

Jayasuriya, K. (2004). The new regulatory state and relational capacity. *Policy & Politics, 32*(4), 487–501.

Jayasuriya, K. (2008). Regionalising the state: Political topography of regulatory regionalism. *Contemporary Politics, 14*(1), 21–35.

Jayasuriya, K. (2009). Regulatory regionalism in the Asia-Pacific: Drivers, instruments and actors. *Australian Journal of International Affairs, 63*(3), 335–347.

Jayasuriya, K. (2010a). The emergence of regulatory regionalism. *Global Asia, 4*(4), 102–107.

REFERENCES

Abbott, K., & Snidal, D. (2000). Hard and soft law in international governance. *International Organisation, 54*(3), 421–456.

Abimanyu, A. (2011). *Refleksi dan gagasan fiskal (Reflection and ideas of fiscal policy)*. Jakarta: Gramedia Pustaka Utama.

Acharya, A. (2002). *Regionalism and multilaterism: Essays on cooperative security in the Asia Pacific*. Singapore: Times Academic Press.

Acharya, A. (2004). How ideas spread: Whose norms matter? Norm localisation and institutional change in Asian regionalism. *International Organization, 58*(Spring), 239–275.

Acharya, A. (2005). Do norms and identity matter? Community and power in Southeast Asia's regional order. *The Pacific Review, 18*(1), 95–118.

Acharya, A. (2011a). *Asia is not one: Regionalism and the ideas of Asia*. Singapore: Institute of Southeast Asian Studies.

Acharya, A. (2011b). ASEAN's dilemma: Courting Washington without hurting Beijing. *Asia Pacific Bulletin*, Vol. 133.

Acharya, A. (2014). *Indonesia matters: Asia's emerging democratic power*. Singapore: World Scientific Publishing Co. Pte. Ltd.

ACMF. (2011). *ASEAN and Plus Standards*. ASEAN Capital Market Forum. Retrieved November 22, 2011, from http://www.theacmf.org/ACMF/webcontent.php?content_id=00015

Adiningsih, S., & Devi, L. Y. (2010). Dinamika koordinasi kebijakan fiskal-moneter in Indonesia [The dynamics of fiscal-monetary policy coordination in Indonesia]. In S. Adiningsih (Ed.), *Koordinasi dan interaksi kebijakan fiskal-moneter: tantangan ke depan (Fiscal-monetary policy coordination and interaction: Future challenge)* (pp. 13–42). Jogjakarta: Kanisius.

© The Author(s) 2017
E. Saputro, *Indonesia and ASEAN Plus Three Financial Cooperation*,
DOI 10.1007/978-981-10-3029-1

Aggarwal, V. K., & Koo, M. G. (2007). The evolution of regionalism in East Asia. *Journal of East Asian Studies, 7*(3), 360–369.

Akrasanee, N., & Prasert, A. (2003). The evolution of ASEAN-Japan Economic Cooperation. In *ASEAN-Japan cooperation: A foundation for East Asian community* (pp. 63–74). Tokyo: Japan Center for International Exchange.

Alam, B. (2001). Indonesian public opinion mixed toward Japan. *The Asahi Shimbun*. Retrieved May 21, 2012, from http://www.asahi.com/english/asianet/column/eng_010907.html

Alami, A. N. (2008). Landasan dan prinsip politik luar negeri Indonesia (Foundation and principle of Indonesian foreign politics). In G. Wuryandari (Ed.), *Politik luar negeri Indonesia di tengah pusaran politik domestik (Indonesian foreign politics at the centre of domestic politics)*. Yogyakarta: Pustaka Pelajar.

Alamsyah, H. (2012). *Perkembangan dan prospek perbankan syariah Indonesia: tantangan dalam menyongsong MEA 2015 (The development and prospect of Indonesian Sharia-banking sector: A challenge in heading ASEAN Economic Community 2015)*. Paper presented to the 8th Indonesian Islamic-Economy Experts Association (IAEI), Jakarta, April 13.

Alatas, A. (2001). *ASEAN Plus Three: Equals peace plus prosperity*. Paper presented to the 2001 Regional Outlook Forum, Bangkok.

Alvstam, C. G. (2001). Regionalization still waiting to happen? In M. Schulz, F. Soderbaum, & J. Ojendal (Eds.), *Regionalization in a globalizing world* (pp. 173–195). London and New York: Zed Books.

Amako, S. (2007). *The idea of new international order China is seeking and East Asia Community*. GIARI Working Papers, Vol. 2007, No. 1.

AMRO. (2011). Press release appointment of the AMRO Director, April 6. Retrieved March 10, 2013, from http://www.amro-asia.org/wp-content/uploads/2011/11/AFDM+3-PR-2011-000-20110406-Appointmeent-of-the-AMRO-Director-PR20110503.pdf

Amyx, J. A. (2004). Political dynamics of regional financial cooperation in East Asia. *Japanese Economy, 32*(2), 98–112.

Amyx, J. A. (2005). What motivates regional financial cooperation in East Asia today? *Asia Pacific Issues*, (76), 1–8.

Anas, T., & Atje, R. (2005). *Economic surveillance and policy dialogue in East Asia: Making the ASEAN surveillance process a new*. Jakarta: Centre for Strategic and International Studies.

Anas, T., & Friawan, D. (2008). *The future role of the IMF: Asian perspectives*. Singapore: Friedrich Ebert Stiftung.

Antique & Latif, S. (2011). Anggito: BI tak perlu intervensi rupiah. *VivaNews*. Retrieved December 19, 2011, from http://us.fokus.vivanews.com/news/read/196636-anggito--bi-tak-perlu-lagi-intervensi-rupiah

Anwar, D. F. (1990). Indonesia's relations with China and Japan: Images, perception and realities. *Contemporary Southeast Asia, 12*(3), 225–246.

Anwar, D. F. (1994). *Indonesia in ASEAN: Foreign policy and regionalism.* New York: St. Martin's Press.

Anwar, D. F. (2003). Megawati's search for an effective foreign policy. In H. Soesastro, A. L. Smith, & H. M. Ling (Eds.), *Governance in Indonesia: Challenges facing the Megawati presidency* (pp. 70–90). Singapore: Institute of Southeast Asian Studies.

APEC. (1997a). *Second APEC Finance Ministers Meeting: Joint ministerial statement.* Retrieved November 28, 2011, from http://apec.org/Meeting-Papers/Ministerial-Statements/Finance/1997_finance.aspx

APEC. (1997b). *Vancouver declaration.* Retrieved September 30, 2014, from http://www.apec.org/Meeting-Papers/Leaders-Declarations/1997/1997_aelm.aspx

APEC. (2010a). *APEC at a glance, 2011.* Singapore: APEC Secretariat.

APEC. (2010b). Yokohama declaration. Retrieved September 15, 2014, from http://www.apec.org/Meeting-Papers/Leaders-Declarations/2010/2010_aelm.aspx

ASEAN. (1977). *Memorandum of understanding on the ASEAN swap arrangements.* Retrieved November 1, 2011, from http://www.aseansec.org/1388.htm

ASEAN. (1978). *The supplementary agreements to memorandum of understanding on the ASEAN swap arrangements.* Retrieved November 1, 2011, from http://www.asean.org/1394.htm

ASEAN. (1981). *Amendements to the memorandum of understanding on the ASEAN swap arrangement.* Retrieved November 3, 2011, from http://www.asean.org/1392.htm

ASEAN. (1982). *Third supplementary agreement to the memorandum of understanding on the ASEAN swap arrangement.* Retrieved November 3, 2011, from http://www.aseansec.org/6301.htm

ASEAN. (1987). *Fourth supplementary agreement to the memorandum of understanding on the ASEAN swap arrangement.* Retrieved November 3, 2011, from http://www.aseansec.org/1390.htm

ASEAN. (1997). *Joint ministerial statement of the special ASEAN Finance Ministers Meeting.* Retrieved November 7, 2011, from http://www.asean.org/6333.htm

ASEAN. (1998). *Terms of understanding on the establishment of the ASEAN surveillance process.* Retrieved November 9, 2011, from http://www.asean.org/739.htm

ASEAN. (1999). *Joint ministerial statement of the 3rd ASEAN Finance Ministers Meeting.* Retrieved November 10, 2011, from http://www.aseansec.org/6311.htm

ASEAN. (2003). *Joint ministerial statement 7th ASEAN Finance Ministers' Meeting.* Retrieved November 22, 2011, from http://www.asean.org/15028.htm

ASEAN. (2006). *Joint ministerial statement of the 10th ASEAN Finance Ministers'Meeting.* Retrieved November 22, 2011, from http://59.77.27.55/Article/ShowArticle.asp?ArticleID=639

ASEAN. (2009). *Joint media statement of the 13th ASEAN Finance Ministers' Meeting.* Retrieved November 22, 2011, from http://www.asean.org/22483.htm

ASEAN. (2013). 2011/2012 ASEAN+3 Research Group final report and summary. Retrieved August 14, 2013, from http://www.asean.org/communities/asean-economic-community/item/20112012-asean3-research-group-final-report-and-summary

ASEAN. (2014). ASEAN+3 Research Group studies. Retrieved October 1, 2014, from http://www.asean.org/news/item/external-relations-asean-3-asean3-research-group-studies

ASEAN Plus Three. (1999). *The joint statement on East Asia cooperation.* Manila: ASEAN Plus Three.

ASEAN Plus Three. (2000). *The joint ministerial statement of the 4th ASEAN Plus Three Finance Ministers' Meeting.* Bandar Seri Begawan: ASEAN Plus Three.

ASEAN Plus Three. (2007). *The joint ministerial statement of the 10th ASEAN Plus Three Finance Ministers' Meeting.* ASEAN Plus Three. Retrieved December 9, 2011, from http://www.mof.go.jp/english/international_policy/convention/asean_plus_3/as3_070505.htm

ASEAN Plus Three. (2008). *The joint ministerial statement of the 11th ASEAN Plus Three ASEAN Ministers Meeting.* Retrieved December 12, 2011, from http://www.asean.org/21502.htm.

ASEAN Plus Three. (2009a). *The joint media statement of the special AFMM Plus Three, action plan to restore economic and financial stability of the Asian region.* Retrieved December 12, 2011, from http://www.asean.org/22158.htm

ASEAN Plus Three. (2009b). *The joint media statement of the 12th ASEAN Plus Three Finance Ministers' Meeting.* Bali: ASEAN Plus Three.

ASEAN Plus Three. (2010a). *Articles of agreement of Credit Guarantee and Investment Facility.* Retrieved February 25, 2013, from http://www.cgif-abmi.org/cgif/pdf/CGIF_Articles_of_Agreement.pdf.

ASEAN Plus Three. (2010b). *The joint ministerial statement of the 13th ASEAN Plus Three Finance Ministers' Meeting.* Tashkent: ASEAN Plus Three.

ASEAN Plus Three. (2011). *The joint ministerial statement of the 14th ASEAN Plus Three Finance Ministers' Meeting.* Ha Noi: ASEAN Plus Three.

ASEAN Plus Three. (2012a). *ASEAN Plus Three New ABMI Roadmap.* Retrieved February 27, 2013, from http://asianbondsonline.adb.org/publications/adb/2008/abmi_roadmap.pdf

ASEAN Plus Three. (2012b). *The joint statement of the 15th ASEAN Plus Three Finance Ministers and Central Bank Governors' Meeting*. Manila: ASEAN Plus Three.

ASEAN Plus Three. (2014). *The joint statement of the 17th ASEAN Plus Three Finance Ministers and Central Bank Governors' Meeting*. Astana: ASEAN Plus Three.

ASH Center for Democratic Governance Innovation. (2010). *From reformasi to institutional transformation: A strategic assessment of Indonesia's prospects for growth, equity and democratic governance*. Jakarta: Harvard Kennedy School/ ASH Center for Democratic Governance and Innovation.

Asian Development Bank. (2008). *Bond financing for infrastructure projects in the ASEAN+3 Region (Financed by the Japan Special Fund)*. Manila: Asian Development Bank.

Asian Development Bank. (2010). ADB to contribute to ASEAN+3 Credit Guarantee Facility, April 14. Retrieved March 11, 2013, from http://www.adb.org/news/adb-contribute-asean3-credit-guarantee-facility

Asian Development Bank. (2012a). *ASEAN+3 Bond Market Guide*. Manila: Asian Development Bank.

Asian Development Bank. (2012b). *Asia Bond Monitor*. Manila: Asian Development Bank.

Azis, I. J. (2012). Asian financial safety nets? Don't hold your breath. *Public Policy Review, 8*(3), 321–340.

Balfas, H. M. (2012). *Hukum pasar modal Indonesia (Indonesian capital market law)*. Jakarta: Tatanusa.

Bank Indonesia. (2009). Establishment of a bilateral currency swap arrangement between People's Bank of China and Bank Indonesia, March 23. Retrieved May 13, 2014, from http://www.bi.go.id/en/iru/highlight-news/Pages/bilateral%20swap%20agreement%20China%20Indonesia.aspx

Bank Indonesia. (2011). Special topics. *Financial Stability Review*, No. 17, Jakarta.

Bank Indonesia. (2012). *Menjaga keseimbangan, mendukung pembangunan ekonomi yang berkelanjutan (Keeping the balance, supporting the sustainable economic development)*. Jakarta: Bank Indonesia.

Bank Indonesia. (2014). Bank Indonesia's function. Retrieved October 24, 2014, from http://www.bi.go.id/en/tentang-bi/fungsi-bi/tujuan/Contents/Default.aspx

Bank of Japan. (2013). *Signing of bilateral swap arrangement between Japan and Indonesia*. Retrieved January 31, 2014, from https://www.boj.or.jp/en/announcements/release_2013/rel131213b.pdf

Bapepam. (2006). Siaran Pers akhir tahun 2006 (the 2006 end of year press release). Retrieved May 12, 2014, from www.bapepam.go.id/bapepamlk/siaran_pers

Bapepam. (2008). *Studi tentang liberalisasi jasa keuangan non-bank di Indonesia (A study on non-banking services liberalisation in Indonesia).* Jakarta: Bapepam.

Bapepam-LK. (2010). *The capital market and non-bank financial industry master plan 2010–2014.* Jakarta: Bapepam-LK.

BBC World Service. (2013). The 2013 BBC country rating pool, May 22. Retrieved October 2, 2014, from http://www.worldpublicopinion.org/pipa/2013%20Country%20Rating%20Poll.pdf

Beeson, M. (2003). ASEAN Plus Three and the rise of reactionary regionalism. *Contemporary Southeast Asia, 25*(2), 251–268.

Beeson, M. (2006). American hegemony and regionalism: The rise of East Asia and the end of the Asia-Pacific. *Geopolitics, 11*(4), 541–560.

Beeson, M. (2007). *Regionalism and globalisation in East Asia.* Basingstoke: Hampshire Palgrave Macmillan.

Beeson, M. (2009). Geopolitics and the making of regions: The fall and rise of East Asia. *Political Studies, 57*(3), 498–516.

Bergsten, C. F. (1997). Open regionalism. *The World Economy, 20*(5), 545–565.

Bhattacharyay, B. N. (2013). Determinants of bond market development in Asia. *Journal of Asian Economics, 24*, 124–137.

Blizkovsky, P. (2013). Stakeholders of economic governance: European perspective. In S. Biscop (Ed.), *Studia Diplomatica LXVI-1* (pp. 71–92). Belgium: Academia Press.

Bremner, B., & Shameen, A. (2005). Yudhoyono's "Triple-Track Strategy". *Bloomberg Businessweek Magazine.* Retrieved April 4, 2013, from http://www.businessweek.com/stories/2005-07-03/online-extra-yudhoyonos-triple-track-strategy

Breslin, S. (2010). Comparative theory, China, and the future of East Asian regionalism(s). *Review of International Studies, 36*(3), 709–729.

Brodjonegoro, B. (2003). Fiscal decentralisation in Indonesia. In H. Soesastro, A. L. Smith, & H. M. Ling (Eds.), *Governance in Indonesia: Challenges facing the Megawati presidency.* Singapore: Institute of Southeast Asian Studies.

Brodjonegoro, B. (2012). *Indonesian economic outlook and crisis management protocol mechanims.* Paper presented to "Seminar on ASEAN+3 Macroeconomic Research Office (AMRO): Strengthening AMRO for regional surveillance and regional financial arrangement", Jakarta, April 12.

Buckley, R. P., Hu, R. W., & Arner, D. (Eds.). (2011). *East Asian economic integration: Law, trade and finance.* Chentelham: Edward Elgar.

Buzan, B., & Wæver, O. (2003). *Regions and powers: The structure of international security, Cambridge Studies in International Relations.* Cambridge: Cambridge University Press.

Cai, K. G. (2010). *The politics of economic regionalism: Explaining regional economic integration in East Asia, International Political Economy Series.* Basingstoke: Palgrave Macmillan.

Cameron, F. (2010). The geopolitics of Asia—What role for the European Union? *International Politics, 47,* 276–292.

Capling, A., & Low, P. (2010). The domestic politics of trade policy-making: State and non-state actor interactions and forum choice. In A. Capling & P. Low (Eds.), *Governments, non-state actors and trade policy-making* (pp. 4–28). Cambridge: Cambridge University Press.

Chandra, A. C. (2008). *Indonesia and ASEAN free trade agreement: Nationalist and regional integration strategy.* Lexington: Lexington Books/Rowman & Littlefield Pub.

Chandra, A. C., & Hanim, L. (2004). Indonesia's non-state actors in ASEAN: A new regionalism agenda for Southeast Asia? *Contemporary Southeast Asia, 26*(1), 155–174.

Chen, M. X., & Mattoo, A. (2008). Regionalism in standards: Good or bad for trade? *The Canadian Journal of Economics, 41*(3), 838–863.

Chey, H. K. (2009). The changing political dynamics of East Asian financial cooperation: The Chiang Mai Initiative. *Asian Survey, 49*(3), 450–467.

Chirathivat, S. (2005). The ASEAN perspective on East Asian-wide regionalism. In F. Kimura & H.-H. Lee (Eds.), *New East Asian regionalism* (pp. 149–170). Cheltenham: Edward Elgar.

Choi, J. Y. (2013). East Asian financial regionalism and the politics of global financial governance: Structural and institutional power in global and regional governance. *Pacific Focus,* No. 3, p. 411.

Chongbo, W. (2011). Forging closer Sino-Japanese economic relations and policy suggestions. *Ritsumekan International Affairs, 10,* 119–142.

Chung, C. (2013). China and Japan in 'ASEAN Plus' multilateral arrangements: Raining on the other guy's parade. *Asian Survey, 53*(5), 801.

Collins, K. (2009). Economic and security regionalism among patrimonial authoritarian regimes: The case of central Asia. *Europe-Asia Studies, 61*(2), 249–281.

Connelly, A. L. (2014). Indonesian foreign policy under President Jokowi. *Lowy Institute Analyses.* Lowy Institute for International Policy, March 5, 2015. Retrieved from http://www.lowyinstitute.org/files/indonesian-foreign-policy-under-president-jokowi_0.pdf

Craswell, E., & Davis, G. (1994). The search for policy coordination: Ministerial and bureaucratic perceptions of agency amalgamations in a federal parliamentary system. *Policy Studies Journal, 22*(1), 59–73.

Credit Guarantee and Investment Facility. (2013). Progress report 2013. Retrieved December 28, 2014, from http://www.cgif-abmi.org

Crouch, H. A. (2010). *Political reform in Indonesia after Soeharto.* Singapore: Institute of Southeast Asian Studies.

CSIS. (2002). Indonesia's new constitution: A peaceful reform. *The Indonesian Quarterly, XXX*(3), 252–262.

Dalla, I. (2003). *Harmonization of bond market rules and regulations in selected APEC economies.* Manila: Asian Development Bank.

Dalla, I. (2012). *East Asian bond markets in 2020: Progress, prospects, and future challenges.* Working Paper.

Daniel, W. (2012). Jepang masih paling rajin kasih utang ke RI (Japan is the most diligent to lend Indonesia), May 22. Retrieved September 1, 2014, from http://news.detik.com/transisipresiden/read/2012/05/22/103916/1921 504/4/jepang-masih-paling-rajin-kasih-utang-ke-ri

Darbellay, A. (2013). *Regulating credit rating agencies.* Elgar Financial Law Series. Edward Elgar Publishing.

Darmawan, A. D. (2011). Credit guarantee encourages issuance of corporate bonds. *Indonesia Finance Today.* Retrieved December 19, 2011, from http://en.indonesiafinancetoday.com/read/4197/Credit-Guarantee-Encourages-Issuance-of-Corporate-Bonds

Davis, J. R. (2010). East Asian regionalism: Origins, development and prospects for the future. *Politikon, 16*(1), 34–49.

De Brouwer, G. (1999). *Financial integration in East Asia.* Cambridge: Cambridge University Press.

De Brouwer, G. (2002). The IMF and East Asia: A changing regional financial architecture. *Pacific Economic Papers*, Vol. 324.

Dick, H., Houben, V. J. H., Lindblad, J. T., & Wee, T. K. (2002). *The emergence of a national economy, ASAA Southeast Asia Publications Series.* Australia: Allen & Unwin.

Dieter, H. (2000). *Monetary regionalism: Regional integration without financial crises.* CSGR Working Paper, No. 52/00, pp. 1–27.

Dieter, H., & Higgott, R. (2003). Exploring alternative theories of economic regionalism: From trade to finance in Asian co-operation? *Review of International Political Economy, 10*(3), 430–454.

Direktorat Jenderal Pengelolaan Utang (DMO). (2013). *Profil utang pemerintah pusat (Central government debts profile).* Jakarta: Direktorat Jenderal Pengelolaan Utang.

Djiwandono, J. S. (2004). Liquidity support to banks during Indonesia's financial crisis. *Bulletin of Indonesian Economic Studies, 40*(1), 59–75.

Eichengreen, B. (2006). *The development of Asian Bond markets.* Paper presented to BIS/Korea University Conference on Asian Bond Markets: Issues and Prospects, Seoul, March 21–23, 2004.

Eklöf, S. (2004). *Power and political culture in Suharto's Indonesia: The Indonesian Democratic Party (PDI) and decline of the New Order (1986–98).* Copenhagen: NIAS.

Emmerson, D. K. (2008). Critical terms: Security, democracy, and regionalism in Southeast Asia. In D. K. Emmerson (Ed.), *Hard choices: Security, democracy, and regionalism in Southeast Asia.* Stanford, CA: Walter H. Shorenstein Asia-Pacific Research Center.

Emmerson, D. K. (2012). Is Indonesia rising? It depends. In A. Reid (Ed.), *Indonesia rising: The repositioning of Asia's third giant* (pp. 49–76). Singapore: Institute of South Asian Studies.

Fabella, R., & Madhur, S. (2003). *Bond market development in East Asia: Issues and challenges*. Retrieved February 11, 2013, from http://www.adb.org/sites/default/files/publication/28182/wp035.pdf

Gagnon, Y.-C. (2010). *The case study as research method: A practical handbook*. Québec: Presses de l'Université du Québec.

Garnaut, R. (2012). Indonesia in the new world balance. In A. Reid (Ed.), *Indonesia rising: The repositioning of Asia's third giant* (pp. 14–27). Singapore: Institute of South Asian Studies.

Gerring, J. (2007). *Case study research: Principles and practices*. Cambridge: Cambridge University Press.

Gray, S., Felman, J., Carvajal, A., & Jobst, A. A. (2014). Developing ASEAN-5 Bond markets: What needs to be done? *Asian-Pacific Economic Literature, 28*(1), 76–95.

Green, R. A. (2011). *Case study research: A program evaluation guide for librarians*. California: Santa Barbara.

Grimes, W. W. (2008). *Political economy of bond market initiatives in East Asia*. Paper presented to American Political Science Association 2008 Annual Meeting, Boston, MA, August 28.

Grimes, W. W. (2009). *Currency and contest in East Asia: The great power politics of financial regionalism, Cornell Studies in Money*. Ithaca: Cornell University Press.

Grimes, W. W. (2011). The Asian monetary fund reborn? Implications of Chiang Mai Initiative Multilateralization. *Asia Policy, 11*(11), 79–104.

Grimes, W. W. (2012). Financial regionalism after the global financial crisis: Regionalist impulses and national strategies. In W. Grant & G. K. Wilson (Eds.), *The consequences of the global financial crisis: The rhetoric of reforms and regulation*. Oxford: Oxford University Press.

Hall, D. (2002). Environmental change, protest, and havens of environmental degradation: Evidence from Asia. *Global Environmental Politics, 2*(2), 20–28.

Hamilton-Hart, N. (2007). Government and private business: Rents, representation and collective action. In R. H. McLeod & A. J. MacIntyre (Eds.), *Indonesia: Democracy and the promise of good governance* (pp. 63–114). Singapore: Institute of Southeast Asian Studies.

Hameiri, S. (2009). Beyond methodological nationalism, but where to for the study of regional governance? *Australian Journal of International Affairs, 63*(3), 430–441.

Hameiri, S., & Jayasuriya, K. (2011). Regulatory regionalism and the dynamics of territorial politics: The case of the Asia-Pacific region. *Political Studies, 59*(1), 20–37.

Hamid, E. S. (2005). *Globalisasi ekonomi dan ekonomi Pancasila (Economic global-ization and Pancasila economy)*. Retrieved September 15, 2014, from http://www.ekonomikerakyatan.ugm.ac.id/My%20Web/sembul29_1.htm

Hassdorf, W. (2011). Much ado about nothing? Chiang Mai Initiative Multilateralisation and East Asian exchange rate cooperation. *Ritsumeikan Annual Review of International Studies, 10*, 121–142.

Haswidi, A., & Suharmoko, A. (2009). RI, Japan ink fresh 1.5t yen swap deal. *The Jakarta Post*. Retrieved July 22, 2011, from http://www.thejakartapost.com/news/2009/07/07/ri-japan-ink-fresh-15t-yen-swap-deal.html

He, B. (2004). East Asian ideas of regionalism: A normative critique. *Australian Journal of International Affairs, 58*(1), 105–125.

He, B., & Inoguchi, T. (2011). Introduction to ideas of Asian regionalism. *Japanese Journal of Political Science, 12*(2), 165–177.

He, K. (2008). Indonesia's foreign policy after Soeharto: International pressure, democratization, and policy change. *International Relations of the Asia-Pacific, 8*(1), 47–72.

Henning, C. R. (2002). *East Asian financial cooperation* (Vol. 68). Washington, DC: Peterson Institute.

Henning, R. (2009). *The future of the Chiang Mai Initiative: An Asian Monetary Fund?* Washington, DC: Peterson Institute for International Economics.

Hill, H., & Menon, J. (2010). *ASEAN economic integration: Features, fulfilments, failures and the future*. ADB Working Paper Series on Regional Economic Integration, No. 69.

Hix, S. (2010). *Institutional design of regional integration: Balancing delegation and representation*. Manila: Asian Development Bank.

Hurrell, A. (1995). Explaining the resurgence of regionalism in world politics. *Review of International Studies, 21*(4), 331–358.

Hyun, S. (2011). *The Asian Bond Markets Initiative and the Yen, Yuan, and Won*. Korean Capital Market Institute. Retrieved October 7, 2014, from http://www.kcmi.re.kr/eng/periodical/opinion_list.asp?syear=2014&pg=16&zno=375

Hyun, S. (2014). *ABMF and standardisation of the Asian bond market*. Korean Capital Market Institute. Retrieved December 31, 2014, from www.kcmi.re.kr/common/downloadw.asp?fid=17008&fgu=002001

Indrawati, S. M. (2001). Fiscal issues and decentralization. In A. L. Smith (Ed.), *Gus Dur and the Indonesian economy* (pp. 77–82). Singapore: Institute of Southeast Asian Studies.

Indrawati, S. M. (2007a). *Developing broader regional financial integration*. Paper presented to East Asia Summit's regional financial cooperation and integration workshop, Jakarta.

Indrawati, S. M. (2007b). *Opportunities and challenges facing new systemic players*. Paper presented to Institute of International Finance, Washington, DC, October 2007.

Indrawati, S. M. (2007c). "Ten years after the crisis", emerging Asian regionalism. Paper presented to the 40th Annual Asia Development Bank Meeting of the Board of Governors, Kyoto, Japan, May 2007.

Indrawati, S. M. (2008). Perspectives on Asian economic integration and cooperation. Emerging Asian regionalism book launch, 41st Asia Development Bank Annual Meeting of the Board of Governors, Madrid.

Inoguchi, M. (2007). Influence of ADB bond issues and US bonds on Asian government bonds. Asian Economic Journal, 21(4), 387–404.

Inoguchi, T. (2011). Japanese ideas of Asian regionalism. Japanese Journal of Political Science, 12, 233–249.

International Monetary Fund. (1998). Indonesia—Memorandum of economic and financial policies. Retrieved April 23, 2013, from http://www.imf.org/external/np/loi/011598.htm

International Monetary Fund. (2007). The special data dissemination standard: Guide for subscribers and users. Washington, DC: International Monetary Fund.

International Monetary Fund. (2012a). 2012 Article IV Consultation: Indonesia, No. 12/277. Washington, DC: International Monetary Fund.

International Monetary Fund. (2012b). Indonesia: CPSS-IOSCO recommendations for securities settlement systems—The equity and corporate bonds securities settlement systems. Washington, DC: International Monetary Fund.

International Monetary Fund. (2013). Report for selected countries and subjects. World Economic Outlook Database. Retrieved May 13, 2014, from http://www.imf.org/external/pubs/ft/weo/2013/01/weodata/index.aspx

Isaac, G. E. (2003). Food safety and eco-labelling regulations: A case of transatlantic regulatory regionalism? In G. P. Sampson & S. Woolcock (Eds.), Regionalism, multilateralism, and economic integration: The recent experience (pp. 227–252). Tokyo: United Nations University Press.

Ito, T., Ogawa, E., Kawai, M., Kawasaki, K., & Murase, T. (2005). Research papers and policy recommendations on economic surveillance and policy dialogue in East Asia. Tokyo: Institute for International Monetary Affairs.

Japan External Trade Organisation. (2012). Japan's outward and inward foreign direct investment. Retrieved June 25, 2014, from https://www.jetro.go.jp/en/reports/statistics/

Jayasuriya, K. (2003). Introduction: Governing the Asia Pacific beyond the new regionalism. Third World Quarterly, 24(2), 199–215.

Jayasuriya, K. (2004). The new regulatory state and relational capacity. Policy & Politics, 32(4), 487–501.

Jayasuriya, K. (2008). Regionalising the state: Political topography of regulatory regionalism. Contemporary Politics, 14(1), 21–35.

Jayasuriya, K. (2009). Regulatory regionalism in the Asia-Pacific: Drivers, instruments and actors. Australian Journal of International Affairs, 63(3), 335–347.

Jayasuriya, K. (2010a). The emergence of regulatory regionalism. Global Asia, 4(4), 102–107.

Jayasuriya, K. (2010b). Learning by the market: Regulatory regionalism, Bologna, and accountability communities. *Globalisation, Societies and Education, 8*(1), 7–22.

Jayasuriya, K., & Robertson, S. (2010). Regulatory regionalism and the governance of higher education. *Globalisation, Societies and Education, 8*(1), 1–6.

Jhaveri, R. (2005). PBOC and Bank Indonesia sign bilateral swap agreement. *Risk.Net*. Retrieved December 19, 2011, from http://www.risk.net/asia-risk/news/1509309/pboc-bank-indonesia-sign-bilateral-swap-agreement

Jiabo, W. (2011). Remarks by His Excellency Wen Jiabao Premier of the People's Republic of China. China-Indonesia Strategic Business Dialogue, Jakarta.

Jiang, Y. (2010). Response and responsibility: China in East Asian financial cooperation. *Pacific Review, 23*(5), 603–623.

Jize, Q. (2005). Indonesia now a strategic partner. *China Daily*. Retrieved September 17, 2013, from http://www.chinadaily.com.cn/english/doc/2005-04/25/content_437349.htm

Johansson, A. C. (2008). Interdependencies among Asian bond markets. *Journal of Asian Economics, 19*(2), 101–116.

Johansson, A. C. (2012). China's growing influence in Southeast Asia—Monetary policy and equity markets. *World Economy, 35*(7), 816–837.

Jones, P. (2010). Regulatory regionalism and education: The European Union in central Asia. *Globalisation, Societies and Education, 8*(1), 59–85.

Kanithasen, P., & Watjannapukka, K. (2011). The ASEAN economic community in 2015: Some steps move forward but no giant leap. *Focused and Quick*, No. 35.

Kartasasmita, A. G. (2005). Diplomasi dan restrukturisasi Deplu (Diplomacy and restructurisation on the Ministry of Foreign Affairs). *Suara Karya Online*. Retrieved April 24, 2013, from http://www.suarakarya-online.com/news.html?id=118419

Katada, S., & Sohn, I. (2014). Regionalism as financial statecraft: China and Japan's pursuit of counterweight strategies. In L. E. Armijo & S. Katada (Eds.), *The financial statecraft of emerging powers: Shield and sword in Asia and Latin America*. Hampshire: Palgrave Macmillan.

Katzenstein, P. J. (2000). Regionalism and Asia. *New Political Economy, 5*(3), 353–368.

Kawai, M. (2005). East Asian economic regionalism: Progress and challenges. *Journal of Asian Economics, 16*(1), 29–55.

Kawai, M. (2010). *East Asian financial co-operation and the role of the ASEAN+3 Macroeconomic Research Office*. Bonn: German Development Institute.

Kawai, M., & Houser, C. (2007). *Evolving ASEAN+3 ERPD: Toward peer reviews or due diligence?* Tokyo: Asian Development Bank Institute.

Kawai, M., & Takagi, S. (2012). A proposal for exchange rate policy coordination in East Asia. In M. Kawai, P. J. Morgan, & S. Takagi (Eds.), *Monetary and currency policy management in Asia*. Cheltenham: Edward Elgar.

Keohane, R. O. (2005). *After hegemony: Cooperation and discord in the world political economy.* Princeton, NJ: Princeton University Press.

Kerwer, D. (2005). Rules that many use: Standards and global regulation. *Governance, 18*(4), 611–632.

Kirschner, V., & Stapel, S. (2012). Does regime type matter? Regional integration from the nation states perspectives in ECOWAS. In T. A. Borzel, L. Goltermann, M. Lohaus, & K. Striebinger (Eds.), *Roads to regionalism: Genesis, design, and effects of regional organization* (pp. 141–157). Farnham: Asghate.

Kirton, J. J., & Trebilcock, M. J. (2004). *Hard choices, soft law: Voluntary standards in global trade, environment, and social governance.* Brookfield: Ashgate.

Komori, Y. (2009). Regional governance in East Asia and the Asia-Pacific. *East Asia: An International Quarterly, 26*(4), 321–341.

Krismantari, I. (2009). Foreign investor dominate Indonesia stock market. *Jakarta Post.* Retrieved September 29, 2014, from http://www.thejakartapost.com/news/2009/01/02/foreign-investors-dominate-indonesia-stock-market.html

Kuncoro, M. (2007). APEC dan kepentingan Indonesia (APEC and Indonesia's interests). *Seputar Indonesia.* Retrieved July 18, 2011, from http://www.seputar-indonesia.com/edisicetak/ekonomi-bisnis/analisis-apec-dan-kepentingan-indo.html

Kurihara, T. (2012). *Achievements of Asian Bond Markets Initiative (ABMI) in the last decade and future challenges.* Paper presented to OECD-ADBI 12th Roundtable on Capital Market Reform in Asia, Tokyo, February 7.

Kurniati, Y., & Budiman, A. S. (2011). Embracing ASEAN economic integration 2015: A quest for an ASEAN business cycle from Indonesia's point of view. In A. Ananta, M. Soekarni, & S. Arifin (Eds.), *The Indonesian economy: Entering new era* (pp. 31–344). Singapore: Institute of Southeast Asian Studies.

Kusumaningtyas, D. A., & Theo, R. (2012). *Yield obligasi Indonesia terseksi di Asia Tenggara (Indonesia government bond's yield is the sexiest in Southeast Asia).* Kontan. Retrieved October 10, 2014, from http://investasi.kontan.co.id/news/yield-obligasi-indonesia-terseksi-di-asia-tenggara

Lahat, L. (2011). How can leaders' perceptions guide policy analysis in an era of governance? *Policy Sciences, 44*(2), 135–155.

Laksmana, E. A. (2011). Variations on a theme: Dimensions of ambivalence in Indonesia-China relations. *Harvard Asia Quarterly, 13*(1), 24–31.

Lee, I. (2012). *Ten Years of the Asian Bond Markets Initiative (ABMI).* Korean Capital Market Institute. Retrieved February 25, 2013, from http://www.kcmi.re.kr

Lee, J. W. (2008). *Harmonization of bond standards in ASEAN+3.* Manila: Asian Development Bank.

Levinger, H. (2014). *What's behind recent trends in Asian corporate bond markets?* Frankfurt: Deutsche Bank Research.

Lewer, J. J., & Terry, N. (2003). Capital account and foreign direct investment policies in the late nineties: What effect on trade? *Asean Economic Bulletin, 20*(3), 256–271.

Lubis, T. M. (2003). Constitutional reforms. In H. Soesastro, A. L. Smith, & H. M. Ling (Eds.), *Governance in Indonesia: Challenges facing the Megawati presidency* (pp. 106–113). Singapore: Institute of Southeast Asian Studies.

MacDonald, K., & Woolcock, S. (2007). Non-State actors in economic diplomacy. In N. Bayne & S. Woocock (Eds.), *The new economic diplomacy* (pp. 77–103). London: Ashgate.

Mahoney, J. (2015). Process tracing and historical explanation. *Security Studies, 24*(2), 200–218.

Mansfield, E. D., & Milner, H. V. (1999). The new wave of regionalism. *International Organization, 53*(3), 589–627.

Mansfield, E. D., Milner, H. V., & Rosendorff, B. P. (2002). Why democracies cooperate more: Electoral control and international trade agreements. *International Organization, 56*(3), 477–513.

Manupipatpong, W. (2002). The ASEAN surveillance process and the East Asian Monetary Fund. *Asean Economic Bulletin, 19*(1), 111–122.

Mariyono, J., & Saputro, E. N. (2009). Political determinants of regional economic growth in Indonesia. *The Asia Pacific Journal of Public Administration, 31*(1), 39–56.

Martinez-Diaz, L., & Woods, N. (2009). *Networks of influence? Developing countries in a networked global order.* Oxford: Oxford University Press.

Martowardojo, A. (2011). *Speech from the Minister of Finance of the Republic of Indonesia.* Presented to the launching of ASEAN exchanges website, Bali, April 8.

Marulitua, R. (2008). *Bursa efek Indonesia masih belum bergairah (Indonesian stock exchange not passionate yet).* Kompas.com. Retrieved January 15, 2012, from http://bisniskeuangan.kompas.com/read/2008/10/30/07343536/Bursa.Efek.Indonesia.Masih.Belum.Bergairah

Maswood, S. J. (2001a). *Japan and East Asian regionalism, The Nissan Institute/Routledge Japanese Studies Series.* London: Routledge.

Maswood, S. J. (2001b). Japanese foreign policy and regionalism. In S. J. Maswood (Ed.), *Japan and East Asian regionalism.* London: Routledge.

Mattli, W. (2001). The politics and economics of international institutional standards setting: An introduction. *Journal of European Public Policy, 8*(3), 328–344.

McLeod, R. H. (1999). Crisis-driven changes to the banking laws and regulations. *Bulletin of Indonesian Economic Studies, 35*(2), 147–154.

Mearsheimer, J. J. (1990). Back to the future: Instability in Europe after the Cold War. *International Security,* (1), 5–56.

Mietzner, M. (2009). *Military politics, Islam, and the state in Indonesia: From turbulent transition to democratic consolidation.* Singapore: Institute of Southeast Asian Studies.

Milner, H. (2002). Regional economic co-operation, global markets and domestic politics: A comparasion of NAFTA and the Maastricht Treaty. In W. D. Coleman & G. R. D. Underhill (Eds.), *Regionalism and global economic integration: Europe, Asia, and the Americas.* London: Routledge.

Ministry of Finance of Japan. (2009). Joint press release on the signing of the agreement on an increase in the maximum amount of the Bilateral Swap Arrangements between Japan and Indonesia under the Chiang Mai Initiative, April 6. Retrieved May 13, 2014, from http://www.mof.go.jp/english/international_policy/financial_cooperation_in_asia/regional_financial_cooperation/pcmie/090406press_release.pdf

Ministry of Finance of Japan. (2011). *Japan's Bilateral Swap Arrangements (BSAs) under the Chiang Mai Initiative (CMI).* Retrieved December 19, 2011, from http://www.mof.go.jp/english/international_policy/financial_cooperation_in_asia/regional_financial_cooperation/pcmie/index.htm

Ministry of Foreign Affairs of Japan. (2008). Joint press statement on the occasion of the entry into force of the Agreement between Japan and the Republic of Indonesia for an Economic Partnership, July 1. Retrieved May 13, 2014, from http://www.mofa.go.jp/region/asia-paci/indonesia/joint0807.html

Ministry of Foreign Affairs of Japan. (2011a). Japan's official development assistance white paper 2010. Retrieved May 13, 2014, from http://www.mofa.go.jp/policy/oda/white/2010/

Ministry of Foreign Affairs of Japan. (2011b). Japan-Indonesia relations. Retrieved July 22, 2011, from http://www.mofa.go.jp/region/asia-paci/indonesia/index.html

Ministry of Foreign Affairs of Japan. (2012). Japan's ODA: Rolling plan for the Republic of Indonesia. Retrieved May 13, 2014, from http://www.mofa.go.jp/policy/oda/rolling_plans/pdfs/indonesia.pdf

Mittelman, J. H. (2000). *The globalization syndrome: Transformation and resistance.* Princeton: Princeton University Press.

Mok, K. H. (2010). Emerging regulatory regionalism in university governance: A comparative study of China and Taiwan. *Globalisation, Societies and Education, 8*(1), 87–103.

Moon, W. (2012). The G20 and Asian monetary cooperation. In J. Park, T. J. Pempel, & G. Xiao (Eds.), *Asian responses to the global financial crisis: The impact of regionalism and the role of the G20* (pp. 104–119). Cheltenham: Edward Elgar.

Murase, T. (2007). Economic surveillance in East Asia and prospective issues. *The Kyoto Economic Review, 76*(1), 67–101.

Murray, P. (2010a). Comparative regional integration in the EU and East Asia: Moving beyond integration snobbery. *International Politics, 47*(3/4), 308–323.

Murray, P. (2010b). East Asian regionalism and EU Studies. *Journal of European Integration, 32*(6), 597–616.

Nabbs-Keller, G. (2013). Reforming Indonesia's foreign ministry: Ideas, organization and leadership. *Contemporary Southeast Asia: A Journal of International & Strategic Affairs, 35*(1), 56–82.

Nanto, D. K. (2006). *East Asian regional architecture: New economic and security arrangements and U.S. policy.* Paper presented to members and committes of US Congress, Washington, DC.

Nemoto, Y., & Nakagawa, S. (2013). Regional financial cooperation in East Asia: Development and challenges. In T. Shiraishi & T. Kojima (Eds.), *ASEAN-Japan Relations* (pp. 184–206). Singapore: Institute of Southeast Asia Studies.

Nesadurai, H. S. (2003). *Globalisation, domestic politics, and regionalism: The ASEAN Free Trade Area.* London: Routledge.

Nesadurai, H. S. (2009a). Economic surveillance as a new mode of regional governance: Contested knowledge and the politics of risk management in East Asia. *Australian Journal of International Affairs, 63*(3), 361–375.

Nesadurai, H. S. (2009b). Finance ministers and central bankers in East Asian financial cooperation. In L. Martinez-Diaz & N. Woods (Eds.), *Networks of influence? Developing countries in a networked global order* (pp. 63–94). Oxford and New York: Oxford University Press.

Nomura Research Institute. (2009). *Technical assistance for "promotion of Asian medium Term Note (MTN) program".* Japan: Nomura Research Institute.

Novotny, D. (2010). *Torn between America and China: Elite perceptions and Indonesian foreign policy.* Singapore: Institute of Southeast Asian Studies.

OECD. (2010). *OECD investment policy reviews Indonesia 2010.* Organisation for Economic Co-operation and Development. OECD: Paris.

Pacheco, A. A. (2006). *Mutual recognition agreements and trade diversion: Consequences for developing nations.* Geneva: Geneva Graduate Institute.

Parinduri, R. A., Thangavelu, S., & Rajan, R. S. (2009). *Exchange rate, monetary and financial issues and policies in Asia.* Singapore: World Scientific.

Park, D., & Park, Y. C. (2004). Toward developing regional bond markets in East Asia. *Asian Economic Papers, 3*(2), 183–209.

Park, S.-H., & Lee, J. Y. (2009). APEC at a crossroads: Challenges and opportunities. *Asian Perspective, 33*(2), 97–124.

Park, Y. C., & Bae, K.-H. (2002). *Financial liberalisation and economic integration in East Asia.* Paper presented to PECC Finance Forum Conference on Issues and Prospects for Regional Cooperation for Financial Stability and Development, Hilton Hawaiian Village, Honolulu, August 11–13.

Park, Y. C., & Takagi, S. (2011). *Creating an integrated market by 2015: Capital account liberalisation in ASEAN.* Paper presented to The 9th NIPFP-DEA Research Meeting on Capital Flows, New Delhi, March 15–16.

Park, Y.-J., & Oh, Y. (2010). *East Asian financial and monetary cooperation and Its prospect: Beyond the CMI.* KIEP Working Paper, Vol. 10, No. 4.

Pascha, W. (2007). The role of regional financial arrangements and monetary integration in East Asia and Europe in relations with the United States. *The Pacific Review, 20*(3), 423–446.

Pempel, T. J. (2010). Soft balancing, hedging, and institutional Darwinism: The economic-security nexus and East Asian regionalism. *Journal of East Asian Studies, 10,* 209–238.

Pepinsky, T. B. (2010). Openness without liberalization: Why bankers in developing countries support financial internationalization. In *APSA 2010 Annual Meeting Paper.*

Pew Research Centre. (2011). Pew Research Global Attitudes Project, July 13. Retrieved July 7, 2012, from http://www.pewglobal.org/2011/07/13/chapter-1-the-global-balance-of-power

Pincus, J., & Ramli, R. (2004). Deepening of hollowing out: Financial liberalisation, accumulation and Indonesia's economic crisis. In K. S. Jomo (Ed.), *After the storm: Crisis, recovery, and sustaining development in four Asian economies* (pp. 116–149). Singapore: Singapore University Press.

Putnam, R. D. (1988). Diplomacy and domestic politics: The logic of two-level games. *International Organization, 42*(3), 427–460.

Rahmi, M. (2009). *Asean Plus 3 tinggalkan ketergantungan pada IMF (ASEAN Plus Three leaves its dependency on IMF).* Retrieved December 19, 2011, from http://economy.okezone.com/read/2009/05/06/277/217032/asean-plus-3-tinggalkan-ketergantungan-pada-imf

Rajan, R., & Sen, R. (2002). *Liberalisation of financial services in Southeast Asia under the ASEAN Framework Agreement on Services (AFAS).* Centre for International Economic Studies (CIES) Discussion Paper, Vol. 226.

Rana, P. B. (2002). *Monetary and financial cooperation in East Asia: The Chiang Mai and beyond.* Asian Development Bank.

Rathus, J. (2010). *Affordable delays for the Chiang Mai Initiative?* East Asia Forum. Retrieved May 31, 2012, from http://www.eastasiaforum.org/2010/12/24/affordable-delays-for-the-chiang-mai-initiative/

Rathus, J. (2011). *Japan, China, and networked regionalism in East Asia, Critical Studies of the Asia Pacific Series.* Hampshire: Palgrave Macmillan.

Rathus, J. (2012). *ASEAN's Macroeconomic Research Office: Open for business.* East Asia Forum. Retrieved August 26, 2012, from http://www.eastasiaforum.org/2012/05/23/aseans-macroeconomic-research-office-open-for-business/

Ravenhill, J. (2002). A three Bloc World? The new East Asian regionalism. *International Relations of the Asia-Pacific, 2,* 167–195.

Ravenhill, J. (2006). Regionalism and state capacity in East Asia. In I. Marsh (Ed.), *Democratisation, governance and regionalism in East and Southeast Asia* (pp. 177–203). New York: Routledge.

Ravenhill, J. (2011). *Global political economy* (3rd ed.). Oxford: Oxford University Press.

Rethel, L. (2010). The new financial development paradigm and Asian bond markets. *New Political Economy, 15*(4), 493–517.

Robertson, S. (2010). The EU, 'regulatory state regionalism' and new modes of higher education governance. *Globalisation, Societies and Education, 8*(1), 23–37.

Rosser, A. (2004). Coalitions, convergence and corporate governance reform in Indonesia. In K. Jayasuriya (Ed.), *Governing the Asia Pacific: Beyond the 'new regionalism'*. New York: Palgrave Macmillan.

Samboh, E. (2011). ASEAN's AMRO may 'replace' IMF financial role. *The Jakarta Post*, April 8. Retrieved July 7, 2011, from http://www.thejakartapost.com/news/2011/04/08/asean%E2%80%99s-amro-may-%E2%80%98replace%E2%80%99-imf-financial-role.html

Saparini, H. (2009). *Policy response to overcome crisis: A lesson from Indonesian case.* Paper presented to International conference on "Re-regulating global finance in the light of the global crisis", Beijing, China.

Saputro, E. (2011). *Where to for ASEAN+3's macroeconomic research office?* East Asia Forum, June 18. Retrieved June 29, 2011, from http://www.eastasiaforum.org/2011/06/18/where-to-for-asean3-s-macroeconomic-research-office/

Saputro, E. (2012). *ASEAN+3 financial cooperation enters a new phase.* East Asia Forum, May 26. Retrieved November 26, 2013, from http://www.eastasiaforum.org/2012/05/26/asean3-financial-cooperation-enters-a-new-phase/

Saputro, E. (2014). Transforming popularity into confidence. *The Jakarta Post*, October 27. Retrieved March 3, 2015, from http://www.thejakartapost.com/news/2014/10/27/transforming-popularity-confidence.html

Schirm, S. A. (2002). *Globalization and the new regionalism: Global markets, domestic politics and regional cooperation.* Cambridge: Polity.

Scott, P. D. (1985). The United States and the overthrow of Sukarno, 1965–1967. *Pacific Affairs, 58*, 239–264.

Sharma, K. (2001). The underlying constraints on corporate bond market development in Southest Asia. *World Development, 29*(8), 1405–1419.

Sheng, A. (2009). *From Asian to global financial crisis: An Asian regulator's view of unfettered finance in the 1990s and 2000s.* New York: Cambridge University Press.

Shimizu, S. (2013). *Japan's bilateral financial cooperation with ASEAN members progressing.* Retrieved April 16, 2014, from http://ajw.asahi.com/article/views/opinion/AJ201309250045

Shin, D. C., & Cho, Y. (2010). How East Asians understand democracy: From a comparative perspective. *ASIEN, 116*, 21–40.

Shiraishi, T. (1997). Japan and Southeast Asia. In T. Shiraishi & P. J. Katzenstein (Eds.), *Network power: Japan and Asia*. Ithaca: Cornell University Press.

Shiraishi, T., & Katzenstein, P. J. (1997). *Network power: Japan and Asia*. Ithaca: Cornell University Press.

Shrader, L. (2013). *Latest on branchless banking from Indonesia*. Retrieved November 18, 2014, from http://www.cgap.org/blog/latest-branchless-banking-indonesia

Simon, S. (2008). ASEAN and multilateralism: The long, bumpy road to community. *Contemporary Southeast Asia, 30*(2), 264–292.

Singh, D. R. A. (2009). ASEAN capital market integration: Issues and challenges. Retrieved October 10, 2014, from http://www.lse.ac.uk/IDEAS/publications/reports/pdf/SR002/SR002_singh.pdf

Siregar, M. (2011). Indonesia's structural reform. *The Indonesian Quarterly, 39*(3), 249–255.

Siregar, R., & Chabchitrchaidol, A. (2013). *Enhancing the effectiveness of CMIM and AMRO: Selected immediate challenges and tasks*. ADBI Working Paper 403. Tokyo: Asian Development Bank Institute.

Smith, A. L. (1999). Indonesia's role in ASEAN: The end of leadership? *Contemporary Southeast Asia, 21*(2), 238–260.

Smith, A. L. (2000). Indonesia's foreign policy under Abdurrahman Wahid: Radical or status quo state? *Contemporary Southeast Asia, 22*(3), 498–526.

Soekarnoputri, M. (2001). *Pidato Presiden Republik Indonesia pada Sidang Tahunan MPR 2001 (Presidential speech at the annual meeting of People Assembly 2001)*. Retrieved November 25, 2014, from http://kepustakaan-presiden.pnri.go.id/uploaded_files/pdf/speech/normal/megawati16.pdf

Soesastro, H. (2000). The Indonesian economy under Abdurrahman Wahid. *Southeast Asian Affairs*, 134–144.

Soesastro, H. (2003). An Asean economic community and ASEAN+3: How do they fit together? *Pacific Economic Papers*, Vol. 338.

Soesastro, H. (2004). *Kebijakan persaingan, daya saing, liberalisasi, globalisasi, regionalisasi dan semua itu (Competition policy, competitiveness, liberalisation, globalisation, regionalisation, and so on)*. CSIS Working Paper Series, Vol. 82.

Soesastro, H. (2006). Regional integration in East Asia: Achievements and future prospects. *Asian Economic Policy Review, 1*(2), 215–234.

Soesastro, H. (2007). Macroeconomic policy reform strategy for regional cooperation. *The Indonesian Quarterly, 35*(2), 167–173.

Sohn, I. (2005). Asian financial cooperation: The problem of legitimacy in global financial governance. *Global Governance, 11*, 487–504.

Sprague, J. (2010). Statecraft in the global financial crisis: An interview with Kaniskha Jayasuriya. *Journal of Critical Globalisation Studies*, (3), 127–138.

Statistics Indonesia. (2011). Perkembangan ekspor dan impor Indonesia April 2011 (The development of Indonesian export-import in April 2011). *Berita Resmi Statistik, 35*(6), 1–11 Retrieved July 22, 2011, from, http://www.bps.go.id/brs_file/exim-01jun11.pdf.

Stone, D. (2008). Global public policy, transnational policy communities, and their networks. *Policy Studies Journal, 36*(1), 19–38.

Storey, I. J. (2000). Indonesia's China policy in the new order and beyond: Problems and prospects. *Contemporary Southeast Asia, 22*(1), 145–174.

Stubbs, R. (2002). Asean Plus Three: Emerging East Asian regionalism? *Asian Survey, 42*(3), 440–455.

Suharmoko, A. (2010). ASEAN+3 backs firms with $700m credit guarantee. *Jakarta Post*, April 15. Retrieved December 19, 2011, from http://www.the-jakartapost.com/news/2010/04/15/asean3-backs-firms-with-700m-credit-guarantee.html

Sujatmiko. (1999). Japan's role in overcoming the Indonesian economic crisis. *Asia-Pacific Review, 6*(1), 109–131.

Sukma, R. (2009). Indonesia-China relations: The politics of re-engagement. *Asian Survey, 49*(4), 591–608.

Sukma, R. (2012). Domestic politics and international posture: Constraints and possibilities. In A. Reid (Ed.), *Indonesia rising: The repositioning of Asia's third giant* (pp. 77–92). Singapore: Institute of South Asian Studies.

Surbakti, R. (1999). Formal political institutions. In R. W. Baker, H. Soesastro, J. Kristiadi, & D. E. Ramage (Eds.), *Indonesia: The challenge of change*. New York: St. Martin's Press.

Suryadinata, L. (1996). *Indonesia's foreign policy under Suharto: Aspiring to international leadership*. Singapore: Times Academic Press.

Sussangkarn, C. (2010). *The Chiang Mai Initiative Multilateralisation: Origin, development, and outlook*. ADBI Working Paper Series, No. 230.

Sussangkarn, C. (2012). *Toward a functional Chiang Mai Initiative*. East Asia Forum. Retrieved July 26, 2013, from http://www.eastasiaforum.org/2012/05/15/toward-a-functional-chiang-mai-initiative/

Suzuki, S. (2004). *East Asian cooperation through conference diplomacy: Institutional aspects of the ASEAN Plus Three (APT) framework*. IDE APEC Study Center Working Paper Series, Vol. 3/4, No. 7.

Takagi, S. (2010). *Regional surveillance for East Asia: How can it be designed to complement global surveillance?* Tokyo: Asian Development Bank Institute.

Taufik, S. (2009). Kronologi aliran Rp 6,7 triliun ke Bank Century (The cronology of IDR 6.7 trillion injection to Century Bank). *Tempo Interaktif*. Retrieved February 12, 2014, from http://www.tempo.co/read/news/2009/11/14/063208353/Kronologi-Aliran-Rp-67-Triliun-ke-Bank-Century

Terada, T. (2007). *Japan and the evolution of Asian regionalism*. GIARI Working Paper, Vol. 2007-E-3.

Terada, T. (2009). *The rise of China: The impetus behind Japanese regionalism.* East Asia Forum. Retrieved May 29, 2012, from http://www.eastasiaforum.org/2009/07/26/the-rise-of-china-the-impetus-behind-japanese-regionalism/

Theo, R. (2011). *SBY: ASEAN motor pertumbuhan ekonomi dunia (SBY: ASEAN the engine of growth for the world).* Kontan. Retrieved May 27, 2011, from http://nasional.kontan.co.id/v2/read/Nasional/64339/SBY-ASEAN-motor-pertumbuhan-ekonomi-dunia

Tongzon, J. L. (2004). ASEAN + 3 and ASEAN economic integration. In K. P. Schönfisch & B. Seliger (Eds.), *ASEAN Plus Three (China, Japan, Korea)—Toward an economic union in East Asia?* Seoul: Hanns Seidel Stiftung.

Tsuneki, A. (2012). Japanese bureaucracy. *Japanese Economy, 39*(3), 49–68.

Vaughn, B. (2007). Indonesia: Domestic politics, strategic dynamics, and American interests. In E. F. McFlynn (Ed.), *Economics and geopolitics of Indonesia* (pp. 79–104). New York: Nova.

Väyrynen, R. (2003). Regionalism: Old and new. *International Studies Review, 5*(1), 25–51.

Vogtle, E. M., & Martens, K. (2014). The Bologna Process as a template for transnational policy oordination. *Policy Studies, 35*(3), 246–263.

Waldner, D. (2015). Process tracing and qualitative causal inference. *Security Studies, 24*(2), 239–250.

Walt, S. M. (1987). *The origins of alliances, Cornell Studies in Security Affairs.* Ithaca: Cornell University Press.

Walter, A. (2008). *Governing finance: East Asia's adoption of international standards, Cornell Studies in Money.* Ithaca: Cornell University Press.

Wanandi, J. (2002). The rise of China: A challenge for East Asia. *The Indonesian Quarterly, XXX*(3), 224–233.

Wang, J. Y. (2011a). China and East Asian regionalism. *European Law Journal, 17*(5), 611–629.

Wang, Y. (2004). Financial cooperation and integration in East Asia. *Journal of Asian Economics, 15*(5), 939–955.

Wang, Y. Z. (2011b). China, economic regionalismand East Asian integration. *Japanese Journal of Political Science, 12*, 195–212.

Wibawa, A. A. (2012). *Bapepam-LK resmi beralih tangan ke OJK (Bapapem-LK formally hand overed to OJK).* Kontan, December 28. Retrieved December 29, 2014, from http://keuangan.kontan.co.id/news/bapepam-lk-resmi-beralih-tangan-ke-ojk

Wie, T. K. (1994). Interactions of Japanese aid and direct investment in Indonesia. *Asean Economic Bulletin, 11*(1), 25–35.

Wie, T. K. (2012). *Indonesia's economy since independence.* Singapore: Institute of Southeast Asian Studies.

Wihardja, M. M. (2011). *2011 East Asia Summit: New members, challenges and opportunities*. East Asia Forum. Retrieved June 1, 2011, from http://www.eastasiaforum.org/2011/06/01/2011-east-asia-summit-new-members-challenges-and-opportunities/

Wong, C. M. (2012). Asean+3 to mimic EU's common currency bond issuance. *Asiamoney, 23*(9), 55.

Woolcock, S. (2007). Theoritical analysis of economic diplomacy. In N. Bayne & S. Woolcock (Eds.), *The new economic diplomacy: Decision-making and negotiation in international economic relations*. Aldershot: Ashgate.

Wuragil, Z. (2001). *Tiga Dirjen di Departemen Luar Negeri dihapus (Three director-generals of the Ministry of Foreign Affairs abolished)*. Tempo Interaktif. Retrieved April 23, 2013, from http://www.tempointeractive.com/hg/nasional/2001/10/28/brk,20011028-07,id.html

Yamadera, S. (2011). *Harmonization of bond standards: ASEAN+3 Bond Market Forum (ABMF)*. Paper presented to FSD CoP Seminar, September 1. Retreived November 15, 2012, from http://www.aric.adb.org/pdf/FSD_CoP_Seminar_1Sept2011.pdf

Yamadera, S., Hahm, J. H., & Hyun, S. (2010). *Harmonization of bond standards in ASEAN+3: Report to the Task Force 3 of the Asian Bond Market Initiative*. Manila: Asian Development Bank.

Yeo, L. H. (2010). Institutional regionalism versus networked regionalism: Europe and Asia compared. *International Politics, 47*(3–4), 324–337.

Yoshimatsu, H. (2008a). Japan and regional governance in East Asia. In N. Thomas (Ed.), *Governance and regionalism in Asia* (pp. 66–88). London: Routledge.

Yoshimatsu, H. (2008b). *The political economy of regionalism in East Asia: Integrative explanation for dynamics and challenges*. Hamsphire: Palgrave Macmillan.

Yoshimatsu, H. (2010). Understanding regulatory governance in Northeast Asia: Environmental and technological cooperation among China, Japan and Korea. *Asian Journal of Political Science, 18*(3), 227–247.

Yoshimatsu, H. (2014). *Comparing institution-building in East Asia: Power politics, governance, and critical junctures*. Palgrave Macmillan.

Yudhoyono, SB 2004, *Pidato Presiden RI: Mengenali masalah, menetapkan agenda dan arah (Speech of Indonesian President: Identifying the problem, setting the agenda and direction)*, Bogor, Indonesia.

Yue, C. S., & Pangestu, M. (2006). Rise of East Asian regonalism. In H. Soesastro & C. Findlay (Eds.), *Reshaping the Asia Pacific economic order* (pp. 123–141). Abingdon: Routledge.

Index

Note: Page number followed by 'n' refers to notes.

© The Author(s) 2017

E. Saputro, *Indonesia and ASEAN Plus Three Financial Cooperation,*
DOI 10.1007/978-981-10-3029-1